High Integrity Compilation

A case study

Susan Stepney

PRENTICE HALL

New York · London · Toronto · Sydney · Tokyo · Singapore

First published 1993 by
Prentice Hall International (UK) Ltd
Campus 400, Maylands Avenue
Hemel Hempstead
Hertfordshire, HP2 7EZ
A division of
Simon & Schuster International Group

Printed and bound in Great Britain by
Dotesios Ltd, Trowbridge, Wilts

Library of Congress Cataloging-in-Publication Data

Stepney, Susan, 1958–
    High integrity compilation : a case study / Susan Stepney.
       p.   cm.
    Includes index.
    ISBN 0-13-381039-9
    1. Compilers (Computer programs)   2. Compiling (Electronic
computers) I. Title.
QA76.76.C65S75 1993
005.4′53–dc20   92-38799
                                      CIP

British Library Cataloguing in Publication Data

A catalogue record for this book is available from
the British Library

ISBN 0-13-381039-9 (pbk)

1 2 3 4 5 97 96 95 94 93

Contents

Preface

Software is increasingly being used in applications where failure could result in injury or loss of life, significant damage to equipment, severe financial loss, or environmental damage. These applications continue to grow in size and complexity, increasing the risk of such failures.

High level languages are often not trusted for these critical applications: they can have complex features that are difficult to understand, and their compilers are not developed to the high degree of assurance required. Thus critical applications tend to be coded in assembly language. But as these applications grow in size using assembly language becomes infeasible; high level languages will have to be used.

To obtain an acceptable level of assurance for a high integrity compiler, it is necessary to have a mathematical specification of the source and target languages, and a formal development of the compiler that translates between them. In this book I illustrate a route for achieving a high integrity compiler by means of a small case study. Note that this is *not* a book about classical compiler development, and so some topics, perhaps surprisingly at first sight, are not covered. There is no treatment of parsing, nor of optimization, for example. The former is a well-understood and solved problem, adequately addressed elsewhere. The latter is not appropriate in high integrity applications, where a clear and traceable link between source code and target code is required for validation.

Part I introduces the problems posed by the requirement for high integrity compilation, and overviews a route to developing such a compiler. Part II specifies a small example language for which the case study compiler, and three static checkers, are developed. Part III specifies the target language and the compiler itself, proves that the compiler's specification correctly implements the high level language semantics, and describes a means of directly implementing the specification to produce an executable compiler. Part IV winds up the discussion by describing the extra components needed for producing a high integrity compiler for a full high level language, and evaluating the proposed approach.

The method for developing a high integrity compiler outlined in this book makes use of many concepts and notations from computer science, including denotational semantics, the Z formal specification language, and the Prolog programming language. Because of this, there is no way the discussion can be stand-alone: it would have to be the size of three tutorial books before I could start talking about high integrity compilers. There are many tutorials on these subjects available, however, and I provide appropriate references to them. Rather than scattering follow-up references throughout the text, I gather them together at the end of relevant chapters, in 'further reading' sections.

This book has evolved from a study originally carried out by Logica into implementation techniques that could be used to build a trustworthy Spark compiler for the formally developed Viper microprocessor. The study was commissioned by RSRE (the Royal Signals and Radar Establishment, which has lately metamorphosed into DRA Malvern), and I would like to thank the staff of RSRE for their input to that early work. In particular, detailed technical assistance was provided by John Kershaw, Clive Pygott and Ian Currie, and technical background was provided by Nic Peeling and Roger Smith. That early work was reported in [Stepney *et al.* 1991].

I would like to thank David Brazier, Jon Brumfitt, David Cooper, Mike Flynn, Colin Grant, Tim Hoverd, Ian Nabney and Dave Whitley of Logica for helpful discussions, and for careful reading of various versions of this work. I would also like to thank the anonymous referees, whose detailed comments helped me to clarify and expand the exposition in places. Last but not least, my thanks also to Helen Martin of Prentice Hall for her encouragement and patience, and to Logica management for providing much of the support, both moral and financial, that enabled me to write this book.

Part I

Introduction and Background

Chapter 1

Introduction

1.1 The problem

If the failure of a piece of software could result in injury or loss of life, significant damage to equipment, severe financial loss, or environmental damage, then that software is *safety critical*. Because the failure of such software is potentially so harmful, it is essential to minimize the chance of its failure—it becomes a *high integrity* application.

It has been argued that the only 'safe' way to write high integrity applications is by using assembly language, because only assembly language is close enough to the hardware that one can be sure about what is supposed to happen during program execution, and because only assemblers (that translate assembly language to machine code) are simple enough to be validated, and hence trusted.

There are two major reasons given for distrusting high level languages, which are further removed from the hardware than assembly languages. Firstly, high level languages are complex and poorly defined. Their involved and ambiguous semantics makes it impossible to know what a program written in such a language means, to know what it is supposed to do when it is executed. So it is impossible to know, looking at a program written in such a language, how it should be translated to execute on the 'real' machine; in some cases the only way to find out what a piece of code does is to 'run it and see'. Secondly, a compiler is itself necessarily a large complex piece of software, and will have bugs. So, even if it were possible to have some idea of the meaning of high level language programs, it is impossible to have any confidence that a compiler correctly implements this meaning. The problem is not restricted to just high level languages; some modern chips have such large complex instruction sets that their assembly languages and assemblers are not trusted for high integrity applications.

There is more than a grain of truth in this argument: some programming languages do have notoriously baroque semantics, and their respective compilers are large complex pieces of software, with all the corresponding potential for errors that implies. But as high integrity applications grow larger and more complex, use of assembly language is becoming infeasible; the large assembly language programs can exhibit as many bugs as the prohibition of high level languages sought to avoid. High level languages, with all their software engineering advantages, are becoming essential. How can these conflicting requirements be reconciled?

As a first step along the way (at least) the following conditions need to be met:

1. The high level source language must have a target-independent meaning; it must be possible to deduce the logical behaviour of any particular program, independent of its execution on a particular target machine.

2. This implies, among other things, that the source language must have a *mathematically defined semantics*. Otherwise it is impossible to deduce even what *should* be the effect of executing a particular program.

3. The target machine language must also have a mathematically defined semantics. Otherwise it is impossible to *prove* that the compilation translation is correct.

4. The compiler from the source to the target language must be correct. Hence it must be derived from the semantics of *both* the source language *and* the target machine's language.

5. To permit *validation*, the compiler for a high integrity language must be *seen to be correct*. It must be written clearly, and must be clearly related to the semantics.

6. The target code produced by the compiler must be clear, and easily related to the source code. This gives the *visibility* to the compilation process that is a requirement for high integrity applications.

7. The semantics for both the source and target languages must be made available for peer review and criticism.

The last three points are important for high integrity applications, in order to conform with the much more stringent validation and visibility requirements these have.

The requirement for a visible link between the source code and target code is most easily met by imperative-style source languages, because their state-based models map well onto most underlying hardware. Higher level languages, such as declarative languages, are much further removed from the machine, and it is correspondingly harder to demonstrate the link. Hence the source language described later in this book is an imperative one.

In addition to the above requirements, the equally thorny problems of proving correct the high integrity *application* being written in the high level language, and of showing that the physical *hardware* correctly implements the meaning of its assembly language, must be addressed. These are beyond the scope of this book.

One approach for constructing a high assurance compiler from the mathematical specifications of the semantics of the source and target languages is described in this book. This is done by defining Tosca, a small, but non-trivial, high level language, and Aida, a typical assembly language, then constructing a compiler using their definitions. Note that this is not a proposal for a new high integrity language, nor is it a claim that this approach is the way to write general-purpose compilers. Rather, it demonstrates how the mathematical specification of a given language can be used in high integrity compiler development.

1.2   Semantics

In order to write a correct compiler, it is necessary to have a mathematically defined semantics of both the source and the target languages. There are several ways of defining the semantics of programming languages, each appropriate for different purposes. Not every form is equally suitable for the purpose of defining a language in such a way that a high integrity compiler can be clearly derived from it.

1.2.1   Axiomatic semantics—too abstract

Axiomatic semantics defines a language by providing assertions and inference rules for reasoning about programs.

Assertions can be expressed as 'Hoare triples':

$$\{P\}S\{Q\}$$

where S is a program fragment, and P and Q are predicates over program states. The triple asserts that if the pre-condition P holds before the execution of program fragment S, and if S terminates, then the post-condition Q holds afterwards.

Inference rules look like

$$\frac{H_1, H_2, \ldots, H_n}{H}$$

This states that if $H_1, H_2, \ldots, H_n$ are true, then H is also true. So, when reasoning about a program, in order to prove H, it is sufficient to prove $H_1, H_2, \ldots, H_n$. This defines the meaning of H.

For example, the inference rule for an **if** construct might be given as something such as

$$\frac{\{P \text{ and } \epsilon\}\gamma_t\{Q\}, \{P \text{ and not } \epsilon\}\gamma_f\{Q\}}{\{P\}\textbf{if } \epsilon \textbf{ then } \gamma_t \textbf{ else } \gamma_f\{Q\}}$$

This rule states that, when reasoning about an **if** construct, in order to prove the post-condition Q is established, it is sufficient to prove that it is established by γ_t whenever ϵ holds, and that it is established by γ_f whenever ϵ does not hold (in each case, assuming the common pre-condition P holds, too).

Such a style of definition is appropriate for showing that two programs have the same meaning, for example, that they establish the same post-condition. This is useful, for example, for reasoning about programs, such as defining meaning-preserving program transformations for the purpose of correct optimization. However, it is an indirect form of definition, and is not so useful for defining a language in a form suitable for direct implementation in a high integrity compiler. It is rather too abstract for our purposes.

1.2.2   Operational semantics—too concrete

Operational semantics defines a language in terms of the operation of a (possibly abstract) machine executing the program, and so is mostly concerned with implementations. For example, it might define the meaning of an **if** construct such as

> **if** ϵ **then** γ_t **else** γ_f

in terms of labels and jumps

```
        < ε >
        JUMP label1
        < γt >
        GOTO label2
label1:
        < γf >
label2:
```

where the program fragments in angle brackets should be replaced with their operational semantics definitions, recursively. JUMP transfers control to the relevant label if the previous expression evaluates to *false*; GOTO is an unconditional jump.

Such a definition is useful, for example, when writing a compiler for that particular machine. However, it is not so good for defining what that meaning actually is, because it is defined only in terms of another programming language, which itself needs a definition. Also, a separate operational semantics is needed for each target machine. There then arises the problem of consistency: how can you be sure all the various semantics are defining the same high level language?

So, although such a definition is ultimately required for defining a compiler, it is too concrete to be an appropriate starting point: a machine-independent definition of the language.

1.2.3 Denotational semantics—just right

Denotational semantics defines a language by mapping it to mathematics. Such a mathematical definition should be better-understood and better-defined. So the language is defined by building a mathematical model that defines 'meaning functions'. Each meaning function maps a type of language construct to a mathematical value. The mathematical values used can have simple types like numbers, and also more structured types like state transition functions. The language construct *denotes* this mathematical value; the value is the 'meaning' of the construct.

The mathematical model suitable for such an imperative language is one of states and state transitions. For example, the denotation of an **if** construct would be defined in terms of the mathematical meanings of its component constructs:

$$D[\![\text{if } \epsilon \text{ then } \gamma_t \text{ else } \gamma_f]\!] \rho\, \sigma = \begin{cases} D[\![\gamma_t]\!]\,\rho\,\sigma, & \text{if } D[\![\epsilon]\!]\,\rho\,\sigma = \textit{true} \\ D[\![\gamma_f]\!]\,\rho\,\sigma, & \text{if } D[\![\epsilon]\!]\,\rho\,\sigma = \textit{false} \end{cases}$$

Here ρ is the environment, a mapping of program identifiers to abstract locations, and σ is the state, a mapping from abstract locations to mathematical values. $D[\![\,]\!]$ is a function that maps program language commands, in an environment and state, to a new state. Hence, it maps program syntax to mathematical values. (The full notation is defined in later chapters.)

The denotational approach of modelling abstract meanings of programs, independent of any machine implementation, satisfies the requirement that a program must have the same logical behaviour no matter what hardware it runs on. It is also at just the right level of abstraction to the starting point for specifying a high integrity compiler.

In later chapters, the denotational semantics of two example languages, the source language Tosca and the target language Aida, are specified.

1.2.4 Non-standard semantics

The denotational semantics described above is a 'standard' semantics: it describes the standard meaning usually associated with a program, that of program execution. It is also called 'dynamic' semantics, because it defines the dynamic changes of state that occur as a program executes.

But it is up to the language designer what the meaning of the language is chosen to be; other 'non-standard' meanings can equally well be defined. Each different meaning thus specified provides a different semantics for a language; the dynamic semantics is just one possible semantics, with a meaning that determines the output values when a program is executed. The best known non-standard meaning defines a type, rather than a value, to be associated with each construct. This 'type-semantics' can be used to determine whether a program type checks. Other non-standard meanings can be defined and used to determined other well-formedness conditions on a program, for example, that every variable is initialized to some value before it is used in an expression. These sort of semantics are called 'static semantics', because they define 'static checks', checks that can be made without executing the program, for example, at compile time.

This is described in more detail in later chapters. In particular, three static semantics for Tosca are specified—declaration-before-use, type checking, and initialization-before-use—and used to implement three static checkers.

1.2.5   Size of task

Before deciding to go the fully formal route of specifying source and target languages, and deriving a correct compiler, we need to know that the task is feasible. How big is the task of mathematically specifying a programming language?

Consider Modula-2, whose denotational semantics have been specified in VDM (more accurately, in the functional subset of Meta-IV, which is essentially a programming language); its specification runs to hundreds of pages. But remember, Modula-2 was specified retrospectively, and its definition was required to keep close to the existing semantics as defined operationally by its various compilers. Features that were difficult or 'messy' to specify had to be included, even where a different approach could have led to a simpler, cleaner, more understandable specification.

For high integrity applications, it is imperative that every potential for misunderstanding and error be reduced to a minimum. So the application language needs to be designed with a coherent and intelligible semantics. It can be argued that if a language feature is difficult to specify cleanly, it is difficult to understand, and hence should not be included in a language used for writing high integrity applications. Note that the converse does not apply: that a particular feature is easy to specify is not sufficient reason for including it in a high integrity language. Although the design of such a language could start from scratch, it is probably more practical to subset an existing language, slicing away those areas of ambiguity and confusion, not fossilizing them in the final definition. Such a language, although probably of a similar size to Modula-2 in terms of *syntax*, would be much smaller and simpler *semantically*.

Tosca itself is smaller than a real high level language, but even so still has quite a substantial specification, including as it does one dynamic and three static semantics.

The target language can be very small. Although many microprocessors have elaborate instruction sets, it is not necessary to specify the semantics of every one of these instructions. Only the subset of the instructions needed to implement the high level language need be specified. No static semantics need be defined either; all the static checks can be done in the high level language, and a correct translation introduces no new errors, so only the dynamic meaning need be considered. Even so, the specification tends to be more complex: the instruction set contains jump instructions, and the semantics of jumps are difficult to specify. Aida is typical of a pruned instruction set language.

1.3   From semantics to a compiler

The compiler's job is to translate each high level construct, such as

> **if** $< test\_expr >$ **then** $< then\_cmd >$ **else** $< else\_cmd >$

into a corresponding target language template, such as

```
        <test_expr translation>
        JUMP label1
        <then_cmd translation>
        GOTO label2
label1:
        <else_cmd translation>
label2:
```

where the program fragments in angle brackets are similarly translated, recursively. Specifying the compiler from a source to a target language consists of defining an operational semantics, in the form of a target language template for each source language construct. An obvious question arises: how can one have any confidence that these are the *correct* target language templates? For example, how can one have any confidence that the **if** statement above and its compiled translation have the same meaning?

It is possible to answer this question. Given the denotational semantics of the target language, it is possible to *calculate* the meaning of the template in the target language. This can be compared with the meaning of the corresponding high level fragment, and be shown to be the same (see Chapter 13). Proving that the correct templates have been specified reduces to calculating the meaning of every template, and showing it to be the same as the meaning of the source language construct. Notice that this approach provides a *structuring* mechanism for the proof process. Arguments are advanced on a construct-by-construct basis, using structural induction over the source language. The complete proof is constructed by working through the syntax tree of the language, until all constructs have a suitable argument supporting them; this then completes the argument in support of the compiler specification as a whole. Hence the complete proof is composed, using a divide-and-conquer strategy, from a number of smaller, independent subproofs. This structure makes the total proof much more tractable, and more understandable, than would a single monolithic approach. Structure is indispensable when doing a large proof.

1.4   Executable specification language—Prolog

There are various notations available for writing denotational semantics, including the conventional mathematical notation, convenient for reasoning about the correctness of the compiler templates.

If the denotational semantics specification is translated into an executable language, then executing it provides an *interpreter* for the specified language. This interpreter can, if desired, be used as a *validation tool* for checking that the formal mathematical specification defines a language with the appropriate informally expected behaviour.

It is possible, given a denotational semantics in some abstract notation, to translate it into an imperative language, such as Pascal, in order to produce an interpreter. However, because the style of such a language is so far removed from the style of the denotational specification, the mapping from the specification to the resulting implementation is very complex. Such a complex mapping process is in itself potentially error-prone, and does not produce an interpreter that is a transparently correct implementation of its specification. Furthermore, the correspondence between it and the operational semantics needed for the associated *compiler* is not obvious.

A better approach is to translate the denotational semantics into a much higher level programming language, one that closely matches the style of specification. This drastically reduces the complexity of the translation step, enabling the semantics to be written clearly and abstractly, in order to provide a transparently correct implementation of the interpreter. A functional language or logic language seems a natural choice.

Prolog is used here as the executable specification language for the Tosca compiler; there is a natural mapping from the denotational semantics into Prolog clauses. Also, an important consideration for a high integrity compiler that must be seen to be correct, Prolog is a mature language that is well supported and has a large user community. The use of an unproven Prolog system, however, is a weak link in the development process, as is the use of an unproven operating system and unproven hardware. The various sources of errors are discussed more fully in Chapter 15. What is being described here is how to strengthen one of the currently weakest links in the process.

Prolog does have some features whose misuse could obscure the mapping from specification to compiler. The most notorious of these is the 'cut' (written !). Cuts are used to increase execution efficiency by controlling backtracking and execution order, and are considered by some as the Prolog equivalent of the 'goto'. However, some cuts are worse than others. Prolog has two semantics: a simple declarative semantics, which is independent of the order in which clauses and goals are written, and is used to reason about the meaning of a program, and a more complex operational semantics, which defines an execution order, and says what happens when a program is executed. It is important for understandability that these two semantics give a program the same meaning. So-called 'green' cuts do maintain this property. 'Red' cuts, on the other hand, result in the two meanings being different. The operational one is (presumably) the desired meaning, but the simpler declarative reading can no longer be used to determine what this meaning is. In order to understand the program it becomes necessary, for example, to know in what order goals are evaluated.

It is important that the Prolog form of a high integrity compiler has the same declarative reading (equivalent to the specification) as operational reading (which provides the executable compiler). So the Prolog must be written in a disciplined manner, eschewing red cuts and other tricks, if necessary sacrificing speed of execution.

1.5 Further reading

Early work on compiler correctness includes [McCarthy and Painter 1966], [Milner and Weyhrauch 1972], [Morris 1973], [Cohn 1979], [Polak 1981]. Work on automatically generating a compiler from a definition of the language's semantics includes [Mosses 1975], [Paulson 1981], [Paulson 1982], [Wand 1984], [Lee 1989] and [Tofte 1990]. The Esprit supported ProCoS (Provably Correct Systems) project has investigated an algebraic approach to correct compilation, described in [Hoare 1991].

Many seminal papers on the axiomatic style of defining programming languages can be found in [Hoare and Jones 1989]. [Tennent 1991] describes the connection between denotational, operational and axiomatic semantics.

For an introduction to denotational semantics, see, for example [Gordon 1979], [Allison 1986] and [Schmidt 1988]. The classic description is [Stoy 1977]. Various static semantic analyses are described in [Cousot and Cousot 1977], [Bramson 1984] and [Bergeretti and Carré 1985]. [Allison 1986] gives examples of translating denotational semantics definitions into Pascal to provide an interpreter. [Stepney and Lord 1987] describes an example of executing a specification in order to validate it.

The formal specification of Modula-2 can be found in [Andrews *et al.* 1991]. [Carré 1989] discusses criteria for including features in high integrity languages.

Anyone still not convinced that natural language is totally unsuitable for rigorously and unambiguously specifying even a simple problem should read [Meyer 1985]. This is an entertaining account of the repeated failed attempts to use English to specify a seemingly trivial problem, and how formalism can help.

There are many good books introducing Prolog. See, for example [Sterling and Shapiro 1986] and [Clocksin and Mellish 1987]. The former discusses green and red cuts.

Chapter 2

Specifying a Language— by Example

2.1 Introduction

This chapter briefly explains the steps involved in the denotational specification of a programming language, using a trivial example language, Turandot ('Tiny, Unfinished, Restricted, and Overly Terse'). This illustrative example is by no means complete; the explanation is intended solely to give an overview of the process of specifying and proving a compiler, in order to motivate the larger complete specifications and proofs in the later chapters.

The denotational semantics definition of a sizable programming language requires the use of a branch of mathematics known as *domain theory*. However, for the simple languages described below, the extra capability, and consequent complexity, provided by domains is not necessary. Set theory provides a sufficient basis for the specifications, and, since it is conceptually simpler, its use clarifies some of the later discussions.

It is necessary to use some particular notation to write a denotational semantics specification. Many programming language specifications introduce their notation for domains in a somewhat *ad hoc* manner; using the simpler set-based approach has the advantage that the well-defined formal specification language Z can be used as the specification notation. Section 2.6 describes a small liberty taken with the syntax of Z that helps improve the clarity of programming language specifications.

Note: in this chapter some of the syntactic categories are decorated with numerical subscripts. These decorations are purely a technical device to distinguish the tutorial definitions from each other and from the later 'true' definitions of Tosca and Aida; they have no further significance.

2.2 Syntax

The first step in specifying a language is a specification of its *syntax*. Such a specification gives rules for well-formed 'sentences' in the language. An example of a badly formed, or syntactically incorrect, English sentence is Douglas Hofstadter's example; *This sentence no verb.*

Traditionally, a programming language's syntax is defined concretely, in terms of well-formed strings of characters. A program text consists of such a string, which first has to be lexically analyzed into a sequence of tokens (keywords, identifiers, and so on), then these tokens have to be parsed into a tree structure or *abstract syntax*. However, lexing and parsing are solved problems, discussed at great length in many classic texts, and so are not addressed yet again here. The specification of the semantics is clearer if it is given directly in terms of the abstract syntax, rather than in concrete terms of strings, which can become cluttered with disambiguation mechanisms like parentheses, keywords, and operator precedence rules. This sort of separation of concerns also allows the concrete syntax to be changed without needing to change the abstract syntax, the semantics definitions or the correctness proofs.

2.2.1 Structure of a syntax specification

Syntax can be defined using three classes of construct: compounds, lists and selection.

A *compound* has a fixed number of components, usually of different types. Compounds can be modelled abstractly in Z using a Cartesian product of the components. For example, a choice command consisting of a test expression, and two branch commands, and an assignment command consisting of an identifier and an expression, can be defined as

$$Choice == EXPR_0 \times CMD_0 \times CMD_0$$
$$Assign == NAME_0 \times EXPR_0$$

The symbol '$==$' is Z's *abbreviation definition*, a way of providing a meaningful name for a more complicated expression. The name can be used to stand for the expression anywhere in the specification.

A *list* has an arbitrary number of components of the same type. Lists are modelled in Z using a sequence. For example, a list of commands, and a list of declarations, can be defined as

$$CMDLIST_0 == \text{seq}_1 CMD_0$$
$$DECLLIST_0 == \text{seq } DECL_0$$

This says that a command list is a non-empty sequence of commands, and a declaration list is a possibly empty sequence of declarations. A block command, consisting of a list of declarations and commands, can be defined using a compound whose components are lists:

$$Block == DECLLIST_0 \times CMDLIST_0$$

A *selection* comprises a set of possible constructs of a particular type. Selections can be modelled in Z using its free type (disjoint union) definition. For example, defining a command to be a choice or an assignment or a block:

$$CMD_0 ::= choice_0 \langle\!\langle Choice \rangle\!\rangle$$
$$|\quad assign_0 \langle\!\langle Assign \rangle\!\rangle$$
$$|\quad block_0 \langle\!\langle Block \rangle\!\rangle$$

The free type notation is explained in Appendix C.

A syntax specification can be shortened by including the compounds and lists directly in the selections. The partial example above can be written more succinctly as

$$CMD_0 ::= choice_0 \langle\!\langle EXPR_0 \times CMD_0 \times CMD_0 \rangle\!\rangle$$
$$|\quad assign_0 \langle\!\langle NAME_0 \times EXPR_0 \rangle\!\rangle$$
$$|\quad block_0 \langle\!\langle seq\ DECL_0 \times seq_1\ CMD_0 \rangle\!\rangle$$

2.2.2   Turandot's abstract syntax

Turandot has only three types of construct: binary operators, expressions, and commands.

$$OP_1 ::= plus$$
$$|\quad lessThan$$
$$|\quad equalTo$$
$$|\quad \ldots$$

This is a typical non-recursive free type definition, and can be thought of as a simple 'enumerated type', listing all Turandot's binary operators, which include comparison and arithmetic operators.

Turandot's expression syntax is

$$EXPR_1 ::= number \langle\!\langle \mathbb{Z} \rangle\!\rangle$$
$$|\quad variable \langle\!\langle NAME_1 \rangle\!\rangle$$
$$|\quad negate \langle\!\langle EXPR_1 \rangle\!\rangle$$
$$|\quad operation \langle\!\langle EXPR_1 \times OP_1 \times EXPR_1 \rangle\!\rangle$$

This is a typical recursive free type definition. It has two base cases (an expression can be an integer or a variable name) and two recursive cases (a new expression can be formed from another by negating it, or from two others by combining them with a binary operator). Note that all values in Turandot are just numbers; the value 1 is also used to indicate 'true' and 0 to indicate 'false'.

Turandot's command syntax is

$$CMD_1 ::= skip$$
$$| \quad assign \langle\!\langle NAME_1 \times EXPR_1 \rangle\!\rangle$$
$$| \quad choice \langle\!\langle EXPR_1 \times CMD_1 \times CMD_1 \rangle\!\rangle$$
$$| \quad compose \langle\!\langle CMD_1 \times CMD_1 \rangle\!\rangle$$

Again, this is a recursive definition. The base cases are the *skip* command, and the assignment command, which assigns the value of an expression to a variable. The others build new commands from smaller commands: *choice* chooses between two commands based on the value of expression, and *compose* composes two commands.

2.2.3 Turandot's concrete syntax

It is quite possible to specify a variety of concrete syntaxes from a single abstract syntax. For example, the concrete choice command can easily be defined as any one of the following:

- if test then then_branch else else_branch

- if test then then_branch else else_branch endif

- test ? then_branch : else_branch

- then_branch ◁ test ▷ else_branch

Using the abstract syntax when specifying the semantics literally abstracts away from these unimportant typographical details. Unimportant for specifying the semantics, that is. Concrete syntax *is* important for making a particular language usable, and so should be chosen with care.

A concrete syntax can be specified by mapping each construct in the abstract syntax to a string of characters. For example, a concrete syntax for Turandot's commands can be specified by

$$\text{CMD} \langle\!| \_ |\!\rangle : CMD_1 \longrightarrow String$$

$$\forall \xi : NAME_1; \; \epsilon : EXPR_1; \; \gamma_1, \gamma_2 : CMD_1 \; \bullet$$

$$\text{CMD} \langle\!| \, skip \, |\!\rangle = \text{``skip''}$$

$$\wedge \; \text{CMD} \langle\!| \, assign(\xi, \epsilon) \, |\!\rangle = \text{NAME} \langle\!| \, \xi \, |\!\rangle \; \frown \; \text{``:=''} \; \frown \; \text{EXPR} \langle\!| \, \epsilon \, |\!\rangle$$

$$\wedge \; \text{CMD} \langle\!| \, choice(\epsilon, \gamma_1, \gamma_2) \, |\!\rangle =$$
$$\text{``if''} \; \frown \; \text{EXPR} \langle\!| \, \epsilon \, |\!\rangle \; \frown \; \text{``then''} \; \frown \; \text{CMD} \langle\!| \, \gamma_1 \, |\!\rangle$$
$$\frown \text{``else''} \; \frown \; \text{CMD} \langle\!| \, \gamma_2 \, |\!\rangle \; \frown \; \text{``endif''}$$

$$\wedge \; \text{CMD} \langle\!| \, compose(\gamma_1, \gamma_2) \, |\!\rangle = \text{CMD} \langle\!| \, \gamma_2 \, |\!\rangle \; \frown \; \text{``;''} \; \frown \; \text{CMD} \langle\!| \, \gamma_1 \, |\!\rangle$$

This specifies a function called CMD (it assumes that functions called NAME and EXPR are also specified) using a Z axiomatic definition. The part above the horizontal line declares the signature of the function: CMD maps elements of the syntactic category CMD_1 to strings. The parts below the line provide the definition of the function, by structural induction over the structure of the language syntax. There is one term for each sort of command in the abstract syntax, and the definition is recursive in terms of the translation of subcomponents of a particular command. The infix operator '⌢' is Z's *concatenation* operator for joining sequences.

Aside—a more thorough definition of concrete syntax would be broken down into steps: defining a mapping from abstract syntax to sequences of tokens, defining the character strings used to represent tokens, and defining how tokens may be separated by white space (spaces, tabs and newlines) and comment strings. The simpler treatment given here is adequate for my purpose: defining a concrete syntax in which to write example Tosca programs.

2.3   Semantics

In the specification of Turandot's syntax, the 'meaning' of each construct is given informally in natural language, if at all. It relies heavily on our intuitive understanding of phrases such as "assigns the value of an expression to a variable". Problems can arise if the intuition of language designer, implementor and user differ, or if areas of ambiguity are resolved differently. What if the expression refers to some variable that has not been assigned a value? Should some default value be assumed, and if so, what value, or should this be an error? In a typed language (like Tosca, but unlike Turandot), what if the expression and variable have a different type? Should the expression's type be silently coerced to that of the variable, or should this be an error?

The denotational approach to providing a mathematical specification is to define *meaning functions*, which map syntactic constructs to what they denote: mathematical values. Appeals to intuition and common understanding can be replaced by mathematical manipulations of these formal definitions.

2.3.1   A mathematical model of Turandot

Different kinds of mathematical model are appropriate for different classes of programming languages. A statement in a declarative language reports a fact about the world, for example, "the cat is on the mat". Reporting a fact does not change the state of the world. A statement in an imperative language, on the other hand, can change the state of the world, for example, "I name this ship the *Blaise Pascal*". An appropriate model for an imperative language (the kind considered in this book) is a state, and a set of state transition functions.

An appropriate state for Turandot is a mapping from variables' names to their current values:

$$State_1 == NAME_1 \nrightarrow \mathbb{Z}$$

$State_1$ is the set of all functions that map names to integers. A particular function σ_1 of type $State_1$ can be declared as $\sigma_1 : State_1$.

Z models functions as sets of pairs; for state functions of the type given above, the first element of each pair is a name, the second is an integer. A particular state σ_1, which has two variables, x with the value 3, and y with the value 9, is

$$\sigma_1 = \{x \mapsto 3, y \mapsto 9\}$$

The *maplet* notation $x \mapsto 3$, an alternative form of the more conventional notation for a pair $(x, 3)$, highlights the 'mapping' nature of the term.

In Z, functions are *partial*: a state need map only some names to values, not all of them. The domain of a state is the set of all those names that have values defined, so $\operatorname{dom}\sigma_1 = \{x, y\}$. The range is the set of all those values that are mapped to, so $\operatorname{ran}\sigma_1 = \{1, 9\}$. If some function was required to be *total*, to map *every* name to a value, it would be declared using an undecorated arrow:

$$\mid \sigma_t : NAME_1 \longrightarrow \mathbb{Z}$$

In this case, $\operatorname{dom}\sigma_t = NAME_1$.

Because a state is a function, applying it to a variable yields the value of that variable: $\sigma_1 x = 3$.

The simplest state change is to update the value of a single variable. The Z way to do this is by *overriding* the value, using the '$\oplus$' operator: for values in the domain of σ_b the function $\sigma_a \oplus \sigma_b$ agrees with σ_b, and elsewhere it agrees with σ_a.

Thus, $\sigma \oplus \{a \mapsto v\}$ produces a new state. If a was in the old state, its value in the new state is changed to v; if it was not, it is added to the new state. So

$$\sigma_1 \oplus \{x \mapsto 1\} = \{x \mapsto 1, y \mapsto 9\}$$
$$\sigma_1 \oplus \{z \mapsto 1\} = \{x \mapsto 3, y \mapsto 9, z \mapsto 1\}$$

In Turandot, each binary operator denotes the corresponding mathematical operator, an expression denotes a value in the context of a state, and a command denotes a state transition function. (Tosca requires a slightly more elaborate model, with an environment as well as a state, as discussed in Chapter 7.)

2.3.2 The meaning of Turandot's binary operators

Let's take Turandot's operators first. Each operator denotes a corresponding mathematical operator. A mathematical binary operator is a function that maps two numbers, its arguments, to another number, the result. Hence it has the type

$\mathbb{Z} \times \mathbb{Z} \nrightarrow \mathbb{Z}$. The operator meaning function that maps syntactic operators onto the corresponding mathematical function is specified as

$$\mathcal{D}\mathcal{O}\mathcal{P}[\![\_]\!] : OP_1 \longrightarrow \mathbb{Z} \times \mathbb{Z} \nrightarrow \mathbb{Z}$$

$$\forall\, x, y : \mathbb{Z} \bullet$$

$$\mathcal{D}\mathcal{O}\mathcal{P}[\![plus]\!](x, y) = x + y$$

$$\wedge\, \mathcal{D}\mathcal{O}\mathcal{P}[\![less\,Than]\!](x, y) = \textbf{if } x < y \textbf{ then } 1 \textbf{ else } 0$$

The function is specified for all Turandot's binary operators by specifying it for each branch of the OP_1 free type definition. Remember that Turandot uses the value 1 for 'true' and 0 for 'false'.

2.3.3   The meaning of Turandot's expressions

An expression denotes a value; what value is denoted can depend on the values of the variables in the current state. The expression meaning function maps an expression to the value it denotes in the context of a state

$$\mathcal{D}\mathcal{E}\mathcal{X}\mathcal{P}\mathcal{R}[\![\_]\!] : EXPR_1 \longrightarrow State_1 \nrightarrow \mathbb{Z}$$

$$\forall\, \chi : \mathbb{Z};\, \xi : NAME_1;\, \epsilon, \epsilon_1, \epsilon_2 : EXPR_1;\, \omega : OP_1;\, \sigma : State_1 \bullet$$

$$\mathcal{D}\mathcal{E}\mathcal{X}\mathcal{P}\mathcal{R}[\![number\ \chi]\!]\sigma = \chi$$

$$\wedge\, \mathcal{D}\mathcal{E}\mathcal{X}\mathcal{P}\mathcal{R}[\![variable\ \xi]\!]\sigma = \sigma\xi$$

$$\wedge\, \mathcal{D}\mathcal{E}\mathcal{X}\mathcal{P}\mathcal{R}[\![negate\ \epsilon]\!]\sigma = -(\mathcal{D}\mathcal{E}\mathcal{X}\mathcal{P}\mathcal{R}[\![\epsilon]\!]\sigma)$$

$$\wedge\, \mathcal{D}\mathcal{E}\mathcal{X}\mathcal{P}\mathcal{R}[\![operation(\epsilon_1, \omega, \epsilon_2)]\!]\sigma =$$
$$\mathcal{D}\mathcal{O}\mathcal{P}[\![\omega]\!](\mathcal{D}\mathcal{E}\mathcal{X}\mathcal{P}\mathcal{R}[\![\epsilon_1]\!]\sigma, \mathcal{D}\mathcal{E}\mathcal{X}\mathcal{P}\mathcal{R}[\![\epsilon_2]\!]\sigma)$$

The semantic definition follows the recursive structure of the $EXPR_1$ abstract syntax. The meaning of an expression consisting of a number is just that number, irrespective of the state. The meaning of an expression consisting of a variable name is the value that name denotes in the current state, found by applying the state function σ to the name. (A variable that has not previously been assigned a value is not in the domain of the state function, and the result of applying the state function is undefined. A resolution of this problem is discussed below, in section 2.4.) The meaning of a *negate* expression is the mathematical negation of the meaning of the subexpression. The meaning of an *operation* expression is found by using the meaning of the operator to combine the meanings of the subexpressions.

2.3.4   The meaning of Turandot's commands

A command denotes a state transition. Hence, the command meaning function
maps a command to a state transition function:

$$\mathcal{D}\mathit{C}\mathit{MD}[\![\_]\!] : CMD_1 \longrightarrow State_1 \rightarrow\!\!\!\rightarrow State_1$$

$$\forall\, \xi : NAME_1;\ \epsilon : EXPR_1;\ \gamma_1, \gamma_2 : CMD_1;\ \sigma : State_1 \bullet$$

$$\mathcal{D}\mathit{C}\mathit{MD}[\![skip]\!]\sigma = \sigma$$

$$\wedge\ \mathcal{D}\mathit{C}\mathit{MD}[\![assign(\xi, \epsilon)]\!]\sigma = \sigma \oplus \{\xi \mapsto \mathcal{D}\mathit{E}\mathit{X}\mathit{P}\mathit{R}[\![\epsilon]\!]\sigma\}$$

$$\wedge\ \mathcal{D}\mathit{C}\mathit{MD}[\![choice(\epsilon, \gamma_1, \gamma_2)]\!]\sigma =$$
$$\quad \text{if } \mathcal{D}\mathit{E}\mathit{X}\mathit{P}\mathit{R}[\![\epsilon]\!]\sigma = 1 \text{ then } \mathcal{D}\mathit{C}\mathit{MD}[\![\gamma_1]\!]\sigma \text{ else } \mathcal{D}\mathit{C}\mathit{MD}[\![\gamma_2]\!]\sigma$$

$$\wedge\ \mathcal{D}\mathit{C}\mathit{MD}[\![compose(\gamma_1, \gamma_2)]\!]\sigma = (\mathcal{D}\mathit{C}\mathit{MD}[\![\gamma_2]\!] \circ \mathcal{D}\mathit{C}\mathit{MD}[\![\gamma_1]\!])\sigma$$

The semantic definition follows the recursive structure of the CMD_1 abstract syntax. *skip* is the identity function; it leaves the state unchanged. *assign* changes the value of one component of the state; the new state maps the relevant name to its new value. *choice* chooses between the two commands based on the value of the expression (remember that the value 1 is used to indicate 'true'). Composing commands composes the state transition functions that they denote.

Notice that the words in the paragraph accompanying the mathematical specification of the semantics are very similar to the words that accompanied the syntax specification. But now they have a mathematical meaning, too. This mathematical meaning can be referred to in case of ambiguity, and can be formally manipulated if necessary, to discover the precise meaning of complex constructs.

2.4   Static semantics

Some sentences in a language can be syntactically correct, but meaningless. For example, in English, Chomsky's famous sentence *Colourless green ideas sleep furiously* is syntactically well-formed, but does not mean anything. In many programming languages, a statement like x := 1 + true might be parsed according to the syntax rules, but might have no meaning, because numbers cannot be added to booleans. In the denotational approach, rules for meaningless constructs can be formalized by providing various static semantics. These look similar to the specifications above, but instead of saying an expression means something like '4', say an expression means 'badly typed'.

We can do this because the interpretation of the meaning of a piece of syntax is up to the specifier, and so we can choose alternative meaning functions for our different purposes. The meaning defined above specifies Turandot's dynamic semantics, the meaning we would expect to be associated with the executing program. But we can associate other, non-standard, meanings, too. For example, we

can choose the state to be those names that have been assigned a value, ignoring what that value might be. Call this the s-state:

$$SState_1 == \mathbb{P}\ NAME_1$$

$\mathbb{P}$ is Z's *power set* constructor, so any state of type $SState_1$ has the type 'set of $NAME_1$'.

Let's define a flag to determine whether or not variables are being used before they are assigned a value:

$$SET_1 ::= yes \mid no$$

Then we can specify an alternative meaning function for expressions, one that maps them to *yes* or *no*, to indicate whether the variables to which they refer have been properly assigned a value or not:

$$\mathcal{S}_{\mathcal{E}\mathcal{X}\mathcal{P}\mathcal{R}}[\![\_]\!] : EXPR_1 \longrightarrow SState_1 \nrightarrow SET_1$$

$\forall \chi : \mathbf{Z};\ \xi : NAME_1;\ \epsilon, \epsilon_1, \epsilon_2 : EXPR_1;\ \omega : OP_1;\ \sigma : SState_1 \bullet$

$\quad \mathcal{S}_{\mathcal{E}\mathcal{X}\mathcal{P}\mathcal{R}}[\![number\ \chi]\!]\sigma = yes$

$\quad \wedge\ \mathcal{S}_{\mathcal{E}\mathcal{X}\mathcal{P}\mathcal{R}}[\![variable\ \xi]\!]\sigma = \mathbf{if}\ \xi \in \sigma\ \mathbf{then}\ yes\ \mathbf{else}\ no$

$\quad \wedge\ \mathcal{S}_{\mathcal{E}\mathcal{X}\mathcal{P}\mathcal{R}}[\![negate\ \epsilon]\!]\sigma = \mathcal{S}_{\mathcal{E}\mathcal{X}\mathcal{P}\mathcal{R}}[\![\epsilon]\!]\sigma$

$\quad \wedge\ \mathcal{S}_{\mathcal{E}\mathcal{X}\mathcal{P}\mathcal{R}}[\![operation(\epsilon_1, \omega, \epsilon_2)]\!]\sigma =$
$\qquad \mathbf{if}\ \mathcal{S}_{\mathcal{E}\mathcal{X}\mathcal{P}\mathcal{R}}[\![\epsilon_1]\!]\sigma = yes \wedge \mathcal{S}_{\mathcal{E}\mathcal{X}\mathcal{P}\mathcal{R}}[\![\epsilon_2]\!]\sigma = yes\ \mathbf{then}\ yes\ \mathbf{else}\ no$

This defines a different meaning for Turandot's expressions: let's call it the s-meaning. So the s-meaning of an expression consisting of a number is always *yes*, irrespective of the s-state. The s-meaning of an expression consisting of a variable name is *yes* if and only if that name is in the current s-state (as we will see in the definition of $\mathcal{S}_{\mathcal{C}\mathcal{M}\mathcal{D}}[\![\_]\!]$, the assignment statement adds names to the state). The s-meaning of a *negate* expression is the same as the s-meaning of the subexpression. The s-meaning of an operation expression is *yes* if and only if the s-meanings of both subexpressions are *yes*.

The s-meaning of a command is an s-state transition:

$$\mathcal{S}_{\mathcal{C}\mathcal{M}\mathcal{D}}[\![\_]\!] : CMD_1 \longrightarrow SState_1 \nrightarrow SState_1$$

$\forall \xi : NAME_1;\ \epsilon : EXPR_1;\ \gamma_1, \gamma_2 : CMD_1;\ \sigma : SState_1 \bullet$

$\quad \mathcal{S}_{\mathcal{C}\mathcal{M}\mathcal{D}}[\![skip]\!]\sigma = \sigma$

$\quad \wedge\ \mathcal{S}_{\mathcal{C}\mathcal{M}\mathcal{D}}[\![assign(\xi, \epsilon)]\!]\sigma = \sigma \cup \{\xi\}$

$\quad \wedge\ \mathcal{S}_{\mathcal{C}\mathcal{M}\mathcal{D}}[\![choice(\epsilon, \gamma_1, \gamma_2)]\!]\sigma = \mathcal{S}_{\mathcal{C}\mathcal{M}\mathcal{D}}[\![\gamma_1]\!]\sigma \cap \mathcal{S}_{\mathcal{C}\mathcal{M}\mathcal{D}}[\![\gamma_2]\!]\sigma$

$\quad \wedge\ \mathcal{S}_{\mathcal{C}\mathcal{M}\mathcal{D}}[\![compose(\gamma_1, \gamma_2)]\!]\sigma = (\mathcal{S}_{\mathcal{C}\mathcal{M}\mathcal{D}}[\![\gamma_2]\!] \circ \mathcal{S}_{\mathcal{C}\mathcal{M}\mathcal{D}}[\![\gamma_1]\!])\sigma$

Notice that the only time a new name is added to the environment is by the *assign* meaning function. The *choice* s-meaning takes the intersection of the states for each branch: a new variable must be assigned a value in both branches before it is considered to be assigned by the whole command.

Such a specification can be used to provide a static check of whether variables are referenced before they are assigned a value. It is called static, because it can be done without actually executing the program (for example, at compile time). Hence such a non-standard interpretation of the meaning of a program is called *static semantics*. Various alternative meanings can be defined to provide various different static semantics. This is described in much more detail in Chapter 8. Tosca has three different static semantics in addition to its dynamic semantics.

2.5 Operational semantics

The target language itself can be specified in the same manner. For example, the target language's syntax may include instructions such as

$$INSTR_1 ::= store \langle\!\langle NAME_1 \rangle\!\rangle$$
$$| \quad jump \langle\!\langle LABEL_1 \rangle\!\rangle$$
$$| \quad goto \langle\!\langle LABEL_1 \rangle\!\rangle$$
$$| \quad label \langle\!\langle LABEL_1 \rangle\!\rangle$$

The informal meanings of these instructions are as follows: *store* stores the value currently in the accumulator (a special location) in the location corresponding to a name; *jump* jumps to its label if the value in the accumulator is 'false', otherwise it does nothing; *goto* jumps unconditionally to its label. Other instructions are also needed, to load values and to combine and compare values. These meanings need to be defined formally, too, by specifying some appropriate meaning function $\mathcal{INSTR}[\![\_]\!]$, that maps syntactic instructions to mathematical values. These further definitions are omitted here for brevity. See Chapter 10 for the specification of Aida, the 'real' target language.

The operational semantics (that is, the specification of the translations from source to target language) is defined in a similar manner. However, the 'operational meaning' function is a purely syntactic definition: it maps source language constructs not to mathematical values, but to sequences of target language instructions.

For example, the definition of the translation of Turandot's commands into the target language might look something like

$\mathcal{O}_{CMD}\langle\!\langle\,\_\,\rangle\!\rangle : CMD_1 \longrightarrow \text{seq } INSTR_1$

$\forall \xi : NAME_1;\ \epsilon : EXPR_1;\ \gamma, \gamma_1, \gamma_2 : CMD_1 \bullet$

$\quad \mathcal{O}_{CMD}\langle\!\langle\, skip\,\rangle\!\rangle = \langle\,\rangle$

$\quad \wedge\ \mathcal{O}_{CMD}\langle\!\langle\, assign(\xi, \epsilon)\,\rangle\!\rangle = \mathcal{O}_{EXPR}\langle\!\langle\,\epsilon\,\rangle\!\rangle \frown \langle\, store\ \xi\,\rangle$

$\quad \wedge\ \mathcal{O}_{CMD}\langle\!\langle\, choice(\epsilon, \gamma_1, \gamma_2)\,\rangle\!\rangle =$
$\qquad\qquad \mathcal{O}_{EXPR}\langle\!\langle\,\epsilon\,\rangle\!\rangle \frown \langle\, jump\ \phi_1\,\rangle \frown \mathcal{O}_{CMD}\langle\!\langle\,\gamma_1\,\rangle\!\rangle$
$\qquad\qquad \frown \langle\, goto\ \phi_2, label\ \phi_1\,\rangle \frown \mathcal{O}_{CMD}\langle\!\langle\,\gamma_2\,\rangle\!\rangle \frown \langle\, label\ \phi_2\,\rangle$

$\quad \wedge\ \mathcal{O}_{CMD}\langle\!\langle\, compose(\gamma_1, \gamma_2)\,\rangle\!\rangle = \mathcal{O}_{CMD}\langle\!\langle\,\gamma_1\,\rangle\!\rangle \frown \mathcal{O}_{CMD}\langle\!\langle\,\gamma_2\,\rangle\!\rangle$

skip does nothing, so translates to an empty sequence of instructions. The expression in an *assign* is translated to the appropriate sequence of instructions (the definition of $\mathcal{O}_{EXPR}\langle\!\langle\,\_\,\rangle\!\rangle$ is not given), and a *store* instruction is concatenated, in order to store the result of the expression at the relevant location. For a *choice* command, the expression is translated, then a *jump on false* instruction is added to jump to the *false* branch. This is followed by a translation of the *true* branch, and an unconditional *goto*, to jump over the *false* branch to the end. Then we get the *false* branch label, and the translation of the *false* branch itself. Finally, the *end* label is added. The instruction list for a *compose* command simply consists of the concatenation of the instruction lists of the composed commands.

This example has been simplified for brevity. The real definition is more involved: it needs to maintain a 'translation environment' to hold the mapping from variables to their storage locations, and to note what labels have been allocated. This is described in detail in Chapter 11. The overview here is merely intended to give a flavour, to motivate future definitions.

This translation to sequences of instructions is purely syntactic. However, given the denotational specification of the target language semantics, as a specification of a meaning function $INSTR[\![\_]\!]$, it is possible to calculate the meaning of this translated sequence of instructions. The proof of correctness becomes a proof that the meaning of a Turandot construct is the same as the meaning of the sequence of instructions that results from translating it:

$$\gamma : CMD_1 \vdash \mathcal{D}_{CMD}[\![\gamma]\!] = INSTR[\![\mathcal{O}_{CMD}\langle\!\langle\,\gamma\,\rangle\!\rangle]\!]$$

The Tosca compiler specification is proved correct in Chapter 13.

2.6   A liberty with Z

As illustrated above, Z is used to specify the various languages and their semantics. However, in order to minimize clutter in the definitions, a small liberty is taken with its syntax when defining Tosca and Aida below.

The definitions of the semantics functions are quantified over all the variables appearing on the left-hand side of the equation. For example, the meaning of Turandot's commands is defined for all possible values of names, expressions, commands, and state variables:

$$\mathcal{D}_{CMD}[\![\_]\!] : CMD_1 \longrightarrow State_1 \rightarrowtail State_1$$

$$\forall \xi : NAME_1;\ \epsilon : EXPR_1;\ \gamma_1, \gamma_2 : CMD_1;\ \sigma : State_1 \bullet$$

$$\mathcal{D}_{CMD}[\![skip]\!]\sigma = \sigma$$

$$\wedge\ \mathcal{D}_{CMD}[\![assign(\xi, \epsilon)]\!]\sigma = \ldots$$

$$\wedge\ \mathcal{D}_{CMD}[\![choice(\epsilon, \gamma_1, \gamma_2)]\!]\sigma = \ldots$$

The continual occurrence of such quantifications tends to clutter the specification. So this is abbreviated, by omitting the declarations of all the arguments of the meaning functions (but not of any other functions), whose types can easily be deduced. You should assume an implicit quantification over all these arguments when reading a definition such as

$$\mathcal{D}_{CMD}[\![\_]\!] : CMD_1 \longrightarrow State_1 \rightarrowtail State_1$$

$$\mathcal{D}_{CMD}[\![skip]\!]\sigma = \sigma$$

$$\mathcal{D}_{CMD}[\![assign(\xi, \epsilon)]\!]\sigma = \ldots$$

$$\mathcal{D}_{CMD}[\![choice(\epsilon, \gamma_1, \gamma_2)]\!]\sigma = \ldots$$

To reduce any confusion this style of abbreviation might cause, the same symbols are consistently used to refer to things of the same type: this usage is summarized in Appendix D.

2.7 Distinguishing syntax from semantics

There is potential for confusion in distinguishing syntactic and semantic values, because some syntax is needed in order to write down the semantic value! For example, assume the value meaning function for Turandot values has been declared as

$$\mathcal{D}_{VAL}[\![\_]\!] : VALUE_1 \longrightarrow \mathbb{Z}$$

Then the meaning of a particular value might look something like $\mathcal{D}_{VAL}[\![42]\!] = 42$. At first sight, this looks rather odd. However, the explanation is straightforward. The digit sequence appearing on the left, inside the special double square brackets, is merely syntax (the value consisting of the character '4' followed by the character '2') whereas the one on the right is the corresponding mathematical *number* (forty two). The syntax can take a variety of forms, for example, *XLII* in Roman numerals, or 101010 in binary, but the mathematical value is the same in each case. The confusion occurs because the concrete syntaxes chosen to write programming language syntax and to write mathematical values can have strings in common.

It is possible to map syntactic numerals to mathematical numbers by defining a mapping from character strings to integers, *String* $\nrightarrow$ **Z**, but this is not very illuminating, since the integers tend themselves to be written as character strings, as above. So the syntactic and semantic domains corresponding to *VALUE*s, or to *NAME*s are not distinguished.

Because of this potential confusion, denotational semantics uses a typographical convention to distinguish syntactic arguments from mathematical values. Special double square brackets are used consistently to enclose syntactic arguments, for example, $\mathcal{M}[\![3]\!] = 3$. Although this convention is not standard Z, it is used here for functions that return mathematical values. Z uses this form of bracket for bags (multisets); there is no potential for confusion here since bags are not used in the following specifications. In addition, special triangular brackets are used to distinguish the syntactic arguments in functions that return *syntactic* results (the concrete syntax and translation functions), for example, $\mathcal{C}(\!|3|\!) =$ "**three**".

2.8   Further reading

See [Meyer 1990] and [Tennent 1991] for further discussion on the use of set theory and partial functions, instead of domain theory, in denotational semantics.

Descriptions of lexing and parsing can be found in many classic texts on compiler writing; see, for example, [Aho and Ullman 1977].

The Z language is described in [Spivey 1992]. [Hayes 1987] contains many case studies, using a slightly older variant of Z. There are many tutorial introductions to Z, for example, [Potter *et al.* 1991].

[Austin 1976] gives an account of how English can be considered an 'imperative' language.

Chapter 3

Using Prolog

3.1 Modelling Z in Prolog

The specification of the operational semantics, the translation from source to target language, specifies the compiler. A Prolog version of the specification directly gives a compiler. If we can find a clear translation from Z to Prolog, this strengthens one of the links in the chain of developing a high integrity compiler: the implementation follows directly from the formal specification.

Later sections in this chapter illustrate a direct translation of the specification of Turandot's commands into Prolog, and explains why this approach needs to be extended by a structuring mechanism: DCTGs. But first, let's see how Z sets are modelled in Prolog.

Z's sets are modelled as Prolog lists. So, for example, the Z set $\{1, 2, 3\}$ can be represented in Prolog as the list [1, 2, 3]. Z functions are also sets (of pairs); they too can be modelled as Prolog lists (of lists). So the state function $\{x \mapsto 3, y \mapsto 9\}$ can be represented in Prolog as [[x,3], [y,9]].

Various predicates to manipulate such lists representing sets, such as union and intersection, are supplied in many Prolog libraries. These have been written to ensure that the order inherent in a Prolog list is not significant when it is used to model a set. Other predicates to perform Z-specific operations must be specially written. For example, a definition to update a state with a (name, value) pair can be written as

```
updatestate(Name, Value, Pre, Post) :-
    setminus(Pre, [Name, _], Mid ),
    union(Mid, [ [Name, Value] ], Post).
```

(In Prolog, names beginning with capital letters are variables.) Here setminus(A, B, C) is a previously-written clause that obeys $A \setminus \{B\} = C$. If the clause is executed with A and B given, C will be instantiated to the set A with element B removed. `Mid` is instantiated to `Pre` with pairs whose first element is `Name` and second is anything (indicated by the underscore) removed.

Similarly, `union(A, B, C)` obeys $A \cup B = C$. If the clause is executed with `A` and `B` given, `C` will be instantiated to the set union of `A` and `B`. `Post` is instantiated with the union of `Mid` and the set containing the single pair `[Name, Value]` (that the second parameter is a set, not an element, explains the double pair of square brackets).

Prolog has the powerful feature that, if a different selection of parameters is provided, the remaining ones will be instantiated. So if `union` is provided with `B` and `C`, it will instantiate `A` so that $A \cup B = C$ is true. Powerful though this feature is, it is not exploited in the following definitions, where the parameters are always supplied in the 'forward' order corresponding to program execution.

3.2   Writing semantics in Prolog—a first attempt

With a suitable set of library definitions like those above, there is a straightforward translation from the semantics definitions in Z to ones in Prolog. (The rules for this translation in the case of Tosca are explained in Chapter 14.)

3.2.1   Dynamic semantics—an interpreter

Consider the Turandot example from Chapter 2. The specification of the dynamic semantics of Turandot's commands (section 2.3.4) can be written in Prolog as follows.

For commands, the Prolog form is

```
command(gamma, PreState, PostState) :-
    expression relating PreState and PostState
```

with one clause for each sort of command `gamma` in the abstract syntax definition. `PreState` is the state before the command, `PostState` is the state that results from executing the command.

skip is the easiest to translate, because the state is not changed:

```
command(skip, PreState, PostState) :-
    PreState = PostState.
```

This clause declares that, for a `skip` command, the `PreState` and `PostState` have the same value, whatever that value is. If the clause is being executed, as part of a Turandot interpreter, a value would be supplied for `PreState`, and `PostState` would become instantiated with the same value:

```
command(assign(Name,Expr), PreState, PostState) :-
    expr(Expr, PreState, Value),
    updatestate(Name, Value, PreState, PostState).
```

This clause declares that, for an `assign` command, `Value` is the value of `Expr` in the `PreState`, and that the `PreState` updated with `Name` and `Value` is the `PostState`. If the clause was being executed, the values for `Name`, `Expr` and `PreState` would be supplied, and used to instantiate `Value` and `PostState` appropriately.

The choice command becomes

```
command(choice(Expr,Then,Else), PreState, PostState) :-
    expr(Expr, PreState, Value),
    (   Value = 1,
        command(Then, PreState, PostState)
    ;
        Value = 0,
        command(Else, PreState, PostState)
    ).
```

`Value` is the value of `Expr` in the `PreState`. Depending on the value of `Value`, either the `PostState` is found using the `Then` parameter, or (as indicated by the Prolog ';') by using the `Else` parameter:

```
command(compose(Cmd1,Cmd2), PreState, PostState) :-
    command(Cmd1, PreState, MidState),
    command(Cmd2, MidState, PostState).
```

The `MidState` is found from the `PreState` using `Cmd1`, and is used along with `Cmd2` to produce the `PostState`.

If these clauses are read declaratively, they provide a Prolog specification of the dynamic semantics. If they are read operationally (or executed), they directly provide an interpreter for the language. To illustrate this dichotomy, the English explanation given above changes tone from declarative to operational as the example progresses.

3.2.2 Static semantics—a use checker

Turandot's static semantics can be written in Prolog in a very similar manner. The s-meaning of its commands (section 2.4) can be written as:

```
scommand(skip, PreSState, PostSState) :-
    PreSState = PostSState.

scommand(assign(Name,Expr), PreSState, PostSState) :-
    union(PreSState, [Name], PostSState).
```

```
scommand(choice(Expr,Then,Else), PreSState, PostSState) :-
    scommand(Then, PreSState, SStateThen),
    scommand(Else, PreSState, SStateElse),
    intersection(SStateThen, SStateElse, PostSState).

scommand(compose(Cmd1,Cmd2), PreSState, PostSState) :-
    scommand(Cmd1, PreSState, MidSState),
    scommand(Cmd2, MidSState, PostSState).
```

If these clauses are read declaratively, they provide a Prolog specification of the static semantics. If they are read operationally (or executed), they directly provide a static checker for the language.

3.2.3   Code templates—a compiler

The specification of Turandot's compiler can be written in Prolog in an analogous manner. Rather than defining a `PostState`, however, the Prolog translation of the commands (section 2.5) defines a list of target language instructions.

```
compile(skip, [ ]).

compile(assign(Name,Expr), [InstrList, store(Name)]) :-
    compile(Expr, InstrList).

compile(choice(Expr,Then,Else),
        [InstrExpr, jump(L1), InstrThen,
         goto(L2), label(L1), InstrElse, label(L2)]
) :-
    compile(Expr, InstrExpr),
    compile(Then, InstrThen),
    compile(Else, InstrElse).

compile(compose(Cmd1,Cmd2), [InstrList1, InstrList2]) :-
    compile(Cmd1, InstrList1),
    compile(Cmd2, InstrList2).
```

If these clauses are read declaratively, they provide a Prolog specification of the compiler translation. If they are read operationally (or executed), they directly provide the compiler.

3.3   Definite Clause Translation Grammars

Although this sort of translation into Prolog is quite straightforward for such a small example, it soon becomes unwieldy. For example, the syntax and semantics definitions of each construct are closely intertwined, and the syntax has to be repeated in each of the different semantics. A better structuring mechanism is needed for a full language with multiple semantics.

Many standard Prologs have a mechanism called Definite Clause Grammars (DCGs) built into them, to allow expressions such as

```
sentence --> noun_phrase, verb_phrase.
noun_phrase --> determiner, noun.
```

to be manipulated. These are automatically converted, by the Prolog system, into their standard Prolog equivalents with the necessary extra arguments:

```
sentence(S0,S) :- noun_phrase(S0,S1), verb_phrase(S1,S).
noun_phrase(S0,S) :- determiner(S0,S1), noun(S1,S).
```

This approach is suitable for defining syntax. For defining semantics as well, even more arguments are needed in the standard Prolog form. These can be provided automatically by using Definite Clause Translation Grammars (DCTGs).

DCTGs provide a general mechanism for grammar computations. The process of successfully parsing a particular input program causes a *parse tree* to be built. The semantic rules are attached to the non-terminal nodes of this parse tree, and used to define the semantic properties of a node in terms of the semantic properties of its subtrees.

Although not directly supported by the Prolog system in the same way as DCGs, Prolog operators and predicates can be defined to support the DCTG approach. These translate a program written in the DCTG form into an equivalent program in standard Prolog. As with the DCG form, this translation provides the various clauses with extra arguments, which are used to define how to build the annotated parse tree.

As a simple example, consider a possible DCTG definition for adding two expressions to produce an expression:

```
expr ::= expr^^Tree1, tPLUS, expr^^Tree2
<:>
value(V) ::-
    Tree1^^value(V1),
    Tree2^^value(V2),
    V is V1 + V2.
```

The first part of the term (before the <:>) defines the concrete syntax. In this example it says that an expression can be a subexpression, a 'plus' token and another subexpression. The subexpressions are labelled with their parse trees. The second part of the term defines the semantics of the composite expression in terms of its subexpressions. Here it says the value of the composite expression is the arithmetic sum of the values of the two subexpressions.

The translation into plain Prolog looks like:

```
expr( node( expr, [Tree1, Tree2],
        [value(V) ::-
            Tree1^^value(V1),
            Tree2^^value(V2),
            V is V1+V2]
        ),
    S0, S ) :-
        expr(Tree1, S0, S1),
        expr(Tree2, S1, S).
```

At first sight, this technique may look more complicated than using plain Prolog. It does, however, have the advantage of cleanly separating the syntax and semantics. Another important advantage of this approach is that a DCTG can be used to support multiple sets of different semantics attached to each node, as extra elements in the node list. So Turandot's *choice* command can be written using the DCTG formalism, including the code template (compiler), dynamic semantics (interpreter), and static semantics (static checker), as

```
command ::=
    tIF, expr^^E,
    tTHEN, command^^Cthen,
    tELSE, command^^Celse
<:>
    (static(PreSState, PostSState) ::-
        Cthen^^static(PreSState, SState1),
        Celse^^static(PreSState, SState2),
        intersection(SState1, SState2, PostSState)
    ),
    (dynamic(PreState, PostState) ::-
        E^^dynamic(PreState, Value),
        (   Value = 1,
            Cthen^^dynamic(PreState, PostState)
        ;
            Value = 0,
            Celse^^dynamic(PreState, PostState)
        )
    ),
    (compile( [InstrExpr, jump(L1), InstrThen,
        goto(L2), label(L1), InstrElse, label(L2)] )
    ::-
        E^^compile(InstrExpr),
        Cthen^^compile(InstrThen),
        Celse^^compile(InstrElse)
    ).
```

Notice that the non-standard static semantics `static` is attached to the DCTG nodes in the same manner as the dynamic semantics `dynamic` and the operational semantics `compile`. Other non-standard semantics for various other types of analyses can be incrementally added to each node in a similar, consistent manner. When executed, each provides a further static analysis checker.

Notice how, with the DCTG approach, the various semantics are in similar forms, and occur textually close together in the Prolog code. This is of great advantage in the process of demonstrating the correctness of the translation from the mathematical specification to the executable compiler.

Chapter 14 gives the DCTG form of the definition of Tosca's various static and dynamic semantics, and its operational semantics in terms of Aida.

3.4 Further reading

For a good introduction to Prolog, see, for example [Sterling and Shapiro 1986] and [Clocksin and Mellish 1987]. [Clocksin and Mellish 1987, Chapter 9] describes DCGs.

The style used in section 3.2 follows [Warren 1980].

DCTGs are described in [Abramson and Dahl 1989, Chapter 9], and the algorithm to convert a DCTG program to Prolog is listed in [Abramson and Dahl 1989, Appendix II.3]. The DCTG approach is the logic programming equivalent of Attribute Grammars [Knuth 1968]. The DCTG formalism does not distinguish between inherited and synthesized attributes, however, because Prolog's unification mechanism makes such a distinction largely unnecessary.

Part II

Tosca—the High Level Language

Chapter 4

Tosca—Syntax

4.1 Overview

The example hypothetical high level language, Tosca ('*Totally Okay* for *Safety Critical Applications*'), is the sort of simple imperative language subset often preferred for safety critical or high integrity applications, and is a typical 'first step' on the road to a trusted full high level language. Tosca has two types, integer and boolean, and all declarations are global. It has a **while-do** loop and an **if-then-else** choice. Other loops (for example, **repeat-until** or **for** loops) and choices (for example, **case**) have similar specifications, and their inclusion would merely add bulk, not new insight, to the discussion.

Tosca's semantics is specified in Chapter 8, on a construct-by-construct basis. Its abstract syntax is given in this chapter, along with the specification of a mapping to its concrete syntax.

4.2 Strings

Tosca's concrete syntax is produced from the abstract syntax by mapping the constructs to strings of characters. Tosca is given a rather conventional concrete syntax: free format (so white space, including new lines, can be placed between any tokens) with commands and declarations terminated (*not* separated) by semicolons:

$[CHAR]$

$String == \text{seq } CHAR$

Strings are enclosed in quotes, rather than Z's sequence brackets, for clarity:

"this is a string"

rather than

$$\langle \text{'t'}, \text{'h'}, \text{'i'}, \text{'s'}, \text{' '}, \text{'i'}, \text{'s'}, \text{' '}, \text{'a'}, \text{' '}, \text{'s'}, \text{'t'}, \text{'r'}, \text{'i'}, \text{'n'}, \text{'g'} \rangle$$

4.3   Names, types and values

Variable names (identifiers) are treated as a Z given set, so their internal structure is not defined further:

$[NAME]$

Tosca has two types: integer and boolean. A 'dummy' type is also needed for the purposes of specification; it is used only in the static type checking semantics, but has to be given here to complete the definition:

$$TYPE ::= \text{integer}$$
$$| \quad \text{boolean}$$
$$| \quad typeWrong$$

The concrete form of the Tosca types is just a simple keyword. The dummy type is never used in a program text, and so needs no concrete form:

$$\mathcal{C}_T \langle\!\!\langle\, \_ \,\rangle\!\!\rangle : TYPE \nrightarrow String$$

$$\mathcal{C}_T \langle\!\!\langle\, \text{integer} \,\rangle\!\!\rangle = \text{``int''}$$
$$\mathcal{C}_T \langle\!\!\langle\, \text{boolean} \,\rangle\!\!\rangle = \text{``bool''}$$

Z does not have a boolean type, so one must be defined in order to model Tosca's boolean type. Because Z has keywords *true* and *false*, these cannot be used as names for the elements of the new boolean type (not even by using a different style of font, unfortunately):

$$Boolean ::= \mathsf{T} \mid \mathsf{F}$$

Z does have an integer type, which can be used in modelling Tosca's integers. The range of integers supported by Tosca is specified loosely:

$$minInt, maxInt : \mathbb{Z}$$

$$minInt < 0 < maxInt$$

$$Integer == minInt \mathrel{..} maxInt$$

Values in Tosca are either integer or boolean, corresponding to the two types:

$$VALUE ::= int_v \langle\!\langle Integer \rangle\!\rangle$$
$$\mid bool_v \langle\!\langle Boolean \rangle\!\rangle$$

No functions are defined to map abstract Tosca names and values to a concrete representation. Instead, abstract and concrete names are assumed to consist of the same string of characters, concrete boolean values are written as **"true"** and **"false"**, and concrete integer values are written as a base ten digit string. The types of these functions are

$$\mathcal{C}_N \langle\!\{ \_ \}\!\rangle : NAME \longrightarrow String$$
$$\mathcal{C}_V \langle\!\{ \_ \}\!\rangle : VALUE \longrightarrow String$$

4.4 Declarations

A Tosca declaration consists of the name of the declared variable and its type. The syntax for variable declarations is

$$DECL ::= \text{declVar} \langle\!\langle NAME \times TYPE \rangle\!\rangle$$

In concrete form, a variable declaration consists of the variable name and its type, separated by a colon:

$$\mathcal{C}_D \langle\!\{ \_ \}\!\rangle : DECL \longrightarrow String$$
$$\mathcal{C}_D \langle\!\{ \text{declVar}(\xi, \tau) \}\!\rangle = \mathcal{C}_N \langle\!\{ \xi \}\!\rangle \frown \text{":"} \frown \mathcal{C}_T \langle\!\{ \tau \}\!\rangle$$

So, for example,

$$\mathcal{C}_D \langle\!\{ \text{declVar}(x, \text{integer}) \}\!\rangle = \text{"x : int"}$$
$$\mathcal{C}_D \langle\!\{ \text{declVar}(b, \text{boolean}) \}\!\rangle = \text{"b : bool"}$$

Multiple declarations are simply a sequence of variable declarations: seq *DECL*. In concrete form, a multiple declaration list has each declaration terminated by a semicolon:

$$\mathcal{C}_{D*} \langle\!\{ \_ \}\!\rangle : \text{seq } DECL \longrightarrow String$$
$$\mathcal{C}_{D*} \langle\!\{ \langle\rangle \}\!\rangle = \text{" "}$$
$$\mathcal{C}_{D*} \langle\!\{ \langle\delta\rangle \}\!\rangle = \mathcal{C}_D \langle\!\{ \delta \}\!\rangle \frown \text{";"}$$
$$\mathcal{C}_{D*} \langle\!\{ \Delta_1 \frown \Delta_2 \}\!\rangle = \mathcal{C}_{D*} \langle\!\{ \Delta_1 \}\!\rangle \frown \mathcal{C}_{D*} \langle\!\{ \Delta_2 \}\!\rangle$$

For example,

$$\mathcal{C}_{D*} \langle\!\{ \langle \text{declVar}(x, \text{integer}), \text{declVar}(b, \text{boolean}) \rangle \}\!\rangle = \text{"x : int ; b : bool ;"}$$

Aside—at first sight, it might seem simpler to define $\mathcal{C}_{D*}\{\!|\_|\!\}$ using only two cases: the empty case and a single recursive case of the form $\mathcal{C}_{D*}\{\!|\langle\delta\rangle \frown \Delta|\!\}$. Indeed, the three-case definition reduces to this two-case alternative when $\Delta_1 = \langle\delta\rangle$. However, by taking $\Delta_2 = \langle\delta\rangle$ instead, the recursion can also be unwound from the other end, if required. And sometimes it is useful to use the full power of the three-case definition to split a sequence into two pieces both larger than singletons (a style used mainly in the proofs, see Chapter 13). So the more general three-case style is preferred.

That the final result is independent of how the sequence is split into Δ_1 and Δ_2 follows from the associativity of concatenation (and, in later more complicated expressions (sections 8.2.2 and 8.5.2), from the associativity of the operators used to combine their parts).

4.5   Operators

Tosca has unary operators (that take one argument and return a result) and binary operators (that take two arguments and return a result). These are further broken down into arithmetic operators (that take numbers and return numbers), comparison operators (that take numbers and return booleans), and logical operators (that take booleans and return booleans).

The binary arithmetic operators are the standard addition and subtraction (more arithmetic operators could be included in a similar manner):

$$BIN\_ARITH\_OP ::= \mathsf{plus}$$
$$|\quad \mathsf{minus}$$

The binary comparison operators are the standard tests for equality and inequality (again, more operators could be included):

$$BIN\_COMP\_OP ::= \mathsf{less}$$
$$|\quad \mathsf{greater}$$
$$|\quad \mathsf{equal}$$

The binary logical operators are conjunction and disjunction:

$$BIN\_LOGIC\_OP ::= \mathsf{or}$$
$$|\quad \mathsf{and}$$

So the binary operators are

$$BIN\_OP ::= \mathsf{binArithOp}\langle\!\langle BIN\_ARITH\_OP\rangle\!\rangle$$
$$|\quad \mathsf{binCompOp}\langle\!\langle BIN\_COMP\_OP\rangle\!\rangle$$
$$|\quad \mathsf{binLogicOp}\langle\!\langle BIN\_LOGIC\_OP\rangle\!\rangle$$

Similarly, the unary operators are broken down into arithmetic operators and logical operators. Here there is only one in each kind:

$UNY\_ARITH\_OP ::=$ negate

$UNY\_LOGIC\_OP ::=$ not

So the unary operators are

$UNY\_OP ::=$ unyArithOp$\langle\!\langle UNY\_ARITH\_OP \rangle\!\rangle$
     $\mid$ unyLogicOp$\langle\!\langle UNY\_LOGIC\_OP \rangle\!\rangle$

A note on specification style: this treatment of the unary operators may appear a little heavy-handed; why not just say

$UNY\_OP_0 ::=$ negate
     $\mid$ not

However, this approach gives a more uniform treatment to the static semantics of operators (the definitions for unary and binary operators look similar, see section 8.3), and allows any new unary operators to be added to the language more easily. Examples like this, with forward references to the reason why certain choices have been made, indicate that writing a specification is an iterative process: early choices may be changed later when their consequences become apparent.

The concrete form of operators is simply some appropriate string chosen to represent the operator. The unary operators are written as

$\mathcal{C}_U\langle\!(\_)\!\rangle : UNY\_OP \longrightarrow String$

$\mathcal{C}_U\langle\!($ unyArithOp negate $)\!\rangle =$ "$-$"
$\mathcal{C}_U\langle\!($ unyLogicOp not $)\!\rangle =$ "**not**"

and the binary operators as

$\mathcal{C}_B\langle\!(\_)\!\rangle : BIN\_OP \longrightarrow String$

$\mathcal{C}_B\langle\!($ binArithOp plus $)\!\rangle =$ "$+$"
$\mathcal{C}_B\langle\!($ binArithOp minus $)\!\rangle =$ "$-$"

$\mathcal{C}_B\langle\!($ binCompOp less $)\!\rangle =$ "$<$"
$\mathcal{C}_B\langle\!($ binCompOp greater $)\!\rangle =$ "$>$"
$\mathcal{C}_B\langle\!($ binCompOp equal $)\!\rangle =$ "$=$"

$\mathcal{C}_B\langle\!($ binLogicOp or $)\!\rangle =$ "**or**"
$\mathcal{C}_B\langle\!($ binLogicOp and $)\!\rangle =$ "**and**"

Notice that the strings chosen to represent unary negate and binary minus are the same; distinguishing between these in a program text is a parsing problem. These parsing concerns do not occur in the semantics definitions, where we are dealing with unambiguous abstract syntax.

4.6   Expressions

A Tosca expression is either a constant, a named variable, a unary expression, or a binary expression:

$$EXPR ::= \mathsf{const} \langle\!\langle VALUE \rangle\!\rangle$$
$$\mid\ \mathsf{var} \langle\!\langle NAME \rangle\!\rangle$$
$$\mid\ \mathsf{unyExpr} \langle\!\langle UNY\_OP \times EXPR \rangle\!\rangle$$
$$\mid\ \mathsf{binExpr} \langle\!\langle EXPR \times BIN\_OP \times EXPR \rangle\!\rangle$$

Expressions that are constants or variables are written using whatever concrete syntax has been chosen for them. Unary expressions are written with the operator first. Binary expressions are written with the binary operator in infix position, and are parenthesized; parenthesizing all binary expressions is an alternative to defining an operator precedence:

$$\mathcal{C}_E \langle\!\langle \_ \rangle\!\rangle : EXPR \longrightarrow String$$

$$\mathcal{C}_E \langle\!\langle \mathsf{const}\ \chi \rangle\!\rangle = \mathcal{C}_V \langle\!\langle \chi \rangle\!\rangle$$

$$\mathcal{C}_E \langle\!\langle \mathsf{var}\ \xi \rangle\!\rangle = \mathcal{C}_N \langle\!\langle \xi \rangle\!\rangle$$

$$\mathcal{C}_E \langle\!\langle \mathsf{unyExpr}(\psi, \epsilon) \rangle\!\rangle = \mathcal{C}_U \langle\!\langle \psi \rangle\!\rangle \frown \mathcal{C}_E \langle\!\langle \epsilon \rangle\!\rangle$$

$$\mathcal{C}_E \langle\!\langle \mathsf{binExpr}(\epsilon_1, \omega, \epsilon_2) \rangle\!\rangle = \text{``(''} \frown \mathcal{C}_E \langle\!\langle \epsilon_1 \rangle\!\rangle \frown \mathcal{C}_B \langle\!\langle \omega \rangle\!\rangle \frown \mathcal{C}_E \langle\!\langle \epsilon_2 \rangle\!\rangle \frown \text{``)''}$$

For example,

$$\mathcal{C}_E \langle\!\langle \mathsf{const}(int_v\ 9) \rangle\!\rangle = \text{``9''}$$

$$\mathcal{C}_E \langle\!\langle \mathsf{var}\ x \rangle\!\rangle = \text{``x''}$$

$$\mathcal{C}_E \langle\!\langle \mathsf{unyExpr}(\mathsf{unyArithOp}\ \mathsf{negate}, \mathsf{const}(int_v\ 9)) \rangle\!\rangle = \text{``} - \text{ 9''}$$

$$\mathcal{C}_E \langle\!\langle \mathsf{binExpr}(\mathsf{var}\ x, \mathsf{binArithOp}\ \mathsf{plus}, \mathsf{const}(int_v\ 9)) \rangle\!\rangle = \text{``(x + 9)''}$$

4.7   Commands

A Tosca command is either a skip, a block (sequence of commands), an assignment, a conditional choice, a while loop, an input, or an output:

$$CMD ::= \mathsf{skip}$$
$$\mid\ \mathsf{block} \langle\!\langle \mathsf{seq}_1\ CMD \rangle\!\rangle$$
$$\mid\ \mathsf{assign} \langle\!\langle NAME \times EXPR \rangle\!\rangle$$
$$\mid\ \mathsf{choice} \langle\!\langle EXPR \times CMD \times CMD \rangle\!\rangle$$
$$\mid\ \mathsf{loop} \langle\!\langle EXPR \times CMD \rangle\!\rangle$$
$$\mid\ \mathsf{input} \langle\!\langle NAME \rangle\!\rangle$$
$$\mid\ \mathsf{output} \langle\!\langle EXPR \rangle\!\rangle$$

Notice that the block is required to have at least one command in it; this may be a skip.

Multiple commands are simply a sequence of commands: seq CMD. The concrete syntax for commands is a conventional keyword-style syntax. A multiple command list has each command terminated by a semicolon:

$$\mathcal{C}_C \langle\!|\, \_ \,|\!\rangle : CMD \longrightarrow String$$
$$\mathcal{C}_{C*} \langle\!|\, \_ \,|\!\rangle : \text{seq } CMD \longrightarrow String$$

$$\mathcal{C}_C \langle\!|\, \text{block } \Gamma \,|\!\rangle = \text{``begin''} \,\widehat{}\, \mathcal{C}_{C*} \langle\!|\, \Gamma \,|\!\rangle \,\widehat{}\, \text{``end''}$$

$$\mathcal{C}_C \langle\!|\, \text{skip} \,|\!\rangle = \text{``skip''}$$

$$\mathcal{C}_C \langle\!|\, \text{assign}(\xi, \epsilon) \,|\!\rangle = \mathcal{C}_N \langle\!|\, \xi \,|\!\rangle \,\widehat{}\, \text{``:=''} \,\widehat{}\, \mathcal{C}_E \langle\!|\, \epsilon \,|\!\rangle$$

$$\mathcal{C}_C \langle\!|\, \text{choice}(\epsilon, \gamma_1, \gamma_2) \,|\!\rangle =$$
$$\text{``if''} \,\widehat{}\, \mathcal{C}_E \langle\!|\, \epsilon \,|\!\rangle \,\widehat{}\, \text{``then''} \,\widehat{}\, \mathcal{C}_C \langle\!|\, \gamma_1 \,|\!\rangle \,\widehat{}\, \text{``else''} \,\widehat{}\, \mathcal{C}_C \langle\!|\, \gamma_2 \,|\!\rangle$$

$$\mathcal{C}_C \langle\!|\, \text{loop}(\epsilon, \gamma) \,|\!\rangle = \text{``while''} \,\widehat{}\, \mathcal{C}_E \langle\!|\, \epsilon \,|\!\rangle \,\widehat{}\, \text{``do''} \,\widehat{}\, \mathcal{C}_C \langle\!|\, \gamma \,|\!\rangle$$

$$\mathcal{C}_C \langle\!|\, \text{input } \xi \,|\!\rangle = \text{``input''} \,\widehat{}\, \mathcal{C}_N \langle\!|\, \xi \,|\!\rangle$$

$$\mathcal{C}_C \langle\!|\, \text{output } \epsilon \,|\!\rangle = \text{``output''} \,\widehat{}\, \mathcal{C}_E \langle\!|\, \epsilon \,|\!\rangle$$

$$\mathcal{C}_{C*} \langle\!|\, \langle \rangle \,|\!\rangle = \text{`` ''}$$

$$\mathcal{C}_{C*} \langle\!|\, \langle \gamma \rangle \,|\!\rangle = \mathcal{C}_C \langle\!|\, \gamma \,|\!\rangle \,\widehat{}\, \text{``;''}$$

$$\mathcal{C}_{C*} \langle\!|\, \Gamma_1 \,\widehat{}\, \Gamma_2 \,|\!\rangle = \mathcal{C}_{C*} \langle\!|\, \Gamma_1 \,|\!\rangle \,\widehat{}\, \mathcal{C}_{C*} \langle\!|\, \Gamma_2 \,|\!\rangle$$

For example,

$$\mathcal{C}_C \langle\!|\, \text{assign}(x, \text{const}(int_v\, 3)) \,|\!\rangle = \text{``x := 3''}$$

$$\mathcal{C}_C \langle\!|\, \text{choice}(\text{var } b, \text{assign}(x, \text{var } y), \text{skip}) \,|\!\rangle =$$
$$\text{``if b then x := y else skip''}$$

$$\mathcal{C}_C \langle\!|\, \text{loop}(\text{var } b, \text{assign}(x, \text{binExpr}(\text{var } x, \text{binArithOp minus}, \text{const}(int_v\, 1)))) \,|\!\rangle =$$
$$\text{``while b do x := (x − 1)''}$$

$$\mathcal{C}_C \langle\!|\, \text{input } x \,|\!\rangle = \text{``input x''}$$

$$\mathcal{C}_C \langle\!|\, \text{output unyExpr}(\text{minus}, \text{var } y) \,|\!\rangle = \text{``output −y''}$$

$$\mathcal{C}_C \langle\!|\, \text{block}\langle \text{input } x, \text{output}(\text{const}(int_v\, 3)) \rangle \,|\!\rangle =$$
$$\text{``begin input x; output 3; end''}$$

4.8 Program

A Tosca program is a sequence of declarations and a command:

$$PROG ::= \text{Tosca} \langle\!\langle \text{seq } DECL \times CMD \rangle\!\rangle$$

Notice that the declaration list may be empty. It is possible to write correct Tosca programs that declare no variables, but they are not very interesting.

In concrete form, a Tosca program is written by concatenating the declarations and the command:

$$\mathcal{C}_P \langle\!\langle \_ \rangle\!\rangle : PROG \longrightarrow String$$

$$\mathcal{C}_P \langle\!\langle \, \mathsf{Tosca}(\Delta, \gamma) \, \rangle\!\rangle = \mathcal{C}_{D^*} \langle\!\langle \Delta \rangle\!\rangle \frown \mathcal{C}_C \langle\!\langle \gamma \rangle\!\rangle$$

For example,

$$\mathcal{C}_P \langle\!\langle \, \mathsf{Tosca}(\langle\,\rangle, \mathsf{skip}) \, \rangle\!\rangle = \text{``}\mathbf{skip}\text{''}$$

$$\mathcal{C}_P \langle\!\langle \, \mathsf{Tosca}(\langle\,\rangle, \mathsf{output}(\mathsf{const}(int_v\, 3))) \, \rangle\!\rangle = \text{``}\mathbf{output\ 3}\text{''}$$

$$\mathcal{C}_P \langle\!\langle \, \mathsf{Tosca}(\langle \mathsf{declVar}(x, \mathsf{integer})\rangle,$$
$$\mathsf{block}\langle \mathsf{assign}(x, \mathsf{const}(int_v\, 3)), \mathsf{output}(\mathsf{var}\ x))\rangle) \, \rangle\!\rangle =$$
$$\text{``}\mathbf{x\ :\ int\ ;\ begin\ x\ :=\ 3;\ output\ x;\ end}\text{''}$$

Chapter 5

A Running Example—
the 'Square' Program

5.1 Introduction

In order to demonstrate how all the various specifications work, a simple running example is used throughout the book, and is introduced here. The example is a program that inputs a positive integer n, and outputs the squares from one up to n^2. In the interests of simplicity, the example does not validate its input.

The dynamic meaning of the example Tosca program is calculated in section 9.2. It is compiled into the target language in section 12.1, and the meaning of the compiled version is calculated in section 12.2.

5.2 Specification

A specification of the example in Z is

$$
\begin{array}{|l}
square : \mathbb{N}_1 \longrightarrow \operatorname{seq} \mathbb{N} \\
\hline
square\ 1 = \langle 1 \rangle \\
\forall\, n : \mathbb{N} \mid n > 1 \bullet square\ n = square(n-1) \frown \langle n * n \rangle
\end{array}
$$

5.3 Concrete syntax

A suitable program that implements the *square* function, written in Tosca's concrete syntax, is

```
n : int ; sq : int ; limit : int ;
begin
     n := 1 ; sq := 1 ;
     input limit ;
     output sq ;
     while ( n < limit ) do
     begin
          sq := ( ( sq + 1 ) + ( n + n ) ) ;
          n := ( n + 1 ) ;
          output sq ;
     end ;
end
```

5.4   Abstract syntax

In abstract syntax, this program is

square ==

Tosca(⟨declVar(n, integer), declVar(sq, integer), declVar($limit$, integer)⟩,
    block⟨assign(n, const(int_v 1)),
        assign(sq, const(int_v 1)),
        input $limit$, output(var sq),
        loop(binExpr(var n, less, var $limit$),
            block⟨assign(sq,
                binExpr(binExpr(var sq, plus, const(int_v 1)),
                    plus, binExpr(var n, plus, var n))),
            assign(n, binExpr(var n, plus, const(int_v 1))),
            output(var sq)⟩⟩⟩)

which rather graphically illustrates why concrete, not abstract, syntax is used for writing programs!

Chapter 6

Partitioning the Specification

6.1 Undefined meanings

Consider the following highly erroneous Tosca 'program':

```
b : bool;
x : int; y : int;
begin
        x := ;          - - syntax error
        z := 1;         - - z not declared
        x := z;         - - z not declared
        x := b;         - - incompatible types
        x := y;         - - y not initialized
end
```

A program must be syntactically correct before any of its meanings (static or dynamic) are defined. So the meaning of the above fragment is *undefined*.

Even if the syntax error is corrected, there are many other things wrong, and the formal meaning of the program should still be *undefined*. Hence, the semantic meaning function is *partial*; it is defined for only some programs, that satisfy certain well-formedness conditions. For example, the conditions relevant to an assignment command are (informally)

$\mathcal{M}_E[\![assignment]\!] =$
    if (target variable is declared)
        $\wedge$ (source expression has no undeclared variables)
        $\wedge$ (source and target have the same type)
        $\wedge$ (source expression has no uninitialized variables)
    then (definition of meaning)
    else *checkWrong*

Checking that all these conditions are met in one lump, as above, results in a clumsy style of specification that seems to put more emphasis on what does not happen, than on what does. A better approach is to partition the specification into several logically separate static checks and a definition of the dynamic (execution) meaning. Such partitioning means that there is no need to check, for example, in the dynamic semantic definitions, that expressions are of the right type (they are; they have passed the type checking), or that variables have been initialized before they are used (they have; they have passed the initialization checking).

This ability to separate concerns puts structure on an otherwise large monolithic specification. It results in several simpler specifications, one for each semantics, since 'error cases' do not have to be considered each time. It gives a more uniform approach, since it can be clearly seen that each static check has been made for each construct. The separation also serves to highlight each of these semantics, showing its purpose.

Not every language can have its semantics partitioned so neatly; achieving a clean separation in an existing language is more difficult than designing the separation in from the start. Tosca has been designed to be separable in this way, and has defined three static semantics—declaration checking, type checking and use checking—and a dynamic semantics. This chapter gives an overview of the purpose of each of the semantics, by informally describing the kind of conditions that each one is designed to check. The following chapters specify Tosca by formally defining each of its four semantics.

6.2   Syntax

If a Tosca program is not syntactically correct, then its declaration-before-use, type, initialization-before-use and dynamic semantics are *undefined*.

6.3   Declaration-before-use semantics

The first static check made on a syntactically correct Tosca program is a declaration-before-use check, to make sure that any variables used in the program have been correctly declared. For example, an informal reading of type checking an assignment command is

$\mathcal{D}_E[\![assignment]\!] =$
    if (target variable is declared)
        $\wedge$ (source expression has no undeclared variables)
    then *checkOK*
    else *checkWrong*

Only if the whole program passes this static check are the other semantics defined. Because this is the first check done, the declaration check meaning functions are in fact *total*: this semantics is defined for any syntactically correct Tosca program.

If $\mathcal{D}_P[\![program]\!] = checkWrong$, then the program does not pass its declaration-before-use check, and so its type, initialization-before-use and dynamic semantics are *undefined*.

6.4   Type-checking semantics

If a Tosca program passes its declaration-before-use check, it is subject to a type-check. The type-checking semantics defines conditions for a program to be well-typed: in the case of an assignment the check is (informally)

$\mathcal{T}_E[\![assignment]\!] =$
    if (source and target have the same type)
    then *checkOK*
    else *checkWrong*

In this definition, there is no need to first check that the variables have a type: since we know they have been declared, they do. Hence $\mathcal{T}_E[\![\ ]\!]$ is a partial function: it is defined only for declaration-checked expressions, and *undefined* for others.

If $\mathcal{T}_P[\![program]\!] = checkWrong$, then the program does not pass its type check, and so its initialization-before-use and dynamic semantics are *undefined*.

6.5   Initialization-before-use semantics

If a Tosca program passes its type check, it is subject to its final static check, that any variable that is accessed has previously been initialized to some value. For an assignment statement, for example, this consists of checking that there are no uninitialized variables in the source expression. Informally:

$\mathcal{U}_E[\![assignment]\!] =$
    if (source expression has no uninitialized variables)
    then *checkOK*
    else *checkWrong*

This provides a static initialization-before-use semantic check. Note that some of the formal definitions of Tosca provide a rather strict constraint on potentially unused variables (guilty until proven innocent), which eliminates programs that might otherwise be thought to be 'correct'. It is probably appropriate to have such a strict definition for a high integrity language. More to the point, however, it does provide an unambiguous definition, which can be reasoned about, and which provides a basis for criticism if necessary.

If $\mathcal{U}_P[\![program]\!] = checkWrong$, then the program does not pass its initialization-before-use check, and so its dynamic semantics are *undefined*.

6.6   Dynamic semantics

Only if a Tosca program passes its initialization-before-use check (and hence its declaration-before-use and type checks, too), is its dynamic meaning defined:

$$\mathcal{M}_E[\![assignment]\!] = $$
(definition of meaning)

Compare this with the form given on page 46. All the conditions to be satisfied have disappeared, because they have already been checked in the static semantics definitions. Hence, the definition is simpler and clearer.

6.7   Redundancy

Not all programming languages require variables to be declared, typed or initialized. For example, in the awk programming language, the first use of a variable implicitly declares it. If it is assigned a value of a particular type (number or string) it has that type. If its first use is on the right-hand side of an expression, it is automatically initialized to zero, or the empty string, as appropriate. This automatic declaration and initialization allows some very concise awk programs, free of clutter.

So why aren't all languages like this? A famous error occurred in a Fortran program controlling the launch of a Mariner space probe. One line of the program used a full stop instead of a comma. The line should have read

```
DO 100 I = 1,10
```

This is the first line of a Fortran DO loop, and instructs the program to repeat the following code up to the line numbered 100, with I taking the values from 1 to 10. Instead, the line read

```
DO 100 I = 1.10
```

This is an assignment statement, assigning the value 1.10 to the variable DO100I. (Fortran permits, and ignores, spaces in variable names.) If Fortran required variables to be declared before use, this error would have been caught by a static check; the spurious variable DO100I would have been flagged as undeclared. It was not caught, and an expensive spacecraft was lost.

So the main purpose of variable declarations and initializations is to provide a safety net; redundancy allows consistency checks. Static checks, that can be performed without having to execute the program, are particularly valuable.

6.8   Further reading

For a description of the *awk* language, see [Kernighan and Pike 1984, section 4.4] or [Aho *et al.* 1988]. The language's name is an acronym made from the names of its designers Aho, Weinberger and Kernighan.

The journal *ACM SIGSOFT Software Engineering Notes* often has notes and articles about computer-related incidents. The Mariner incident, along with many others, is listed in [Neumann 1985].

Chapter 7

Tosca—States and Environments

7.1 Introduction

There are two obvious ways to organize the specification of each of the four semantics for each of Tosca's various language constructs: either specify each separate semantics completely in turn, or specify each construct completely in turn. After experimenting with both organizations, the latter has been chosen. Specifying all the semantics of each language construct in one place makes it easier to understand that construct as a whole. This approach does have one drawback, however. It becomes necessary to specify quite a few auxiliary Z types and functions before their use may be apparent. These auxiliary definitions are gathered together in this chapter. It may be best to skim through on first reading, noting what things have been defined, but waiting until the next chapter to find out how they are used.

7.2 Semantics—general

7.2.1 Environment and state

A variable that has been declared but not yet initialized has no associated value. So modelling the state as a mapping from variable names to their values is not appropriate. (Using a partial function for the mapping does not help, because it does not distinguish variables not in the domain that have not been declared, from those not in the domain that have been declared, but not yet given a value.) It is conventional to introduce intermediate *locations*, and use an *environment* to map names to locations, and a *store* to map locations to values. A declaration changes the environment by assigning a new variable to a new location. But that location does not become part of the store's domain until the variable is first assigned a

50

value. The evolving *state* of a computation consists of this store, and the input and output streams.

In two of the static semantics, declaration-before-use and type checking, the state of a variable does not change: once declared it stays declared, once typed it retains that type. So for these an environment, but no state, is required. With the other two semantics, initialization-before-use and dynamic, the state of a variable can change. A variable starts out uninitialized when declared, and may later be initialized. In the dynamic case, a variable may take on many values as the computation progresses. So both these definitions require an environment and a state.

The domains of all these various environments are a set of variable names. Since *NAME* is a syntactic, as well as a semantic, domain, when an environment function is applied to a name it is written $\rho[\![\xi]\!]$ rather than $\rho(\xi)$, to highlight this point.

7.2.2 Check status

The purpose of a static semantics is to check whether a construct is okay or wrong

$$CHECK ::= checkOK \mid checkWrong$$

Although *CHECK* has only two values, Z has no boolean type, so *CHECK* cannot be declared as a boolean flag. Even if Z did have such a type, it would be better specification style to make *CHECK* a free type definition as above. If later it were decided to modify the specification by adding an extra check status, for example, *checkWarn*, it would be relatively straightforward to extend the definition given above.

Check results need to be combined. $\bowtie$ is an infix function that combines check results 'pessimistically'; the combination of the check results is *checkOK* only if both the arguments are *checkOK*:

$$
\begin{array}{|l}
\_ \bowtie \_ : CHECK \times CHECK \longrightarrow CHECK \\
\hline
\forall c_1, c_2 : CHECK \bullet \\
\quad c_1 \bowtie c_2 = \\
\qquad \textbf{if } c_1 = checkOK \wedge c_2 = checkOK \\
\qquad \textbf{then } checkOK \textbf{ else } checkWrong
\end{array}
$$

7.2.3 Memory locations

Store locations are modelled as integers.

$$Locn == \mathbb{Z}$$

These numbers could be interpreted as representing memory addresses, for example. Negative locations have been allowed: these could be interpreted as 'special' addresses, for example, registers. The interpretation chosen does not affect Tosca's semantics; it is important only when mapping to a particular low level language.

7.3   Declaration-before-use semantics

For this non-standard interpretation, the declaration environment is a mapping from the names that are referenced in the program to their check status (representing declared or not declared):

$$Env_D == NAME \nrightarrow CHECK$$

7.4   Type checking semantics

The *TYPE* definition given in the abstract syntax is augmented with a *typeWrong* component:

$$TYPE ::= \ldots$$
$$| \quad typeWrong$$

For this non-standard interpretation, the type environment describes the mapping from identifiers to their types:

$$Env_T == NAME \nrightarrow TYPE$$

7.5   Initialization-before-use semantics

A use value is either *checkWrong* (for a variable whose value is used before being initialized, or an expression that uses a *checkWrong* variable in a subexpression) or *checkOK* (for a variable that has been initialized before being used, or an expression that uses only *checkOK* variables in its subexpressions).

The $Store_U$ is the mapping from store locations to the current use state of the variable stored there:

$$Store_U == Locn \nrightarrow CHECK$$

7.5.1   The initialization-before-use state

The $State_U$ has two components, the $Store_U$ and a tag noting the check status. This tag propagates through the definition and becomes the final check result:

$$State_U == Store_U \times CHECK$$

The generic Z functions *first* and *second* extract components of an ordered pair. The query functions $storeOf_U$ and $checkOf_U$ are more meaningful names for these, for use when extracting the store and check components of the state pair:

$$storeOf_U == first[Store_U, CHECK]$$

$$checkOf_U == second[Store_U, CHECK]$$

$\boxplus_v$ updates the store component of a use state:

$$
\begin{array}{|l}
\_\;\boxplus_v\;\_ : State_U \times Store_U \longrightarrow State_U \\
\hline
\forall \varsigma_{v1}, \varsigma_{v2} : Store_U;\; c_1 : CHECK \;\bullet \\
\quad (\varsigma_{v1}, c_1) \boxplus_v \varsigma_{v2} = (\varsigma_{v1} \oplus \varsigma_{v2}, c_1)
\end{array}
$$

updateUse_U changes the use check component of the store to the worse of its current value and that of the input:

$$
\begin{array}{|l}
updateUse_U : CHECK \longrightarrow State_U \longrightarrow State_U \\
\hline
\forall c_1, c_2 : CHECK;\; \varsigma_v : Store_U \;\bullet \\
\quad updateUse_U\; c_1(\varsigma_v, c_2) = (\varsigma_v, c_1 \bowtie c_2)
\end{array}
$$

7.5.2   The initialization-before-use environment

The use environment is a mapping from names (identifiers) to what they denote, locations:

$$Env_U == NAME \rightarrowtail Locn$$

The mapping is an injective (one-to-one) function, which ensures that no two names map to the same location.

7.5.3   Worse use store

The function *worseStore* takes two use stores, ς_{v1} and ς_{v2}, and returns a use store that combines the worst properties of each.

Where the domains of the two use stores coincide, on dom $\varsigma_{v1} \cap$ dom ς_{v2}, *worseStore* is defined by the check status combining function, $\bowtie$.

Where the domains do not overlap, on dom $\varsigma_{v1} \lhd \varsigma_{v2}$ and dom $\varsigma_{v2} \lhd \varsigma_{v1}$, it means that one store has a location that maps to some check status, and the other does not have that location. If that unmatched location maps to *checkWrong*, the worse behaviour is to continue to map to *checkWrong*. If that unmatched location maps to *checkOK* (if, for example, a variable is initialized in one branch of a choice but not in the other), the worse behaviour is to remove the location from the domain of the result; it is worse to have a variable uninitialized than set to something. In either case, this can be achieved by range restricting the non-overlapping parts of the stores to *checkWrong*:

$$\begin{array}{l}
\hline
worseStore : Store_U \times Store_U \longrightarrow Store_U \\
\hline
\forall \varsigma_{v1}, \varsigma_{v2} : Store_U \bullet \\
\quad worseStore(\varsigma_{v1}, \varsigma_{v2}) = \\
\qquad \{ \lambda : Locn \mid \lambda \in \operatorname{dom}\varsigma_{v1} \cap \operatorname{dom}\varsigma_{v2} \bullet \lambda \mapsto (\varsigma_{v1} \lambda \bowtie \varsigma_{v2} \lambda) \} \\
\qquad \cup \operatorname{dom}\varsigma_{v2} \vartriangleleft \varsigma_{v1} \vartriangleright \{ checkWrong \} \\
\qquad \cup \operatorname{dom}\varsigma_{v1} \vartriangleleft \varsigma_{v2} \vartriangleright \{ checkWrong \}
\end{array}$$

$\vartriangleright$ is Z's range restriction: the relation $S \vartriangleright r$ is that subset of the relation S that has its range restricted to the elements in r. $\vartriangleleft$ is Z's domain anti-restriction: the relation $d \vartriangleleft S$ is that subset of the relation S that has its domain restricted to the elements not in d. For example,

$$\{ a \mapsto 1, b \mapsto 2, c \mapsto 3 \} \vartriangleright \{1, 2\} = \{ a \mapsto 1, b \mapsto 2 \}$$

$$\{ a \} \vartriangleleft \{ a \mapsto 1, b \mapsto 2, c \mapsto 3 \} = \{ b \mapsto 2, c \mapsto \}$$

$$\{ a \} \vartriangleleft \{ a \mapsto 1, b \mapsto 2, c \mapsto 3 \} \vartriangleright \{1, 2\} = \{ b \mapsto 2 \}$$

The definition of *worseStore* is one of the more complicated-looking definitions, so, to see how it works, consider two stores:

$$\varsigma_{v1} = \{ \lambda_1 \mapsto checkOK, \lambda_2 \mapsto checkWrong, \lambda_3 \mapsto checkOK \}$$

$$\varsigma_{v2} = \{ \lambda_2 \mapsto checkOK, \lambda_3 \mapsto checkOK, \lambda_4 \mapsto checkWrong \}$$

The overlapping domain is $\operatorname{dom}\varsigma_{v1} \cap \operatorname{dom}\varsigma_{v2} = \{\lambda_2, \lambda_3\}$. λ_2 maps to *checkWrong* in one store, *checkOK* in the other, and so to *checkWrong* in the composed store. λ_3 will continue mapping to *checkOK*.

ς_{v1} has one location not in ς_{v2}, λ_1. This maps to *checkOK*, so will not appear in the combined store:

$$\operatorname{dom}\varsigma_{v2} \vartriangleleft \varsigma_{v1} = \{ \lambda_1 \mapsto checkOK \}$$

$$\operatorname{dom}\varsigma_{v2} \vartriangleleft \varsigma_{v1} \vartriangleright \{ checkWrong \} = \varnothing$$

ς_{v2} has an unmatched location, λ_4. It maps to *checkWrong*, which carries over:

$$\operatorname{dom}\varsigma_{v1} \vartriangleleft \varsigma_{v2} = \{ \lambda_4 \mapsto checkWrong \}$$

$$\operatorname{dom}\varsigma_{v1} \vartriangleleft \varsigma_{v2} \vartriangleright \{ checkWrong \} = \{ \lambda_4 \mapsto checkWrong \}$$

So the worse store that results from combining these is

$$worseStore(\varsigma_{v1}, \varsigma_{v2})$$

$$= \{ \lambda_2 \mapsto checkWrong, \lambda_3 \mapsto checkOK \} \cup \varnothing \cup \{ \lambda_4 \mapsto checkWrong \}$$

$$= \{ \lambda_2 \mapsto checkWrong, \lambda_3 \mapsto checkOK, \lambda_4 \mapsto checkWrong \}$$

7.5.4 Worse use state

The function *worseState* takes two use states and returns a use state that combines the *worst* properties of each:

$$
\begin{array}{|l}
\hline
worseState : State_U \times State_U \longrightarrow State_U \\
\hline
\forall \varsigma_{v1}, \varsigma_{v2} : Store_U;\ c_1, c_2 : CHECK \bullet \\
\qquad worseState((\varsigma_{v1}, c_1), (\varsigma_{v2}, c_2)) = (worseStore(\varsigma_{v1}, \varsigma_{v2}), c_1 \bowtie c_2)
\end{array}
$$

7.6 Dynamic semantics

The *Store* is modelled as a mapping from store locations to values:

$$Store == Locn \nrightarrow VALUE$$

7.6.1 Input and output

Input and output are modelled as lists of integers:

$$Input == \text{seq}\ Integer$$
$$Output == \text{seq}\ Integer$$

7.6.1.1 The dynamic state

The state of a computation has three components, the store mapping, the input, and the output:

$$State == Store \times Input \times Output$$

Z has no generic functions analogous to its *first* and *second* to extract components of an ordered triple. The query functions *storeOf* and *outOf* need to be defined to extract the store and output sequence components of the state tuple:

$$
\begin{array}{|l}
\hline
storeOf : State \longrightarrow Store \\
outOf : State \longrightarrow Output \\
\hline
\forall \varsigma : Store;\ in : Input;\ out : Output \bullet \\
\qquad storeOf(\varsigma, in, out) = \varsigma \\
\qquad \land\ outOf(\varsigma, in, out) = out
\end{array}
$$

$\boxplus$ updates the store component of a dynamic state:

$$
\begin{array}{|l}
\hline
\_ \boxplus \_ : State \times Store \longrightarrow State \\
\hline
\forall \varsigma_1, \varsigma_2 : Store;\ in : Input;\ out : Output \bullet \\
\qquad (\varsigma_1, in, out) \boxplus \varsigma_2 = (\varsigma_1 \oplus \varsigma_2, in, out)
\end{array}
$$

7.6.1.2   The dynamic environment

The environment is a mapping from names (identifiers) to what they denote, locations:

$$Env == NAME \rightarrowtail Locn$$

The mapping is an injective (one-to-one) function, which ensures that no two names map to the same location.

7.7   Aside—using generic definitions

Tosca's syntax includes sequences of declarations and sequences of commands. The meaning of a sequence of such constructs is related to the meaning of a single construct in a uniform manner; all the specifications look boringly similar (see, for example, section 8.2.2).

Thus, it might be thought appropriate to define a generic Z function that maps a meaning function for a single construct to the corresponding meaning function for a sequence of constructs, and instantiate this generic with various actual types when used. But one of the motivations for specifying and building a high integrity compiler in the manner being described here is that the translation from the formal Z specification to the Prolog implementation is as clear as possible; the use of some sorts of generic function can obscure this translation. So the Tosca specification has the definition of each separate function written out fully. To illustrate this point further, a generic form for sequences of declarations is given below, for comparison with the explicit forms given in section 8.2.2.

The meaning of a declaration in all four of Tosca's semantics is an appropriate environment change (expressed as a mapping from environment to environment). The meaning of a sequence of declarations is also an environment change. An empty sequence has no effect on the environment, and hence its meaning is the identity function. A sequence consisting of a single declaration has the same meaning as that declaration. The meaning of a longer sequence can be split up as the meaning of shorter subsequences, joined together by functional composition. So an appropriate definition, generic in the environment variable, that maps the meaning function for a single declaration to one for a sequence of declarations, is

$$
\begin{array}{l}
\rule{5cm}{0.4pt}\,[E]\,\rule{5cm}{0.4pt} \\
SEQ : (DECL \nrightarrow E \nrightarrow E) \longrightarrow (\text{seq } DECL \nrightarrow E \nrightarrow E) \\
\hline
\forall \delta : DECL;\ \Delta_1, \Delta_2 : \text{seq}_1\ DECL;\ \mathcal{F} : DECL \nrightarrow E \nrightarrow E \bullet \\
\quad (SEQ\ \mathcal{F})\langle\,\rangle = \text{id } E \\
\quad \wedge\ (SEQ\ \mathcal{F})\langle\delta\rangle = \mathcal{F}\ \delta \\
\quad \wedge\ (SEQ\ \mathcal{F})(\Delta_1 ^\frown \Delta_2) = (SEQ\ \mathcal{F})\Delta_1 \circ (SEQ\ \mathcal{F})\Delta_2
\end{array}
$$

Each of the four meaning functions for sequences of declarations could be concisely defined, by instantiating SEQ with the appropriate environment, and applying it to the appropriate meaning function for single declarations, thus

$$\mathcal{D}_{D^*} == SEQ[Env_D]\, \mathcal{D}_D$$

$$\mathcal{T}_{D^*} == SEQ[Env_T]\, \mathcal{T}_D$$

$$\mathcal{U}_{D^*} == SEQ[Env_U]\, \mathcal{U}_D$$

$$\mathcal{M}_{D^*} == SEQ[Env]\, \mathcal{M}_D$$

However, the link to the Prolog implementation would be less clear in this form. The style of this particular Z specification is guided by a balance between clarity of specification, ease of proof, and clarity of translation into Prolog. If the same specification were written for a different reason, it might well be written in a different style.

Chapter 8

Tosca—Semantics

8.1 Introduction

This chapter specifies the semantics of Tosca. There is a separate section for each syntactic category: declarations, operators, expressions, commands, and program. For each separate construct in each syntactic category, its abstract syntax is repeated as a reminder, then the four semantics are given in order: declaration-before-use, type-checking, initialization-before-use, and dynamic. The following chapter uses these definitions to calculate the meanings of the example 'square' program.

8.2 Declarations

8.2.1 Variable declarations

$$DECL ::= \mathsf{declVar} \langle\!\langle NAME \times TYPE \rangle\!\rangle$$

8.2.1.1 Variable declaration, declaration-before-use semantics

The meaning function $\mathcal{D}_D[\![\,]\!]$ takes a declaration and name environment, and gives a new name environment, with the declaration added. (A similar function is defined for declaration lists.)

If a new variable is being declared, it is added to the name environment as okay. If a variable with the same name has already been declared (either with the same type, or a different type) it is flagged as wrong:

58

$$\mathcal{D}_D[\![\_]\!] : DECL \longrightarrow Env_D \longrightarrow Env_D$$

$$\mathcal{D}_D[\![\mathsf{declVar}(\xi,\tau)]\!]\,\rho_\delta =$$

    if $\xi \in \mathrm{dom}\,\rho_\delta$
    then $\rho_\delta \oplus \{\xi \mapsto checkWrong\}$
    else $\rho_\delta \oplus \{\xi \mapsto checkOK\}$

8.2.1.2 Variable declaration, type-checking semantics

The meaning function $\mathcal{T}_D[\![\,]\!]$ takes a declaration and type environment, and gives a new type environment, with the declaration added. A declared variable is added to the type environment with its type:

$$\mathcal{T}_D[\![\_]\!] : DECL \rightarrowtail Env_T \longrightarrow Env_T$$

$$\mathcal{T}_D[\![\mathsf{declVar}(\xi,\tau)]\!]\,\rho_\tau = \rho_\tau \oplus \{\xi \mapsto \tau\}$$

Note that ξ is not in the domain of ρ_τ, because variables declared more than once are trapped by the declaration-before-use semantics. So the definition could equivalently be written as $\rho_\tau \cup \{\xi \mapsto \tau\}$. The use of the $\oplus$ operator merely serves to highlight that fact that the final environment is also a function.

8.2.1.3 Variable declaration, initialization-before-use semantics

A declaration changes the environment by adding a new (name, location) pair. The declaration meaning function $\mathcal{U}_D[\![\,]\!]$ maps a declaration to a function that describes the change in the environment caused by the declaration.

A declared variable is added to the environment by mapping it to a previously unallocated location:

$$\mathcal{U}_D[\![\_]\!] : DECL \rightarrowtail Env_U \longrightarrow Env_U$$

$$\exists \lambda : Locn \mid \lambda \notin \mathrm{ran}\,\rho_v \bullet$$

$$\mathcal{U}_D[\![\mathsf{declVar}(\xi,\tau)]\!]\,\rho_v = \rho_v \oplus \{\xi \mapsto \lambda\}$$

8.2.1.4 Variable declaration, dynamic semantics

A declaration changes the environment by adding a new (name, location) pair. The declaration meaning function $\mathcal{M}_D[\![\,]\!]$ maps a declaration to a function that describes the change in the environment caused by the declaration.

A declared variable is added to the environment by mapping its name to an unallocated memory location:

$$\mathcal{M}_D[\![\_]\!] : DECL \rightarrowtail Env \longrightarrow Env$$

$$\exists \lambda : Locn \mid \lambda \notin \mathrm{ran}\,\rho \bullet$$

$$\mathcal{M}_D[\![\mathsf{declVar}(\xi,\tau)]\!]\,\rho = \rho \oplus \{\xi \mapsto \lambda\}$$

Since a declaration does not change the state, λ is not in the domain of *Store* yet. The variable has been declared, but as yet has no associated value.

The choice of the memory location λ is specified only loosely. This permits any suitable allocation strategy to be chosen on implementation, for example, allocation to a register. Later, it is chosen in such a way as to simplify the correctness proofs.

Notice that the type of the variable, τ, is not needed here: it is used only in the static type semantics checks.

8.2.2   Multiple declarations

seq *DECL*

The definition of the meanings of multiple declarations is an inductive extension of the meaning of a single declaration. An empty declaration list has no effect on the environment. Checking a list with one element is done by checking that element. Checking a list of declarations composed of two sublists is done by checking the second sublist in the environment that results from checking the first sublist.

All the definitions below look very similar. See section 7.7 for a discussion of this point.

8.2.2.1   Multiple declarations, declaration-before-use semantics

$$\mathcal{D}_{D^*}[\![\_]\!] : \operatorname{seq} DECL \longrightarrow Env_D \longrightarrow Env_D$$

$$\mathcal{D}_{D^*}[\![\langle\,\rangle]\!] = \operatorname{id} Env_D$$

$$\mathcal{D}_{D^*}[\![\langle\delta\rangle]\!] = \mathcal{D}_D[\![\delta]\!]$$

$$\mathcal{D}_{D^*}[\![\Delta_1 \,\widehat{\ }\, \Delta_2]\!] = \mathcal{D}_{D^*}[\![\Delta_2]\!] \circ \mathcal{D}_{D^*}[\![\Delta_1]\!]$$

8.2.2.2   Multiple declarations, type-checking semantics

$$\mathcal{T}_{D^*}[\![\_]\!] : \operatorname{seq} DECL \nrightarrow Env_T \longrightarrow Env_T$$

$$\mathcal{T}_{D^*}[\![\langle\,\rangle]\!] = \operatorname{id} Env_T$$

$$\mathcal{T}_{D^*}[\![\langle\delta\rangle]\!] = \mathcal{T}_D[\![\delta]\!]$$

$$\mathcal{T}_{D^*}[\![\Delta_1 \,\widehat{\ }\, \Delta_2]\!] = \mathcal{T}_{D^*}[\![\Delta_2]\!] \circ \mathcal{T}_{D^*}[\![\Delta_1]\!]$$

8.2.2.3   Multiple declarations, initialization-before-use semantics

$$\mathcal{U}_{D^*}[\![\_]\!] : \operatorname{seq} DECL \nrightarrow Env_U \longrightarrow Env_U$$

$$\mathcal{U}_{D^*}[\![\langle\,\rangle]\!] = \operatorname{id} Env_U$$

$$\mathcal{U}_{D^*}[\![\langle\delta\rangle]\!] = \mathcal{U}_D[\![\delta]\!]$$

$$\mathcal{U}_{D^*}[\![\Delta_1 \,\widehat{\ }\, \Delta_2]\!] = \mathcal{U}_{D^*}[\![\Delta_2]\!] \circ \mathcal{U}_{D^*}[\![\Delta_1]\!]$$

8.2.2.4   Multiple declarations, dynamic semantics

$$\mathcal{M}_{D^*}[\![\_]\!] : \text{seq } DECL \nrightarrow Env \longrightarrow Env$$

$$\mathcal{M}_{D^*}[\![\langle\,\rangle]\!] = \text{id } Env$$

$$\mathcal{M}_{D^*}[\![\langle\delta\rangle]\!] = \mathcal{M}_D[\![\delta]\!]$$

$$\mathcal{M}_{D^*}[\![\Delta_1 \,\widehat{\,}\, \Delta_2]\!] = \mathcal{M}_{D^*}[\![\Delta_2]\!] \circ \mathcal{M}_{D^*}[\![\Delta_1]\!]$$

8.3   Operators

$UNY\_ARITH\_OP ::= \text{negate}$

$UNY\_LOGIC\_OP ::= \text{not}$

$UNY\_OP \qquad\quad ::= \text{unyArithOp}\langle\!\langle UNY\_ARITH\_OP \rangle\!\rangle$
$\qquad\qquad\qquad | \quad \text{unyLogicOp}\langle\!\langle UNY\_LOGIC\_OP \rangle\!\rangle$

$BIN\_ARITH\_OP ::= \text{plus} \mid \text{minus}$

$BIN\_COMP\_OP ::= \text{less} \mid \text{greater} \mid \text{equal}$

$BIN\_LOGIC\_OP ::= \text{or} \mid \text{and}$

$BIN\_OP \qquad\quad ::= \text{binArithOp}\langle\!\langle BIN\_ARITH\_OP \rangle\!\rangle$
$\qquad\qquad\qquad | \quad \text{binCompOp}\langle\!\langle BIN\_COMP\_OP \rangle\!\rangle$
$\qquad\qquad\qquad | \quad \text{binLogicOp}\langle\!\langle BIN\_LOGIC\_OP \rangle\!\rangle$

8.3.1   Operators, declaration-before-use semantics

No declaration-before-use semantics needs to be defined for operators. All the necessary checking is done in the expressions, because applying an operator to them cannot introduce a further error in this semantics.

8.3.2   Operators, type-checking semantics

The meaning functions $\mathcal{T}_U[\![\,]\!]$ and $\mathcal{T}_B[\![\,]\!]$ map unary and binary operators to functions from the types of the arguments to the types of the results.

Arithmetic operators take integer arguments and return integer results; comparison operators take integers and return booleans; logical operators take booleans and return booleans:

$$\mathcal{T}_U[\![\,\_\,]\!] : UNY\_OP \longrightarrow TYPE \longrightarrow TYPE$$

$\mathcal{T}_U[\![\text{unyArithOp }\psi_\alpha]\!]\tau =$
    if $\tau = $ integer **then** integer **else** *typeWrong*

$\mathcal{T}_U[\![\text{unyLogicOp }\psi_\lambda]\!]\tau =$
    if $\tau = $ boolean **then** boolean **else** *typeWrong*

$$\mathcal{T}_B[\![\,\_\,]\!] : BIN\_OP \longrightarrow TYPE \times TYPE \longrightarrow TYPE$$

$\mathcal{T}_B[\![\text{binArithOp }\omega_\alpha]\!](\tau_1, \tau_2) =$
    if $(\tau_1 = $ integer $\wedge\ \tau_2 = $ integer$)$ **then** integer **else** *typeWrong*

$\mathcal{T}_B[\![\text{binCompOp }\omega_\chi]\!](\tau_1, \tau_2) =$
    if $(\tau_1 = $ integer $\wedge\ \tau_2 = $ integer$)$ **then** boolean **else** *typeWrong*

$\mathcal{T}_B[\![\text{binLogicOp }\omega_\lambda]\!](\tau_1, \tau_2) =$
    if $(\tau_1 = $ boolean $\wedge\ \tau_2 = $ boolean$)$ **then** boolean **else** *typeWrong*

8.3.3   Operators, initialization-before-use semantics

No initialization-before-use semantics needs to be defined for operators. All the necessary checking is done in the expressions, because applying an operator to them cannot introduce a further error in this semantics.

8.3.4   Operators, dynamic semantics

An operator produces a new value from one or two other values. The dynamic meaning functions $\mathcal{M}_U[\![\,]\!]$ and $\mathcal{M}_B[\![\,]\!]$ take unary and binary operators and map them to functions between values.

Tosca operators are defined in terms of the corresponding mathematical operators:

$$\mathcal{M}_U[\![\,\_\,]\!] : UNY\_OP \longrightarrow VALUE \nrightarrow VALUE$$

$\forall\, n : Integer\ \bullet$
    $\mathcal{M}_U[\![\text{unyArithOp negate}]\!](int_v\ n) = int_v(-n)$

$\forall\, b : Boolean\ \bullet$
    $\mathcal{M}_U[\![\text{unyLogicOp not}]\!](bool_v\ b) = bool_v(\text{if } b = \mathsf{T} \text{ then } \mathsf{F} \text{ else } \mathsf{T})$

The functions int_v and $bool_v$ are needed to map integers and booleans to *VALUE*s. In Z, logical operators can be applied only to predicates, not to values, so unfortunately it is not possible to write the meaning of unyLogicOp as $bool_v(\neg\ b)$:

$$\mathcal{M}_B[\![\_]\!] : BIN\_OP \longrightarrow VALUE \times VALUE \nrightarrow VALUE$$

$\forall\, b_1, b_2 : Boolean \bullet$

$\quad \mathcal{M}_B[\![\text{binLogicOp or}]\!](bool_v\, b_1, bool_v\, b_2) =$
$\qquad bool_v(\textbf{if } b_1 = \textsf{T} \vee b_2 = \textsf{T} \textbf{ then } \textsf{T} \textbf{ else } \textsf{F})$

$\quad \wedge\, \mathcal{M}_B[\![\text{binLogicOp and}]\!](bool_v\, b_1, bool_v\, b_2) =$
$\qquad bool_v(\textbf{if } b_1 = b_2 = \textsf{T} \textbf{ then } \textsf{T} \textbf{ else } \textsf{F})$

$\forall\, n_1, n_2 : Integer \bullet$

$\quad \mathcal{M}_B[\![\text{binArithOp plus}]\!](int_v\, n_1, int_v\, n_2) = int_v(n_1 + n_2)$

$\quad \wedge\, \mathcal{M}_B[\![\text{binArithOp minus}]\!](int_v\, n_1, int_v\, n_2) = int_v(n_1 - n_2)$

$\quad \wedge\, \mathcal{M}_B[\![\text{binCompOp less}]\!](int_v\, n_1, int_v\, n_2) =$
$\qquad bool_v(\textbf{if } n_1 < n_2 \textbf{ then } \textsf{T} \textbf{ else } \textsf{F})$

$\quad \wedge\, \mathcal{M}_B[\![\text{binCompOp greater}]\!](int_v\, n_1, int_v\, n_2) =$
$\qquad bool_v(\textbf{if } n_1 > n_2 \textbf{ then } \textsf{T} \textbf{ else } \textsf{F})$

$\quad \wedge\, \mathcal{M}_B[\![\text{binCompOp equal}]\!](int_v\, n_1, int_v\, n_2) =$
$\qquad bool_v(\textbf{if } n_1 = n_2 \textbf{ then } \textsf{T} \textbf{ else } \textsf{F})$

Notice that the effect of arithmetic overflow is undefined. For example, if $n_1 + n_2 > maxInt$, then it is not in the domain of the function int_v, and so the result is not defined. Any implementation is permitted. For example, an interpreter might print an error message, or perform extended precision arithmetic; a compiler might generate code to halt the processor, or perform modulo arithmetic. The compiler correctness proofs apply only to the defined case, where overflow does not occur. Then, for each safety critical application written in Tosca (or any other language!), there needs to be a proof that its arithmetic never overflows.

8.4 Expressions

8.4.1 Meaning functions

The meaning functions for expressions are declared in this section, to show the types of the arguments and results. They are defined in the following sections, inductively over the structure of expressions.

8.4.1.1 *Expression meaning function, declaration-before-use semantics*

An expression is checked in the current environment. The meaning function $\mathcal{D}_E[\![\,]\!]$ maps an expression to its declaration status, in the context of the name environment:

$$\mid \; \mathcal{D}_E[\![\_]\!] : EXPR \longrightarrow Env_D \longrightarrow CHECK$$

8.4.1.2 Expression meaning function, type-checking semantics

The meaning function $\mathcal{T}_E[\![\;]\!]$ maps an expression to its type, in the context of the type environment:

$$\mid \; \mathcal{T}_E[\![\_]\!] : EXPR \nrightarrow Env_T \nrightarrow TYPE$$

8.4.1.3 Expression meaning function, initialization-before-use semantics

The meaning function $\mathcal{U}_E[\![\;]\!]$ takes an expression, a use environment and state, and gives a possibly modified state (which occurs if an uninitialized variable is used in the expression):

$$\mid \; \mathcal{U}_E[\![\_]\!] : EXPR \nrightarrow Env_U \nrightarrow State_U \nrightarrow State_U$$

8.4.1.4 Expression meaning function, dynamic semantics

An expression produces a value that depends on the current state. The meaning function $\mathcal{M}_E[\![\;]\!]$ maps an expression to the value it denotes in the context of an environment and state:

$$\mid \; \mathcal{M}_E[\![\_]\!] : EXPR \nrightarrow Env \nrightarrow State \nrightarrow VALUE$$

Finding the meaning of an expression does not change the state. Hence Tosca expressions have no side effects.

8.4.2 Constant

$$EXPR ::= \mathsf{const}\langle\!\langle VALUE \rangle\!\rangle$$

8.4.2.1 Constant, declaration-before-use semantics

An expression consisting of a constant is always okay:

$$\mid \; \mathcal{D}_E[\![\mathsf{const}\; \chi]\!]\, \rho_\delta = checkOK$$

8.4.2.2 Constant, type-checking semantics

The type of an expression consisting of a constant is boolean for T and F, and integer for a number:

$$\mid \; \mathcal{T}_E[\![\mathsf{const}\; \chi]\!]\, \rho_\tau = \textbf{if } \chi \in \text{ran } bool_v \textbf{ then } \textsf{boolean } \textbf{else } \textsf{integer}$$

8.4.2.3 Constant, initialization-before-use semantics

An expression consisting of a constant is $checkOK$, and leaves the state unchanged:

$$\mid \; \mathcal{U}_E[\![\mathsf{const}\; \chi]\!]\, \rho_v = \text{id } State_U$$

8.4.2.4   Constant, dynamic semantics

The meaning of a constant is just the constant's actual mathematical value:

$$\mid \; \mathcal{M}_E[\![\text{const } \chi]\!] \, \rho \, \sigma = \chi$$

Note that the χ inside the brackets represents the syntactic literal constant, and the one outside the brackets represents its mathematical value.

8.4.3   Named variable

$$EXPR ::= \text{var} \langle\!\langle NAME \rangle\!\rangle$$

8.4.3.1   Named variable, declaration-before-use semantics

An expression consisting of a variable's name is okay if the name has been declared:

$$\mid \; \mathcal{D}_E[\![\text{var } \xi]\!] \, \rho_\delta = \textbf{if } \xi \in \text{dom } \rho_\delta \textbf{ then } \textit{checkOK} \textbf{ else } \textit{checkWrong}$$

8.4.3.2   Named variable, type-checking semantics

The type of an expression consisting of a variable's name is given by the type environment function:

$$\mid \; \mathcal{T}_E[\![\text{var } \xi]\!] \, \rho_\tau = \rho_\tau[\![\xi]\!]$$

8.4.3.3   Named variable, initialization-before-use semantics

The variable in the expression will either be uninitialized (so not in the domain of the store) or set to something (either *checkWrong* or *checkOK*).

If the variable is uninitialized, then the new store is modified to set the identifier to *checkWrong*, and the use value of the state becomes *checkWrong*.

If the variable is in the domain of the store, the store is not changed, and the state's use value is set to the worse of its previous value and that of the variable.

This is the only kind of *expression* that directly changes the store (the assignment command can also change the store):

$$
\begin{aligned}
\mid \; & \mathcal{U}_E[\![\text{var } \xi]\!] \, \rho_v (\varsigma_v, \textit{use}) = \\
& \quad (\textbf{let } \lambda == \rho_v[\![\xi]\!] \bullet \\
& \qquad \textbf{if } \lambda \in \text{dom } \varsigma_v \\
& \qquad \textbf{then } (\varsigma_v, \textit{use} \bowtie \varsigma_v \, \lambda) \\
& \qquad \textbf{else } (\varsigma_v \oplus \{\lambda \mapsto \textit{checkWrong}\}, \textit{checkWrong}) \,)
\end{aligned}
$$

8.4.3.4   Named variable, dynamic semantics

The meaning of an expression consisting of a variable's name is the variable's current value. This is found by first using the environment's variable function to find the memory location, then using the state's store function to get the corresponding value:

$$\mid \ \mathcal{M}_E[\![\mathsf{var}\ \xi]\!]\ \rho\ \sigma = (\mathit{storeOf}\ \sigma)(\rho[\![\xi]\!])$$

8.4.4   Unary expression

$$EXPR ::= \mathsf{unyExpr}\langle\!\langle UNY\_OP \times EXPR\rangle\!\rangle$$

8.4.4.1   Unary expression, declaration-before-use semantics

A unary expression declaration checks the same as its component expression:

$$\mid \ \mathcal{D}_E[\![\mathsf{unyExpr}(\psi, \epsilon)]\!] = \mathcal{D}_E[\![\epsilon]\!]$$

8.4.4.2   Unary expression, type-checking semantics

The type of a unary expression is determined by the type of the component expression, and the definition of $\mathcal{T}_U$ given above:

$$\mid \ \mathcal{T}_E[\![\mathsf{unyExpr}(\psi, \epsilon)]\!]\ \rho_\tau = \mathcal{T}_U[\![\psi]\!](\mathcal{T}_E[\![\epsilon]\!]\ \rho_\tau)$$

8.4.4.3   Unary expression, initialization-before-use semantics

A unary expression use checks the same as its component expression:

$$\mid \ \mathcal{U}_E[\![\mathsf{unyExpr}(\psi, \epsilon)]\!] = \mathcal{U}_E[\![\epsilon]\!]$$

8.4.4.4   Unary expression, dynamic semantics

The meaning of a unary operator applied to a subexpression is the corresponding mathematical operator applied to the value that the subexpression denotes:

$$\mid \ \mathcal{M}_E[\![\mathsf{unyExpr}(\psi, \epsilon)]\!]\ \rho\ \sigma = \mathcal{M}_U[\![\psi]\!](\mathcal{M}_E[\![\epsilon]\!]\ \rho\ \sigma)$$

8.4.5   Binary expression

$$EXPR ::= \mathsf{binExpr}\langle\!\langle EXPR \times BIN\_OP \times EXPR\rangle\!\rangle$$

8.4.5.1   Binary expression, declaration-before-use semantics

A binary expression is *checkOK* if both the subexpressions are *checkOK*:

$$\mathcal{D}_E[\![\mathsf{binExpr}(\epsilon_1, \omega, \epsilon_2)]\!]\, \rho_\delta = \mathcal{D}_E[\![\epsilon_1]\!]\, \rho_\delta \bowtie \mathcal{D}_E[\![\epsilon_2]\!]\, \rho_\delta$$

8.4.5.2   Binary expression, type-checking semantics

The type of a binary operator applied to two subexpressions is determined by the types of the subexpressions, and the definition of $\mathcal{T}_B$ given above:

$$\mathcal{T}_E[\![\mathsf{binExpr}(\epsilon_1, \omega, \epsilon_2)]\!]\, \rho_\tau = \mathcal{T}_B[\![\omega]\!](\mathcal{T}_E[\![\epsilon_1]\!]\, \rho_\tau, \mathcal{T}_E[\![\epsilon_2]\!]\, \rho_\tau)$$

8.4.5.3   Binary expression, initialization-before-use semantics

The use of a binary operator applied to two expressions is *checkOK* only if both expressions are *checkOK*. Notice that the store can be changed if either subexpression uses an uninitialized variable:

$$\mathcal{U}_E[\![\mathsf{binExpr}(\epsilon_1, \omega, \epsilon_2)]\!]\, \rho_v\, \sigma_v = worseState(\mathcal{U}_E[\![\epsilon_1]\!]\, \rho_v\, \sigma_v, \mathcal{U}_E[\![\epsilon_2]\!]\, \rho_v\, \sigma_v)$$

8.4.5.4   Binary expression, dynamic semantics

The value of the expression consisting of a binary operator applied to two subexpressions is the corresponding mathematical operator applied to the values of the subexpressions (remember there are no side effects, so evaluating the first subexpression changes neither the environment nor the store):

$$\mathcal{M}_E[\![\mathsf{binExpr}(\epsilon_1, \omega, \epsilon_2)]\!]\, \rho\, \sigma = \mathcal{M}_B[\![\omega]\!](\mathcal{M}_E[\![\epsilon_1]\!]\, \rho\, \sigma, \mathcal{M}_E[\![\epsilon_2]\!]\, \rho\, \sigma)$$

8.5   Commands

8.5.1   Meaning functions

The meaning functions for commands are declared in this section, to show the types of the arguments and results. They are defined in the following sections, inductively over the structure of commands.

8.5.1.1   Command meaning functions, declaration-before-use semantics

A command is checked in the current environment. The meaning function $\mathcal{D}_C[\![\,]\!]$ maps a command to its check status, in the context of the name environment. Similarly for lists of commands:

$$\mathcal{D}_C[\![\_]\!] : CMD \longrightarrow Env_D \longrightarrow CHECK$$
$$\mathcal{D}_{C^*}[\![\_]\!] : \mathsf{seq}\ CMD \longrightarrow Env_D \longrightarrow CHECK$$

8.5.1.2   Command meaning functions, type-checking semantics

The meaning function $\mathcal{T}_C[\![\,]\!]$ takes a command and type environment, and gives *checkOK* or *checkWrong*, depending on whether the command is well-typed or not. Similarly for lists of commands:

$$\mathcal{T}_C[\![\_]\!] : CMD \twoheadrightarrow Env_T \twoheadrightarrow CHECK$$

$$\mathcal{T}_{C^*}[\![\_]\!] : \text{seq } CMD \twoheadrightarrow Env_T \twoheadrightarrow CHECK$$

8.5.1.3   Command meaning functions, initialization-before-use semantics

The meaning function $\mathcal{U}_C[\![\,]\!]$ takes a command, use environment and store, and gives the new store that results from checking the command. Similarly for lists of commands:

$$\mathcal{U}_C[\![\_]\!] : CMD \twoheadrightarrow Env_U \twoheadrightarrow State_U \twoheadrightarrow State_U$$

$$\mathcal{U}_{C^*}[\![\_]\!] : \text{seq } CMD \twoheadrightarrow Env_U \twoheadrightarrow State_U \twoheadrightarrow State_U$$

8.5.1.4   Command meaning functions, dynamic semantics

A command causes a state change. The command meaning function $\mathcal{M}_C[\![\,]\!]$ maps a command to the relevant state transition function, in the context of an environment. Similarly for lists of commands:

$$\mathcal{M}_C[\![\_]\!] : CMD \twoheadrightarrow Env \twoheadrightarrow State \twoheadrightarrow State$$

$$\mathcal{M}_{C^*}[\![\_]\!] : \text{seq } CMD \twoheadrightarrow Env \twoheadrightarrow State \twoheadrightarrow State$$

8.5.2   Multiple commands

seq *CMD*

The definitions below look very similar. See section 7.7 for a discussion of this point.

8.5.2.1   Multiple commands, declaration-before-use semantics

An empty command list declaration checks okay. A command list with a single command checks the same as that command. Checking a list of commands composed of two sublists is done by checking each sublist, and taking the worse result:

$$\mathcal{D}_{C^*}[\![\langle\rangle]\!]\,\rho_\delta = checkOK$$

$$\mathcal{D}_{C^*}[\![\langle\gamma\rangle]\!]\,\rho_\delta = \mathcal{D}_C[\![\gamma]\!]\,\rho_\delta$$

$$\mathcal{D}_{C^*}[\![\Gamma_1 \,\widehat{}\, \Gamma_2]\!]\,\rho_\delta = (\mathcal{D}_{C^*}[\![\Gamma_1]\!]\,\rho_\delta) \bowtie (\mathcal{D}_{C^*}[\![\Gamma_2]\!]\,\rho_\delta)$$

8.5.2.2   *Multiple commands, type-checking semantics*

An empty command list type checks okay. A command list with a single command type checks the same as that command. Type checking a list of commands composed of two sublists is done by checking each sublist, and taking the worse result:

$$\mathcal{T}_{C^*}[\![\langle\,\rangle]\!]\,\rho_\tau = \mathit{checkOK}$$

$$\mathcal{T}_{C^*}[\![\langle\gamma\rangle]\!]\,\rho_\tau = \mathcal{T}_C[\![\gamma]\!]\,\rho_\tau$$

$$\mathcal{T}_{C^*}[\![\Gamma_1 \frown \Gamma_2]\!]\,\rho_\tau = \mathcal{T}_{C^*}[\![\Gamma_1]\!]\,\rho_\tau \bowtie \mathcal{T}_{C^*}[\![\Gamma_2]\!]\,\rho_\tau$$

8.5.2.3   *Multiple commands, initialization-before-use semantics*

An empty command list has no effect on the use state. A command list with a single command type checks the same as that command. Use checking a list of commands composed of two sublists is done by checking the second sublist in the use state that results from checking the first sublist:

$$\mathcal{U}_{C^*}[\![\langle\,\rangle]\!]\,\rho_v = \mathrm{id}\ State_U$$

$$\mathcal{U}_{C^*}[\![\langle\gamma\rangle]\!]\,\rho_v = \mathcal{U}_C[\![\gamma]\!]\,\rho_v$$

$$\mathcal{U}_{C^*}[\![\Gamma_1 \frown \Gamma_2]\!]\,\rho_v = (\mathcal{U}_{C^*}[\![\Gamma_2]\!]\,\rho_v) \circ (\mathcal{U}_{C^*}[\![\Gamma_1]\!]\,\rho_v)$$

8.5.2.4   *Multiple commands, dynamic semantics*

An empty command list has no effect on the state. A command list with a single command has the same effect as that command. Evaluating a list of commands composed of two sublists is done by evaluating the second sublist in the state that results from evaluating the first sublist:

$$\mathcal{M}_{C^*}[\![\langle\,\rangle]\!]\,\rho = \mathrm{id}\ State$$

$$\mathcal{M}_{C^*}[\![\langle\gamma\rangle]\!]\,\rho = \mathcal{M}_C[\![\gamma]\!]\,\rho$$

$$\mathcal{M}_{C^*}[\![\Gamma_1 \frown \Gamma_2]\!]\,\rho = (\mathcal{M}_{C^*}[\![\Gamma_2]\!]\,\rho) \circ (\mathcal{M}_{C^*}[\![\Gamma_1]\!]\,\rho)$$

8.5.3   Block

$$CMD ::= \mathsf{block}\langle\!\langle \mathrm{seq}_1\ CMD \rangle\!\rangle$$

8.5.3.1   *Block, declaration-before-use semantics*

A block's declaration check status is the result of checking the sequence of body commands:

$$\mathcal{D}_C[\![\mathsf{block}\ \Gamma]\!]\,\rho_\delta = \mathcal{D}_{C^*}[\![\Gamma]\!]\,\rho_\delta$$

8.5.3.2   Block, type-checking semantics

A block's type check status is the result of type checking the sequence of body commands:

$$\mid \; \mathcal{T}_C[\![\text{block }\Gamma]\!]\,\rho_\tau = \mathcal{T}_{C*}[\![\Gamma]\!]\,\rho_\tau$$

8.5.3.3   Block, initialization-before-use semantics

A block's use check status is the result of use checking the sequence of body commands:

$$\mid \; \mathcal{U}_C[\![\text{block }\Gamma]\!]\,\rho_v = \mathcal{U}_{C*}[\![\Gamma]\!]\,\rho_v$$

8.5.3.4   Block, dynamic semantics

A block's dynamic meaning is the meaning of the sequence of body commands:

$$\mid \; \mathcal{M}_C[\![\text{block }\Gamma]\!]\,\rho = \mathcal{M}_{C*}[\![\Gamma]\!]\,\rho$$

8.5.4   Skip

$$CMD ::= \text{skip}$$

8.5.4.1   Skip, declaration-before-use semantics

The skip statement always checks okay:

$$\mid \; \mathcal{D}_C[\![\text{skip}]\!]\,\rho_\delta = checkOK$$

8.5.4.2   Skip, type-checking semantics

The skip statement always type checks *checkOK*:

$$\mid \; \mathcal{T}_C[\![\text{skip}]\!]\,\rho_\tau = checkOK$$

8.5.4.3   Skip, initialization-before-use semantics

The skip statement does nothing; it leaves the store unchanged:

$$\mid \; \mathcal{U}_C[\![\text{skip}]\!]\,\rho_v = \text{id } State_U$$

8.5.4.4   Skip, dynamic semantics

The skip statement does nothing; it leaves the state unchanged:

$$\mid \; \mathcal{M}_C[\![\text{skip}]\!]\,\rho = \text{id } State$$

8.5.5 Assignment

$$CMD ::= \mathsf{assign}\langle\!\langle NAME \times EXPR \rangle\!\rangle$$

8.5.5.1 Assignment, declaration-before-use semantics

Assignment checks *checkOK* if the target variable has been declared and if the source expression checks okay:

$$\mathcal{D}_C[\![\mathsf{assign}(\xi, \epsilon)]\!]\, \rho_\delta =$$
$$(\text{if } \xi \in \mathrm{dom}\, \rho_\delta \text{ then } checkOK \text{ else } checkWrong)$$
$$\bowtie \mathcal{D}_E[\![\epsilon]\!]\, \rho_\delta$$

8.5.5.2 Assignment, type-checking semantics

Assignment type checks *checkOK* if the target variable and the source expression have the same type, and that type is not wrong:

$$\mathcal{T}_C[\![\mathsf{assign}(\xi, \epsilon)]\!]\, \rho_\tau =$$
$$\text{if } \rho_\tau[\![\xi]\!] = \mathcal{T}_E[\![\epsilon]\!]\, \rho_\tau \neq typeWrong \text{ then } checkOK \text{ else } checkWrong$$

Notice that it would not be correct simply to check that the target and source have the same types, in case they were both *typeWrong*.

8.5.5.3 Assignment, initialization-before-use semantics

The final use store depends on the use state of the variable in the store resulting from evaluating the expression (using this intermediate store can catch usage like **x := (x+1)**, where **x** has not previously been initialized).

If the variable has not yet been used (either properly or improperly, possibly in the expression), its use becomes *checkOK*, otherwise its use is left unchanged. Notice this is the case whether the expression is *checkOK* or *checkWrong*—this semantics does not worry if a variable has been set to a *checkWrong* expression, it just notes what variables are used before they are set to anything at all. In the above example, **x** is set to *checkWrong* on evaluating the expression, and hence remains wrong on evaluating the assignment:

$$\mathcal{U}_C[\![\mathsf{assign}(\xi, \epsilon)]\!]\, \rho_v\, \sigma_v =$$
$$(\text{let } \lambda == \rho_v[\![\xi]\!];\ \sigma_{v1} == \mathcal{U}_E[\![\epsilon]\!]\, \rho_v\, \sigma_v \bullet$$
$$\text{if } \lambda \in \mathrm{dom}(storeOf_U\, \sigma_v)$$
$$\text{then } \sigma_{v1}$$
$$\text{else } \sigma_{v1} \boxplus_v \{\lambda \mapsto checkOK\})$$

8.5.5.4 *Assignment, dynamic semantics*

Assignment updates the store. It modifies the value held in the target variable's store location to that of the value of the source expression:

$$\mid \; \mathcal{M}_C[\![\mathsf{assign}(\xi, \epsilon)]\!] \, \rho \, \sigma = \sigma \boxplus \{\rho[\![\xi]\!] \mapsto \mathcal{M}_E[\![\epsilon]\!] \, \rho \, \sigma\}$$

8.5.6   Choice

$$CMD ::= \mathsf{choice}\langle\!\langle EXPR \times CMD \times CMD \rangle\!\rangle$$

8.5.6.1 *Choice, declaration-before-use semantics*

The choice command checks *checkOK* only if the expression and both subcommands check *checkOK*:

$$\mid \; \mathcal{D}_C[\![\mathsf{choice}(\epsilon, \gamma_1, \gamma_2)]\!] \, \rho_\delta = \mathcal{D}_E[\![\epsilon]\!] \, \rho_\delta \bowtie \mathcal{D}_C[\![\gamma_1]\!] \, \rho_\delta \bowtie \mathcal{D}_C[\![\gamma_2]\!] \, \rho_\delta$$

8.5.6.2 *Choice, type-checking semantics*

The choice command type checks *checkOK* only if the expression has type boolean and both subcommands type check *checkOK*:

$$\mathcal{T}_C[\![\mathsf{choice}(\epsilon, \gamma_1, \gamma_2)]\!] \, \rho_\tau =$$

$$(\text{if } \mathcal{T}_E[\![\epsilon]\!] \, \rho_\tau = \mathsf{boolean \ then} \; checkOK \; \mathbf{else} \; checkWrong)$$
$$\bowtie \mathcal{T}_C[\![\gamma_1]\!] \, \rho_\tau$$
$$\bowtie \mathcal{T}_C[\![\gamma_2]\!] \, \rho_\tau$$

8.5.6.3 *Choice, initialization-before-use semantics*

If an uninitialized variable is used in one branch of a choice, it should be mapped to *checkWrong*. But if a variable is initialized in one branch of a choice, it should not be *checkOK*; that branch might never be executed.

For example, if none of **x**, **y** and **z** have been previously initialized, then after the command

if *expr* then
    begin
        x := 0;
        z := 1;
    end
else
    begin
        x := 1;
        y := 1;
        z := (z+1);
    end

we would want **x** to be set to *checkOK* and the others to be set to *checkWrong*, **y** because it is initialized in one branch but not the other, and **z** because it is initialized in one branch but set to something uninitialized in the other.

The new use state is determined by the worse of the two subcommands, evaluated in the possibly changed use state of the expression (which can occur if an uninitialized variable is used in the expression):

$$\mathcal{U}_C[\![\mathsf{choice}(\epsilon, \gamma_1, \gamma_2)]\!]\, \rho_v\, \sigma_v =$$
$$(\,\mathsf{let}\ \sigma_{v1} == \mathcal{U}_E[\![\epsilon]\!]\, \rho_v\, \sigma_v \bullet$$
$$worseState(\mathcal{U}_C[\![\gamma_1]\!]\, \rho_v\, \sigma_{v1},\ \mathcal{U}_C[\![\gamma_2]\!]\, \rho_v\, \sigma_{v1})\,)$$

Notice that the same environment is used in both branches of the choice.

8.5.6.4   *Choice, dynamic semantics*

The meaning of the conditional choice command depends on the value of the test expression. If the value of the expression is T, the *then* command is applied; if the value of the expression is F, the *else* command is applied:

$$\mathcal{M}_C[\![\mathsf{choice}(\epsilon, \gamma_1, \gamma_2)]\!]\, \rho\, \sigma =$$
$$\mathsf{if}\ \mathcal{M}_E[\![\epsilon]\!]\, \rho\, \sigma = bool_v\ \mathsf{T}\ \mathsf{then}\ \mathcal{M}_C[\![\gamma_1]\!]\, \rho\, \sigma\ \mathsf{else}\ \mathcal{M}_C[\![\gamma_2]\!]\, \rho\, \sigma$$

8.5.7   Loop

$$CMD ::= \mathsf{loop}\langle\!\langle EXPR \times CMD \rangle\!\rangle$$

8.5.7.1   *Loop, declaration-before-use semantics*

The loop command checks *checkOK* only if both the expression and the subcommand check *checkOK*:

$$\mathcal{D}_C[\![\mathsf{loop}(\epsilon, \gamma)]\!]\, \rho_\delta = \mathcal{D}_E[\![\epsilon]\!]\, \rho_\delta \bowtie \mathcal{D}_C[\![\gamma]\!]\, \rho_\delta$$

8.5.7.2   *Loop, type-checking semantics*

The loop command type checks *checkOK* only if the expression has type boolean and the subcommand type checks *checkOK*:

$$\mathcal{T}_C[\![\text{loop}(\epsilon, \gamma)]\!]\, \rho_\tau =$$

$$\qquad (\text{if } \mathcal{T}_E[\![\epsilon]\!]\, \rho_\tau = \text{boolean then } checkOK \text{ else } checkWrong)$$
$$\qquad \bowtie \mathcal{T}_C[\![\gamma]\!]\, \rho_\tau$$

8.5.7.3   *Loop, initialization-before-use semantics*

If an uninitialized variable is used in a loop, it should be mapped to *checkWrong*. But if a variable is initialized in a loop, it should not be mapped to *checkOK*: the loop might never be executed. For example, in the program

$$
\begin{aligned}
&\textbf{x : int; y : int; z : int;}\\
&\textbf{while } expr \textbf{ do}\\
&\qquad \textbf{begin}\\
&\qquad\qquad \textbf{z := x;}\\
&\qquad\qquad \textbf{y := 1;}\\
&\qquad \textbf{end}
\end{aligned}
$$

the uninitialized **x** might be used, because the loop body might be executed, and so it should be mapped to *checkWrong*. But the initialization of **y** might not occur, because the loop body might not be executed, and so it should not be mapped to *checkOK*.

   The new use state is determined by the worse of the original state and the one resulting from the body of the command, remembering that the expression (which is guaranteed to be evaluated at least once) might change the state:

$$\mathcal{U}_C[\![\text{loop}(\epsilon, \gamma)]\!]\, \rho_v\, \sigma_v =$$

$$\qquad (\textbf{let } \sigma_{v1} == \mathcal{U}_E[\![\epsilon]\!]\, \rho_v\, \sigma_v \bullet$$
$$\qquad\qquad worseState(\sigma_{v1}, \mathcal{U}_C[\![\gamma]\!]\, \rho_v\, \sigma_{v1}))$$

8.5.7.4   *Loop, dynamic semantics*

The meaning of the while loop command depends on the value of the test expression. If the value of the expression is T, the body command is applied, and then the whole while command is reapplied, to the now modified state. If the value of the expression is F, nothing is done:

$$\mathcal{M}_C[\![\text{loop}(\epsilon, \gamma)]\!]\, \rho\, \sigma =$$

$$\qquad \textbf{if } \mathcal{M}_E[\![\epsilon]\!]\, \rho\, \sigma = bool_v\, \textsf{T}$$
$$\qquad \textbf{then } \mathcal{M}_C[\![\text{loop}(\epsilon, \gamma)]\!]\, \rho\, (\mathcal{M}_C[\![\gamma]\!]\, \rho\, \sigma)$$
$$\qquad \textbf{else } \sigma$$

The definitions of the other Tosca constructs are recursive, but always in terms of their simpler components, and so the recursion terminates. The recursive definition of **loop**, however, is given in terms of itself, and so does not necessarily terminate. It has a solution only if the value of the test becomes false in some state that occurs during the evaluation, otherwise it corresponds to an 'infinite loop'. See Appendix B for further discussion of this point.

8.5.8   Input

$$CMD ::= \mathsf{input}\langle\!\langle NAME \rangle\!\rangle$$

8.5.8.1   *Input, declaration-before-use semantics*

Input checks *checkOK* if the name has been declared:

$\mathcal{D}_C[\![\mathsf{input}\,\xi]\!]\,\rho_\delta =$

   if $\xi \in \mathrm{dom}\,\rho_\delta$ **then** *checkOK* **else** *checkWrong*

8.5.8.2   *Input, type-checking semantics*

Input type checks *checkOK* if the identifier is an integer (input can only be integers in Tosca):

$\mathcal{T}_C[\![\mathsf{input}\,\xi]\!]\,\rho_\tau =$

   if $\rho_\tau[\![\xi]\!] = \mathsf{integer}$ **then** *checkOK* **else** *checkWrong*

8.5.8.3   *Input, initialization-before-use semantics*

The new use state on input depends on the use state of the variable. If it has not yet been used (either properly or improperly), its use becomes *checkOK*, otherwise its use is left unchanged:

$\mathcal{U}_C[\![\mathsf{input}\,\xi]\!]\,\rho_\upsilon\,\sigma_\upsilon =$

   (**let** $\lambda == \rho_\upsilon[\![\xi]\!]$ •

      if $\lambda \in \mathrm{dom}(storeOf_U\,\sigma_\upsilon)$
      then σ_υ
      else $\sigma_\upsilon \boxplus_\upsilon \{\lambda \mapsto checkOK\}$)

8.5.8.4   *Input, dynamic semantics*

Input removes an integer from the input list, and assigns it to the variable:

$\mathcal{M}_C[\![\mathsf{input}\,\xi]\!]\,\rho\,(\varsigma, \langle v \rangle \frown in, out) =$

$(\varsigma \oplus \{\rho[\![\xi]\!] \mapsto int_\upsilon\,v\}, in, out)$

The function int_υ maps the integer to a *VALUE*.

8.5.9 Output

$$CMD ::= \mathsf{output}\langle\!\langle EXPR\rangle\!\rangle$$

8.5.9.1   Output, declaration-before-use semantics

Output type checks *checkOK* if the expression checks okay:

$$\mid \; \mathcal{D}_C[\![\mathsf{output}\;\epsilon]\!]\,\rho_\delta = \mathcal{D}_E[\![\epsilon]\!]\,\rho_\delta$$

8.5.9.2   Output, type-checking semantics

Output type checks *checkOK* if the expression has type integer:

$$\left|\begin{array}{l} \mathcal{T}_C[\![\mathsf{output}\;\epsilon]\!]\,\rho_\tau = \\[4pt] \quad \textbf{if }\; \mathcal{T}_E[\![\epsilon]\!]\,\rho_\tau = \mathsf{integer}\; \textbf{then}\; checkOK\; \textbf{else}\; checkWrong \end{array}\right.$$

8.5.9.3   Output, initialization-before-use semantics

The new use store produced by output depends on that of the expression:

$$\mid \; \mathcal{U}_C[\![\mathsf{output}\;\epsilon]\!] = \mathcal{U}_E[\![\epsilon]\!]$$

8.5.9.4   Output, dynamic semantics

Output appends the value of the expression to the output list:

$$\left|\begin{array}{l} \mathcal{M}_C[\![\mathsf{output}\;\epsilon]\!]\,\rho(\varsigma, in, out) = \\[4pt] \quad (\varsigma, in, out \;\widehat{}\; \langle int_v\widetilde{\;}(\mathcal{M}_E[\![\epsilon]\!]\,\rho(\varsigma, in, out))\rangle) \end{array}\right.$$

The function $int_v\widetilde{\;}$ maps the *VALUE* of the expression to an integer.

8.6   Program

$$PROG ::= \mathsf{Tosca}\langle\!\langle \mathsf{seq}\;DECL \times CMD\rangle\!\rangle$$

8.6.1   Program, declaration-before-use semantics

The declaration meaning of a program maps it to a declaration check. A program's check status is the result of checking the body command in the environment of the declarations:

$$\left|\begin{array}{l} \mathcal{D}_P[\![\_]\!] : PROG \longrightarrow CHECK \\[4pt] \hline \\[-6pt] \mathcal{D}_P[\![\mathsf{Tosca}(\Delta, \gamma)]\!] = \mathcal{D}_C[\![\gamma]\!](\mathcal{D}_{D^*}[\![\Delta]\!]\varnothing) \end{array}\right.$$

A program checks okay if its check value is *checkOK*. So the condition for the rest of the semantics to be defined is

$$\mathcal{D}_P[\![\mathsf{Tosca}(\Delta, \gamma)]\!] = checkOK$$

8.6.2 Program, type-checking semantics

The type meaning of a program maps it to a type check. The command is checked in the environment of the declarations:

$$\begin{array}{|l}
\mathcal{T}_P[\![\_]\!] : PROG \nrightarrow CHECK \\
\hline
\mathcal{D}_P[\![\mathsf{Tosca}(\Delta, \gamma)]\!] = checkOK \Rightarrow \\
\quad \mathcal{T}_P[\![\mathsf{Tosca}(\Delta, \gamma)]\!] = \mathcal{T}_C[\![\gamma]\!](\mathcal{T}_{D*}[\![\Delta]\!]\varnothing)
\end{array}$$

A program type checks okay if its type check value is *checkOK*. So the condition for the initialization before use semantics to be defined is

$$\mathcal{T}_P[\![\mathsf{Tosca}(\Delta, \gamma)]\!] = checkOK$$

8.6.3 Program, initialization-before-use semantics

The use meaning of a program maps it to a use check. Use checking a program means checking the command in the environment of the declarations:

$$\begin{array}{|l}
\mathcal{U}_P[\![\_]\!] : PROG \nrightarrow CHECK \\
\hline
\mathcal{D}_P[\![\mathsf{Tosca}(\Delta, \gamma)]\!] = checkOK \\
\wedge\ \mathcal{T}_P[\![\mathsf{Tosca}(\Delta, \gamma)]\!] = checkOK \Rightarrow \\
\quad \mathcal{U}_P[\![\mathsf{Tosca}(\Delta, \gamma)]\!] = checkOf_U(\mathcal{U}_C[\![\gamma]\!](\mathcal{U}_{D*}[\![\Delta]\!]\varnothing)(\varnothing, checkOK))
\end{array}$$

A program use checks okay if its value is *checkOK*. So the condition for the dynamic semantics to be defined is

$$\mathcal{U}_P[\![\mathsf{Tosca}(\Delta, \gamma)]\!] = checkOK$$

8.6.4 Program, dynamic semantics

A program maps its input to its output. The meaning of a program is simply this mapping. Its body command is executed in the environment and state of the declarations:

$$\mathcal{M}_P[\![\_]\!] : PROG \twoheadrightarrow Input \twoheadrightarrow Output$$

$$\mathcal{D}_P[\![\mathsf{Tosca}(\Delta, \gamma)]\!] = checkOK$$
$$\wedge\ \mathcal{T}_P[\![\mathsf{Tosca}(\Delta, \gamma)]\!] = checkOK$$
$$\wedge\ \mathcal{U}_P[\![\mathsf{Tosca}(\Delta, \gamma)]\!] = checkOK \Rightarrow$$
$$\mathcal{M}_P[\![\mathsf{Tosca}(\Delta, \gamma)]\!]i =$$
$$outOf(\mathcal{M}_C[\![\gamma]\!]\,(\mathcal{M}_{D*}[\![\Delta]\!]\varnothing)\,(\varnothing, i, \langle\,\rangle)\,)$$

Notice that, even if a program passes all its static checks, it may still have errors. It may fail to terminate because of a non-terminating loop, or may fail because of insufficient input.

8.7   Freedom in the definitions

The more programming errors that can be discovered statically, the better. Each of these checks could be specified as a separate static semantics, or added as an extra condition in an existing semantics. There is a great deal of freedom in how many of these various semantics are specified, and in how the checks are distributed between the semantics. Some conditions might have been placed in different semantics, or dropped altogether; other conditions might have been added. Clarity of specification and separation of concerns should be a goal: not only should this make the specification easier to understand, but it should make the effect of the restrictions easier to predict.

A couple of places where the definitions might have been different are discussed below.

8.7.1   Simpler checking

It might seem unnecessary to keep checking that variables are initialized before use once an error has been found. For example, the definition for commands could be modified to

$$\mathcal{U}_C[\![\gamma]\!]\,\rho_v(\varsigma_v, use) =$$

> **if** $use = checkWrong$
> **then** (ς_v, use)
> **else** as before ...

The meaning of an expression might similarly be simplified not to update the store, but merely to propagate a use result.

This conceptually simpler definition results in a check result that is *checkWrong* or *checkOK*, but it gives no indication of *which* variables are being improperly used. The more complicated definition actually used results in a final state that includes information about *all* the improperly used variables. There is a trade-off between complexity of the static semantics definitions and the amount of useful information available in the final state.

8.7.2 Declared without use

Should a variable that is declared but never used be flagged? The current definition of the various static semantics does not define it to be an error. However, for a safety critical language, it might be wise to take a stricter view, and define a static semantics to check for this case. If it were thought to be important to know if variables were not used, but that such a case should not be counted as an error, then a new check status such as *checkWarn* could be introduced.

Chapter 9

Calculating the Meanings of Programs

9.1 Incorrect programs

In order to understand how the various static semantics can be used as checks, let's calculate the static meanings of various short programs that have errors in them.

9.1.1 A variable not declared

Consider the complete Tosca program

    x := true

Notice that **x** has not been declared. The abstract syntax form is

$$declErr == \mathsf{Tosca}(\langle\,\rangle, \mathsf{assign}(x, \mathsf{const}(bool_v\ \mathsf{T})))$$

and the declaration-before-use meaning is

$$\mathcal{D}_P[\![declErr]\!]$$

$$= \mathcal{D}_P[\![\mathsf{Tosca}(\langle\,\rangle, \mathsf{assign}(x, \mathsf{const}(bool_v\ \mathsf{T})))]\!]$$

$$= \mathcal{D}_C[\![\mathsf{assign}(x, \mathsf{const}(bool_v\ \mathsf{T}))]\!](\mathcal{D}_{D*}[\![\langle\,\rangle]\!]\varnothing)$$

$$= \mathcal{D}_C[\![\mathsf{assign}(x, \mathsf{const}(bool_v\ \mathsf{T}))]\!](\mathrm{id}\ Env_D\varnothing)$$

$$= \mathcal{D}_C[\![\mathsf{assign}(x, \mathsf{const}(bool_v\ \mathsf{T}))]\!]\varnothing$$

$$= checkWrong \bowtie \mathcal{D}_E[\![\mathsf{const}(bool_v\ \mathsf{T})]\!]\varnothing$$

$$= checkWrong$$

    □

9.1.2   A type error

Consider the complete Tosca program

> int x ;
> x := true

Now x has been declared, but is assigned to an expression of the wrong type. The abstract syntax form is

$$typeErr \ == \ \mathsf{Tosca}(\langle\mathsf{declVar}(x,\mathsf{integer})\rangle, \mathsf{assign}(x,\mathsf{const}(bool_v\ \mathsf{T})))$$

The declaration-before-use meaning is *checkOK*, and the type checking meaning is

$$\mathcal{T}_P[\![typeErr]\!]$$

$$= \mathcal{T}_P[\![\mathsf{Tosca}(\langle\mathsf{declVar}(x,\mathsf{integer})\rangle, \mathsf{assign}(x,\mathsf{const}(bool_v\ \mathsf{T})))]\!]$$

$$= \mathcal{T}_C[\![\mathsf{assign}(x,\mathsf{const}(bool_v\ \mathsf{T}))]\!](\mathcal{T}_{D^*}[\![\langle\mathsf{declVar}(x,\mathsf{integer})\rangle]\!]\langle\,\rangle)$$

$$= \mathcal{T}_C[\![\mathsf{assign}(x,\mathsf{const}(bool_v\ \mathsf{T}))]\!]\{x \mapsto \mathsf{integer}\}$$

$$= \textbf{if } \mathsf{integer} = \mathcal{T}_E[\![\mathsf{const}(bool_v\ \mathsf{T})]\!]\{x \mapsto \mathsf{integer}\}$$
$$\quad \textbf{then } checkOK$$
$$\quad \textbf{else } checkWrong$$

$$= \textbf{if } \mathsf{integer} = \mathsf{boolean} \textbf{ then } checkOK \textbf{ else } checkWrong$$

$$= checkWrong$$

□

9.1.3   Use without initialization

Consider the complete Tosca program

> int x ;
> output x

x has been declared, and is of the right type to be used in an **output**, but has not been assigned a value before it is used. The abstract syntax form is

$$useErr \ == \ \mathsf{Tosca}(\langle\mathsf{declVar}(x,\mathsf{integer})\rangle, \mathsf{output}(\mathsf{var}\ x))$$

The declaration-before-use meaning, and type checking meaning, are both *check-OK*, and the use checking meaning is

$$\mathcal{U}_P[\![useErr]\!]$$

$$= \mathcal{U}_P[\![\mathsf{Tosca}(\langle\mathsf{declVar}(x,\mathsf{integer})\rangle, \mathsf{output}(\mathsf{var}\ x))]\!]$$

$$= checkOf_U(\mathcal{U}_C[\![output(var\ x)]\!]$$
$$(\mathcal{U}_{D*}[\![\langle declVar(x, integer)\rangle]\!]\varnothing)(\varnothing, checkOK))$$
$$= checkOf_U(\mathcal{U}_C[\![output(var\ x)]\!]\{x \mapsto \lambda_1\}(\varnothing, checkOK))$$
$$= checkOf_U(\mathcal{U}_E[\![var\ x]\!]\{x \mapsto \lambda_1\}(\varnothing, checkOK))$$
$$= checkOf_U(\{\lambda_1 \mapsto checkWrong\}, checkWrong)$$
$$= checkWrong$$

□

9.2   The 'square' program

Now let's consider a bigger, and correct, example—the 'square' program introduced in Chapter 5.

9.2.1   Some convenient abbreviations

Before we start calculating the various static and dynamic meanings of the 'square' program, it is convenient to define some abbreviations.

Let Δ_{all} be the list of all the declarations:

$$\Delta_{all} == \langle declVar(n, integer), declVar(sq, integer), declVar(limit, integer)\rangle$$

Let γ_{loop} be the body of the while loop:

$\gamma_{loop} ==$

    block⟨assign(sq,
          binExpr(binExpr(var sq, plus, const(int_v 1)),
            plus, binExpr(var n, plus, var n))),
       assign(n, binExpr(var n, plus, const(int_v 1))),
       output(var sq) ⟩

Let γ_{body} be the body of the block:

$\gamma_{body} ==$

    block⟨assign(n, const(int_v 1)), assign(sq, const(int_v 1)),
      input $limit$, output(var sq),
      loop(binExpr(var n, less, var $limit$), γ_{loop}) ⟩

So the example program is simply

$$square = \mathsf{Tosca}(\Delta_{all}, \gamma_{body})$$

9.2.2 The 'square' program, declaration-before-use semantics

The declaration-before-use meaning of the square program is

$$\mathcal{D}_P[\![square]\!]$$
$$= \mathcal{D}_P[\![\mathsf{Tosca}(\Delta_{all}, \gamma_{body})]\!]$$

Using the definition of $\mathcal{D}_P[\![\_]\!]$ from section 8.6.1, this becomes

$$= \mathcal{D}_C[\![\gamma_{body}]\!](\mathcal{D}_{D*}[\![\Delta_{all}]\!]\varnothing)$$

Expanding the definition of Δ_{all} gives

$$= \mathcal{D}_C[\![\gamma_{body}]\!](\mathcal{D}_{D*}[\![\langle\mathsf{declVar}(n, \mathsf{integer}),$$
$$\mathsf{declVar}(sq, \mathsf{integer}), \mathsf{declVar}(limit, \mathsf{integer})\rangle]\!]\varnothing)$$

Writing the list as a concatenation of two sublists gives

$$= \mathcal{D}_C[\![\gamma_{body}]\!](\mathcal{D}_{D*}[\![\langle\mathsf{declVar}(n, \mathsf{integer})\rangle$$
$$\frown\langle\mathsf{declVar}(sq, \mathsf{integer}), \mathsf{declVar}(limit, \mathsf{integer})\rangle]\!]\varnothing)$$

Using the definition of $\mathcal{D}_{D*}[\![\Delta_1 \frown \Delta_2]\!]$ (section 8.2.2.1) gives

$$= \mathcal{D}_C[\![\gamma_{body}]\!]((\mathcal{D}_{D*}[\![\langle\mathsf{declVar}(sq, \mathsf{integer}), \mathsf{declVar}(limit, \mathsf{integer})\rangle]\!]$$
$$\circ \mathcal{D}_{D*}[\![\langle\mathsf{declVar}(n, \mathsf{integer})\rangle]\!])\varnothing)$$

Using the definition of $\mathcal{D}_{D*}[\![\langle\delta\rangle]\!]$, and the definition of composition $\circ$ gives

$$= \mathcal{D}_C[\![\gamma_{body}]\!](\mathcal{D}_{D*}[\![\langle\mathsf{declVar}(sq, \mathsf{integer}), \mathsf{declVar}(limit, \mathsf{integer})\rangle]\!]$$
$$(\mathcal{D}_D[\![\mathsf{declVar}(n, \mathsf{integer})]\!]\varnothing))$$

The meaning of the declaration of n is to add the name to the environment, mapping it to $checkOK$ (section 8.2.1.1):

$$= \mathcal{D}_C[\![\gamma_{body}]\!](\mathcal{D}_{D*}[\![\langle\mathsf{declVar}(sq, \mathsf{integer}), \mathsf{declVar}(limit, \mathsf{integer})\rangle]\!]$$
$$\{n \mapsto checkOK\})$$

Repeating this procedure for the other two declarations yields the full environment:

$$= \mathcal{D}_C[\![\gamma_{body}]\!]\rho_\delta$$
$$\text{where } \rho_\delta == \{n \mapsto checkOK, sq \mapsto checkOK, limit \mapsto checkOK\}$$

Expanding the definition of γ_{body} gives

$$= \mathcal{D}_{C*}[\![\langle\mathsf{assign}(n, \mathsf{const}(int_v 1)), \mathsf{assign}(sq, \mathsf{const}(int_v 1)),$$
$$\mathsf{input}\ limit, \mathsf{output}(\mathsf{var}\ sq),$$
$$\mathsf{loop}(\mathsf{binExpr}(\mathsf{var}\ n, \mathsf{less}, \mathsf{var}\ limit), \gamma_{loop})\rangle]\!]\rho_\delta$$

Using the definition of $\mathcal{D}_{C^*}[\![\_]\!]$ (section 8.5.1.1) multiple times:

$$= \mathcal{D}_C[\![\text{assign}(n, \text{const}(int_v\ 1))]\!]\ \rho_\delta$$
$$\bowtie \mathcal{D}_C[\![\text{assign}(sq, \text{const}(int_v\ 1))]\!]\ \rho_\delta$$
$$\bowtie \mathcal{D}_C[\![\text{input } limit]\!]\ \rho_\delta$$
$$\bowtie \mathcal{D}_C[\![\text{output}(\text{var } sq)]\!]\ \rho_\delta$$
$$\bowtie \mathcal{D}_C[\![\text{loop}(\text{binExpr}(\text{var } n, \text{less}, \text{var } limit), \gamma_{loop})]\!]\ \rho_\delta$$

Both the assignments have their target in the environment, and corresponding expressions are *checkOK*, so both assignments are *checkOK*. The input has its variable in the environment, and the output's expression is *checkOK*, so both these commands are *checkOK*, too. Thus, the expression becomes

$$= \mathcal{D}_C[\![\text{loop}(\text{binExpr}(\text{var } n, \text{less}, \text{var } limit), \gamma_{loop})]\!]\ \rho_\delta$$

Using the meaning of the loop command from section 8.5.7.1:

$$= \mathcal{D}_E[\![\text{binExpr}(\text{var } n, \text{less}, \text{var } limit)]\!]\ \rho_\delta$$
$$\bowtie \mathcal{D}_C[\![\gamma_{loop}]\!]\ \rho_\delta$$

Using the meaning of the binary expression from section 8.4.5.1, and expanding the definition of γ_{loop}:

$$= \mathcal{D}_E[\![\text{var } n]\!]\ \rho_\delta$$
$$\bowtie \mathcal{D}_E[\![\text{var } limit]\!]\ \rho_\delta$$
$$\bowtie \mathcal{D}_C[\![\text{block}\langle\text{assign}(sq,$$
$$\text{binExpr}(\text{binExpr}(\text{var } sq, \text{plus}, \text{const}(int_v\ 1)),$$
$$\text{plus}, \text{binExpr}(\text{var } n, \text{plus}, \text{var } n))),$$
$$\text{assign}(n, \text{binExpr}(\text{var } n, \text{plus}, \text{const}(int_v\ 1))),$$
$$\text{output}(\text{var } sq)\rangle]\!]\ \rho_\delta$$

Both the expressions are *checkOK*. Expanding the block's command list gives

$$= \mathcal{D}_C[\![\text{assign}(sq,$$
$$\text{binExpr}(\text{binExpr}(\text{var } sq, \text{plus}, \text{const}(int_v\ 1)),$$
$$\text{plus}, \text{binExpr}(\text{var } n, \text{plus}, \text{var } n)))]\!]\ \rho_\delta$$
$$\bowtie \mathcal{D}_C[\![\text{assign}(n, \text{binExpr}(\text{var } n, \text{plus}, \text{const}(int_v\ 1)))]\!]\ \rho_\delta$$
$$\bowtie \mathcal{D}_C[\![\text{output}(\text{var } sq)]\!]\ \rho_\delta$$

The target of the first assignment is in the environment, so this becomes

$$= \mathcal{D}_E[\![\text{binExpr}(\text{binExpr}(\text{var } sq, \text{plus}, \text{const}(int_v\ 1)),$$
$$\text{plus}, \text{binExpr}(\text{var } n, \text{plus}, \text{var } n))]\!]\ \rho_\delta$$
$$\bowtie \mathcal{D}_C[\![\text{assign}(n, \text{binExpr}(\text{var } n, \text{plus}, \text{const}(int_v\ 1)))]\!]\ \rho_\delta$$
$$\bowtie \mathcal{D}_C[\![\text{output}(\text{var } sq)]\!]\ \rho_\delta$$

$$= \mathcal{D}_E[\![\mathsf{binExpr}(\mathsf{var}\ sq, \mathsf{plus}, \mathsf{const}(int_v\ 1))]\!]\ \rho_\delta$$
$$\bowtie \mathcal{D}_E[\![\mathsf{binExpr}(\mathsf{var}\ n, \mathsf{plus}, \mathsf{var}\ n)]\!]\ \rho_\delta$$
$$\bowtie \mathcal{D}_C[\![\mathsf{assign}(n, \mathsf{binExpr}(\mathsf{var}\ n, \mathsf{plus}, \mathsf{const}(int_v\ 1)))]\!]\ \rho_\delta$$
$$\bowtie \mathcal{D}_C[\![\mathsf{output}(\mathsf{var}\ sq)]\!]\ \rho_\delta$$

$$= \mathcal{D}_E[\![\mathsf{var}\ sq]\!]\ \rho_\delta$$
$$\bowtie \mathcal{D}_E[\![\mathsf{const}(int_v\ 1)]\!]\ \rho_\delta$$
$$\bowtie \mathcal{D}_E[\![\mathsf{var}\ n]\!]\ \rho_\delta$$
$$\bowtie \mathcal{D}_E[\![\mathsf{var}\ n]\!]\ \rho_\delta$$
$$\bowtie \mathcal{D}_C[\![\mathsf{assign}(n, \mathsf{binExpr}(\mathsf{var}\ n, \mathsf{plus}, \mathsf{const}(int_v\ 1)))]\!]\ \rho_\delta$$
$$\bowtie \mathcal{D}_C[\![\mathsf{output}(\mathsf{var}\ sq)]\!]\ \rho_\delta$$

The four individual expressions are *checkOK*, so

$$= \mathcal{D}_C[\![\mathsf{assign}(n, \mathsf{binExpr}(\mathsf{var}\ n, \mathsf{plus}, \mathsf{const}(int_v\ 1)))]\!]\ \rho_\delta$$
$$\bowtie \mathcal{D}_C[\![\mathsf{output}(\mathsf{var}\ sq)]\!]\ \rho_\delta$$

The target of the assignment is in the environment, and the output checks okay, so this becomes

$$= \mathcal{D}_E[\![\mathsf{binExpr}(\mathsf{var}\ n, \mathsf{plus}, \mathsf{const}(int_v\ 1))]\!]\ \rho_\delta$$
$$= \mathcal{D}_E[\![\mathsf{var}\ n]\!]\ \rho_\delta \bowtie \mathcal{D}_E[\![\mathsf{const}(int_v\ 1)]\!]\ \rho_\delta$$

Both these expressions are *checkOK*, so we have the final result

$$\mathcal{D}_P[\![square]\!] = checkOK$$
□

So the 'square' program passes the declaration-before-use static check: it makes no use of any variables it has not declared. The other two static semantics can be calculated similarly, both giving *checkOK*.

9.2.3   The 'square' program, dynamic semantics

Let's calculate the dynamic, or execution, meaning of the 'square' program (which is its output, a sequence of numbers) for an input of 3:

$$\mathcal{M}_P[\![square]\!]\langle 3 \rangle$$
$$= \mathcal{M}_P[\![\mathsf{Tosca}(\Delta_{all}, \gamma_{body})]\!]\langle 3 \rangle$$
$$= outOf(\mathcal{M}_C[\![\gamma_{body}]\!](\mathcal{M}_{D^*}[\![\Delta_{all}]\!]\varnothing)\,(\varnothing, \langle 3 \rangle, \langle\,\rangle)\,)$$

Substituting for Δ_{all} gives

$$= outOf(\,\mathcal{M}_C[\![\gamma_{body}]\!](\mathcal{M}_{D^*}[\![\langle \mathsf{declVar}(n, \mathsf{integer}),$$
$$\mathsf{declVar}(sq, \mathsf{integer}), \mathsf{declVar}(limit, \mathsf{integer})\rangle]\!]\varnothing)$$
$$(\varnothing, \langle 3 \rangle, \langle\,\rangle)\,)$$

The declaration list can be expanded to give

$$= outOf(\,\mathcal{M}_C[\![\gamma_{body}]\!](\mathcal{M}_D[\![\text{declVar}(limit, \text{integer})]\!]$$
$$\mathcal{M}_D[\![\text{declVar}(sq, \text{integer})]\!]\mathcal{M}_D[\![\text{declVar}(n, \text{integer})]\!]\varnothing$$
$$(\varnothing, \langle 3 \rangle, \langle \rangle))\,)$$

Applying these three declarations to the initially empty environment gives

$$= outOf(\,\mathcal{M}_C[\![\gamma_{body}]\!]\,\rho_f(\varnothing, \langle 3 \rangle, \langle \rangle)\,)$$
$$\text{where } \rho_f == \{n \mapsto \lambda_n, sq \mapsto \lambda_{sq}, limit \mapsto \lambda_{limit}\}$$

The command list can now be expanded to give

$$= outOf(\,(\mathcal{M}_C[\![\text{loop}(\text{binExpr}(\text{var } n, \text{less}, \text{var } limit), \gamma_{loop})]\!]\,\rho_f)$$
$$(\mathcal{M}_C[\![\text{output}(\text{var } sq)]\!]\,\rho_f)$$
$$(\mathcal{M}_C[\![\text{input } limit]\!]\,\rho_f)$$
$$(\mathcal{M}_C[\![\text{assign}(sq, \text{const}(int_v\,1))]\!]\,\rho_f)$$
$$(\mathcal{M}_C[\![\text{assign}(n, \text{const}(int_v\,1))]\!]\,\rho_f(\varnothing, i, \langle \rangle))\,)$$

The two assignments update the store so that the location of n and the location of sq map to 1. The input command assigns the head of the input sequence to limit, and modifies the input sequence. The output command then modifies the output sequence:

$$= outOf(\mathcal{M}_C[\![\text{loop}(\text{binExpr}(\text{var } n, \text{less}, \text{var } limit), \gamma_{loop})]\!]\,\rho_f\,\sigma_1)$$
$$\text{where } \sigma_1 == (\{\lambda_n \mapsto int_v\,1, \lambda_{sq} \mapsto int_v\,1, \lambda_{limit} \mapsto int_v\,3\}, \langle \rangle, \langle 1 \rangle)$$

The meaning of the loop depends on the value of the test. The value of the test is

$$\mathcal{M}_E[\![\text{binExpr}(\text{var } n, \text{less}, \text{var } limit)]\!]\,\rho_f\,\sigma_1$$
$$= \mathcal{M}_B[\![\text{less}]\!](\mathcal{M}_E[\![\text{var } n]\!]\,\rho_f\,\sigma_1, \mathcal{M}_E[\![\text{var } limit]\!]\,\rho_f\,\sigma_1)$$
$$= \mathcal{M}_B[\![\text{less}]\!](int_v\,1, int_v\,3)$$
$$= bool_v(\text{if } 1 < 3 \text{ then } \mathsf{T} \text{ else } \mathsf{F})$$
$$= bool_v\,\mathsf{T}$$

The test is T, so the *then* branch of the *loop* definition is used, giving

$$\mathcal{M}_P[\![square]\!]\langle 3 \rangle$$
$$= outOf(\,\mathcal{M}_C[\![\text{loop}(\text{binExpr}(\text{var } n, \text{less}, \text{var } limit), \gamma_{loop})]\!]\,\rho_f$$
$$(\mathcal{M}_C[\![\text{block}\langle\text{assign}(sq,$$
$$\text{binExpr}(\text{binExpr}(\text{var } sq, \text{plus}, \text{const}(int_v\,1)),$$
$$\text{plus}, \text{binExpr}(\text{var } n, \text{plus}, \text{var } n))),$$
$$\text{assign}(n, \text{binExpr}(\text{var } n, \text{plus}, \text{const}(int_v\,1))),$$
$$\text{output}(\text{var } sq)\rangle]\!]\,\rho_f\,\sigma_1)\,)$$

Expanding out the command list in the block gives

$$= outOf(\,(\mathcal{M}_C[\![\text{loop}(\text{binExpr}(\text{var } n, \text{less}, \text{var } limit), \gamma_{loop})]\!]\,\rho_f)$$
$$(\mathcal{M}_C[\![\text{output}(\text{var } sq)]\!]\,\rho_f)$$
$$(\mathcal{M}_C[\![\text{assign}(n, \text{binExpr}(\text{var } n, \text{plus}, \text{const}(int_v\,1)))]\!]\,\rho_f)$$
$$(\mathcal{M}_C[\![\text{assign}(sq,$$
$$\text{binExpr}(\text{binExpr}(\text{var } sq, \text{plus}, \text{const}(int_v\,1)),$$
$$\text{plus}, \text{binExpr}(\text{var } n, \text{plus}, \text{var } n)))]\!]\,\rho_f\,\sigma_1)\,)$$

The meaning of the assignment to sq is

$$\mathcal{M}_C[\![\text{assign}(sq,$$
$$\text{binExpr}(\text{binExpr}(\text{var } sq, \text{plus}, \text{const}(int_v\,1)),$$
$$\text{plus}, \text{binExpr}(\text{var } n, \text{plus}, \text{var } n)))]\!]\,\rho_f\,\sigma_1$$

$$= \sigma_1 \boxplus \{\lambda_{sq} \mapsto$$
$$\mathcal{M}_E[\![\text{binExpr}(\text{binExpr}(\text{var } sq, \text{plus}, \text{const}(int_v\,1)),$$
$$\text{plus}, \text{binExpr}(\text{var } n, \text{plus}, \text{var } n)))]\!]\,\rho_{decl}\,\sigma_1\}$$

$$= \sigma_1 \boxplus \{\lambda_{sq} \mapsto$$
$$\mathcal{M}_B[\![\text{plus}]\!](\mathcal{M}_E[\![\text{binExpr}(\text{var } sq, \text{plus}, \text{const}(int_v\,1))]\!]\,\rho_{decl}\,\sigma_1,$$
$$\mathcal{M}_E[\![\text{binExpr}(\text{var } n, \text{plus}, \text{var } n)]\!]\,\rho_{decl}\,\sigma_1)\}$$

$$= \sigma_1 \boxplus \{\lambda_{sq} \mapsto \mathcal{M}_B[\![\text{plus}]\!](\mathcal{M}_B[\![\text{plus}]\!](storeOf\,\sigma_1\,sq, int_v\,1),$$
$$\mathcal{M}_B[\![\text{plus}]\!](storeOf\,\sigma_1\,n, storeOf\,\sigma_1\,n))\}$$

$$= \sigma_1 \boxplus \{\lambda_{sq} \mapsto \mathcal{M}_B[\![\text{plus}]\!](\mathcal{M}_B[\![\text{plus}]\!](int_v\,1, int_v\,1), \mathcal{M}_B[\![\text{plus}]\!](int_v\,1, int_v\,1))\}$$

$$= \sigma_1 \boxplus \{\lambda_{sq} \mapsto \mathcal{M}_B[\![\text{plus}]\!](int_v(1+1), int_v(1+1))\}$$

$$= \sigma_1 \boxplus \{\lambda_{sq} \mapsto int_v\,4\}$$

So we now have

$$\mathcal{M}_P[\![square]\!]\langle 3\rangle$$
$$= outOf(\,(\mathcal{M}_C[\![\text{loop}(\text{binExpr}(\text{var } n, \text{less}, \text{var } limit), \gamma_{loop})]\!]\,\rho_f)$$
$$(\mathcal{M}_C[\![\text{output}(\text{var } sq)]\!]\,\rho_f)$$
$$\mathcal{M}_C[\![\text{assign}(n, \text{binExpr}(\text{var } n, \text{plus}, \text{const}(int_v\,1)))]\!]\,\rho_f(\sigma_1 \boxplus \{\lambda_{sq} \mapsto int_v\,4\})\,)$$

The assignment increments the value of n, and the output command appends the value of sq to the output list, leaving us back at the loop:

$$= outOf(\mathcal{M}_C[\![\text{loop}(\text{binExpr}(\text{var } n, \text{less}, \text{var } limit), \gamma_{loop})]\!]\,\rho_f\,\sigma_2)$$
$$\text{where } \sigma_2 == (\{\lambda_n \mapsto int_v\,2, \lambda_{sq} \mapsto int_v\,4, \lambda_{limit} \mapsto int_v\,3\}, \langle\rangle, \langle 1, 4\rangle)$$

Evaluating the test in the loop in this new state σ_2 gives

$$\mathcal{M}_E[\![\text{binExpr}(\text{var } n, \text{less}, \text{var } limit)]\!]\,\rho_f\,\sigma_2$$
$$= bool_v(\textbf{if } 2 < 3 \textbf{ then } \mathsf{T} \textbf{ else } \mathsf{F})$$
$$= bool_v\,\mathsf{T}$$

So it's the *then* branch of the loop definition again. This gives the three commands again: the assignment that changes the value of *sq* to $((4+1)+(2+2)) = 9$, the increment of *n* to 3, and the output of *sq*. This leaves the state as σ_3, where

$$\sigma_3 == (\{\lambda_n \mapsto int_v\ 3, \lambda_{sq} \mapsto int_v\ 9, \lambda_{limit} \mapsto int_v\ 3\}, \langle\ \rangle, \langle 1, 4, 9\rangle)$$

and we're back at the loop again. Evaluating the test in the loop in this new state σ_3 gives

$$\mathcal{M}_E[\![\mathsf{binExpr}(\mathsf{var}\ n, \mathsf{less}, \mathsf{var}\ limit)]\!]\ \rho_f\ \sigma_3$$

$$= bool_v(\mathbf{if}\ 3 < 3\ \mathbf{then}\ \mathsf{T}\ \mathbf{else}\ \mathsf{F})$$

$$= bool_v\ \mathsf{F}$$

so this time the *else* branch in the definition of the loop is used: the identity function.

$$\mathcal{M}_P[\![square]\!]\langle 3\rangle$$

$$= outOf(\mathsf{id}\ State\ \sigma_3)$$

$$= outOf\ \sigma_3$$

$$= \langle 1, 4, 9\rangle$$

$\square$

So the meaning of the square program with input of 3 is $\langle 1, 4, 9\rangle$.

This is a lot of effort for such a simple result, and it is not sensible to calculate the meaning of a program in general this way by hand. However, when the specification is translated into Prolog, these are the sort of manipulations being performed by the interpreter. Also, they are sort of manipulations used when calculating the meaning of the compiler templates later on, in order to prove that they are correct.

Part III

The Correct Compiler

Chapter 10

Aida—the Target Language

10.1 Introduction

The example target language, Aida ('An Imaginary Denotational Assembler'), is specified in this chapter. It is closer to a machine language than Tosca, for example, it has low level jump instructions rather than high level structured constructs such as a loop. It can be thought of as the first refinement of the compiler.

Do we have to go through with Aida all that we did with Tosca? Fortunately not. This is the target language, and it is used only in a well-controlled manner. In particular, no equivalent of the use checking or type checking semantics is needed: if the source program is checked, and the translation is done correctly, the target program will be correct, too. Jumps (the dreaded gotos) are handled in a controlled fashion.

If we wanted to define a complete language, rather than just what is sufficient for the target of a translation, much more would be needed, analogous to all the static semantics checks defined for Tosca. For example, static semantics would be defined to check that

- the labels referred to in all jumps and gotos exist,

- if a value is loaded from a location, then an appropriate value has previously been stored in it,

- a value used to control a conditional jump corresponds to a boolean value.

10.2   Abstract syntax

Aida has two syntactic categories: instructions and programs. It also uses labels, which are modelled as numbers:

$Label == \mathbb{N}$

Aida's instructions are goto (an unconditional jump to a label), a conditional jump to a label, a label (the target of jumps), an instruction to load a constant value, an instruction to load a value from a location, an instruction to store a value at a location, various unary and binary arithmetic instructions, an input, and an output:

$INSTR ::=$ goto$\langle\!\langle Label \rangle\!\rangle$
$\qquad\quad |$ jump$\langle\!\langle Label \rangle\!\rangle$
$\qquad\quad |$ label$\langle\!\langle Label \rangle\!\rangle$
$\qquad\quad |$ loadConst$\langle\!\langle VALUE \rangle\!\rangle$
$\qquad\quad |$ loadVar$\langle\!\langle Locn \rangle\!\rangle$
$\qquad\quad |$ store$\langle\!\langle Locn \rangle\!\rangle$
$\qquad\quad |$ unyOp$\langle\!\langle UNY\_OP \rangle\!\rangle$
$\qquad\quad |$ binOp$\langle\!\langle BIN\_OP \times Locn \rangle\!\rangle$
$\qquad\quad |$ input
$\qquad\quad |$ output

An Aida program is a sequence of instructions:

$AIDA\_PROG ::=$ Aida$\langle\!\langle$seq $INSTR \rangle\!\rangle$

There is no need to define a concrete syntax for Aida: its abstract syntax is simple and concise enough to be understandable. For a real compiler, a concrete syntax would need to be defined in terms of the appropriate assembly language mnemonics.

10.3   Aida's domains

Locations are modelled by numbers as in Tosca. Aida's store maps locations to the values held there:

$Store_I == Locn \nrightarrow VALUE$

Note that Aida's store has the same structure as Tosca's dynamic store. In particular, the range of integers that can be stored in an Aida location is the same as can be stored in a Tosca location. Some low level languages correspond to processors that can store only a restricted range of integers in a single location (for example, 8-bit processors). For such a language, $Store_I$ is more complicated, with values mapped to multiple locations; the correctness proofs are correspondingly more complicated. These intricacies are not discussed further here.

10.3.1 Aida's state

Aida's state consists of its store, and the input and output streams:

$State_I == Store_I \times Input \times Output$

Note that Aida's state has the same structure as Tosca's dynamic state. So Tosca's update function $\boxplus$, defined in section 7.6.1.1, can also be used to update Aida's state.

Aida has a special 'accumulator' memory location, which will be used to hold the results of arithmetic operations, and also the value used to control conditional jumps:

$\mid A : Locn$

The query functions $storeOf_I$ and $outOf_I$ return the $Store_I$ and $Output$ components of the $State_I$:

$storeOf_I : State_I \longrightarrow Store_I$
$outOf_I : State_I \longrightarrow Output$

$\forall \varsigma_\iota : Store_I; \ in : Input; \ out : Output \bullet$

$storeOf_I(\varsigma_\iota, in, out) = \varsigma_\iota$
$\wedge \ outOf_I(\varsigma_\iota, in, out) = out$

10.3.2 Continuations and Aida's environment

Because of jumps, the semantics of a language like Aida is not as straightforward as that of one like Tosca. Sequences of commands do not compose in the same way. For example, the meaning of $\langle goto\ \phi, store\ \lambda \rangle$ is not the meaning of $goto\ \phi$ followed by the meaning of $store\ \lambda$; the goto command somehow bypasses the store command. The conventional way to solve this problem is to use a *continuation* semantics. A continuation is the computation that follows a command if it is not a jump; it is the state transition of the rest of the program from that point on. The meaning of a label is then simply a continuation, and a jump to a label means what is expected: the computation given by the rest of the program from that label onwards. The meaning of a jump is the meaning of the label it jumps to. (See section 10.5 for a small example of continuations.)

Hence, a continuation is a computation, that is, a state transition:

$Cont == State_I \nrightarrow State_I$

Aida's environment is a mapping from labels to what they denote, which is the computation that follows from jumping to the label. This computation is a continuation:

$Env_I == Label \nrightarrow Cont$

10.4   Aida's dynamic semantics

10.4.1   Meaning functions

The meaning functions for instructions and sequences of instructions are declared here, and defined in the following sections.

An instruction causes a state change. So the instruction meaning function $\mathcal{M}_I[\![\_]\!]$ maps an instruction to the relevant state transition function, in the context of an environment and continuation. A similar function is defined for lists of instructions.

$$\mathcal{M}_I[\![\_]\!] : INSTR \twoheadrightarrow Env_I \twoheadrightarrow Cont \twoheadrightarrow State_I \twoheadrightarrow State_I$$

$$\mathcal{M}_{I*}[\![\_]\!] : \text{seq } INSTR \twoheadrightarrow Env_I \twoheadrightarrow Cont \twoheadrightarrow State_I \twoheadrightarrow State_I$$

10.4.2   Multiple instructions

The empty list of instructions has no effect. The meaning of the singleton list is the meaning of that instruction. The meaning of a list of instructions composed of two sublists is given by the meaning of the first sublist executed with a continuation given by the second sublist:

$$\mathcal{M}_{I*}[\![\langle\rangle]\!]\,\rho_\iota\,\vartheta\,\sigma_\iota = \vartheta\,\sigma_\iota$$

$$\mathcal{M}_{I*}[\![\langle\iota\rangle]\!]\,\rho_\iota\,\vartheta\,\sigma_\iota = \mathcal{M}_I[\![\iota]\!]\,\rho_\iota\,\vartheta\,\sigma_\iota$$

$$\mathcal{M}_{I*}[\![I_1 \,\widehat{}\, I_2]\!]\,\rho_\iota\,\vartheta\,\sigma_\iota = \mathcal{M}_{I*}[\![I_1]\!]\,\rho_\iota(\mathcal{M}_{I*}[\![I_2]\!]\,\rho_\iota\,\vartheta)\,\sigma_\iota$$

10.4.3   Goto

A `goto` instruction performs its following computation with the continuation denoted by the label:

$$\mathcal{M}_I[\![\text{goto }\phi]\!]\,\rho_\iota\,\vartheta\,\sigma_\iota = \rho_\iota[\![\phi]\!]\,\sigma_\iota$$

10.4.4   Jump

A `jump` instruction is a conditional `goto`. If the value in the accumulator is F, it jumps to the label, performing its following computation with the label's continuation. Otherwise it proceeds with the original continuation:

$$\mathcal{M}_I[\![\text{jump }\phi]\!]\,\rho_\iota\,\vartheta\,\sigma_\iota =$$
$$\textbf{if } storeOf_I\,\sigma_\iota\,A = bool_v\,\textsf{F} \textbf{ then } \rho_\iota[\![\phi]\!]\,\sigma_\iota \textbf{ else } \vartheta\,\sigma_\iota$$

10.4.5   Load a constant

A `loadConst` instruction loads a constant value into the accumulator:

$$\mathcal{M}_I[\![\texttt{loadConst } \chi]\!] \, \rho_\iota \, \vartheta \, \sigma_\iota = \vartheta(\sigma_\iota \boxplus \{A \mapsto \chi\})$$

10.4.6   Load from a memory location

A `loadVar` instruction loads the value stored in a memory location into the accumulator:

$$\mathcal{M}_I[\![\texttt{loadVar } \lambda]\!] \, \rho_\iota \, \vartheta \, \sigma_\iota = \vartheta(\sigma_\iota \boxplus \{A \mapsto \mathit{storeOf}_I \, \sigma_\iota \, \lambda\})$$

10.4.7   Store a value

A `store` instruction stores the value in the accumulator at a memory location:

$$\mathcal{M}_I[\![\texttt{store } \lambda]\!] \, \rho_\iota \, \vartheta \, \sigma_\iota = \vartheta(\sigma_\iota \boxplus \{\lambda \mapsto \mathit{storeOf}_I \, \sigma_\iota \, A\})$$

10.4.8   Unary operator

A `unyOp` instruction changes the value in the accumulator in a way determined by the operator. The unary operators are assumed to have the same meaning as in Tosca.

$$\mathcal{M}_I[\![\texttt{unyOp } \psi]\!] \, \rho_\iota \, \vartheta \, \sigma_\iota = \vartheta(\sigma_\iota \boxplus \{A \mapsto \mathcal{M}_U[\![\psi]\!](\mathit{storeOf}_I \, \sigma_\iota \, A)\})$$

10.4.9   Binary operator

A `binOp` instruction combines the values in the accumulator and a memory location in a way determined by the operator. The resulting value is stored in the accumulator. The binary operators are assumed to have the same meaning as in Tosca:

$$\mathcal{M}_I[\![\texttt{binOp}(\omega, \lambda)]\!] \, \rho_\iota \, \vartheta \, \sigma_\iota =$$
$$\vartheta(\sigma_\iota \boxplus \{A \mapsto \mathcal{M}_B[\![\omega]\!](\mathit{storeOf}_I \, \sigma_\iota \, A, \mathit{storeOf}_I \, \sigma_\iota \, \lambda)\})$$

10.4.10   Input

An `input` instruction chops the the head off the input sequence and loads it into the accumulator:

$$\mathcal{M}_I[\![\texttt{input}]\!] \, \rho_\iota \, \vartheta(\varsigma_\iota, \langle n \rangle \frown \mathit{in}, \mathit{out}) = \vartheta(\varsigma_\iota \oplus \{A \mapsto \mathit{int}_v \, n\}, \mathit{in}, \mathit{out})$$

10.4.11   Output

An output instruction appends the value in the accumulator to the output sequence:

$$\mid \; \mathcal{M}_I[\![\text{output}]\!] \, \rho_\iota \, \vartheta(\varsigma_\iota, in, out) = \vartheta(\varsigma_\iota, in, out \,^\frown \langle int_v{}^\sim(\varsigma_\iota \, A)\rangle)$$

10.4.12   Labels and a program

A complete Aida program is an Aida construct, and maps input to output.

The meanings of the label and Aida constructs are defined together. In the following, it is assumed that none of the commands in the sequence of instructions I_n is a label. The body instructions are executed in an initial state that is empty, except for the input component:

$$\mathcal{M}_A[\![\_]\!] : AIDA\_PROG \rightarrowtail Input \rightarrowtail Output$$

$$\exists \rho_\iota : Env_I; \; \vartheta_1, \vartheta_2, \vartheta_3, \ldots, \vartheta_n : Cont \mid$$
$$\rho_\iota = \{\phi_1 \mapsto \vartheta_1, \phi_2 \mapsto \vartheta_2, \ldots, \phi_n \mapsto \vartheta_n\}$$
$$\wedge \; \vartheta_1 = \mathcal{M}_{I*}[\![I_1]\!] \, \rho_\iota \, \vartheta_2$$
$$\wedge \; \vartheta_2 = \mathcal{M}_{I*}[\![I_2]\!] \, \rho_\iota \, \vartheta_3$$
$$\wedge \ldots$$
$$\wedge \; \vartheta_n = \mathcal{M}_{I*}[\![I_n]\!] \, \rho_\iota (\text{id } State_I) \, \bullet$$

$$\mathcal{M}_A[\![\text{Aida}(I_0{}^\frown$$
$$\langle \text{label } \phi_1 \rangle \,^\frown I_1{}^\frown$$
$$\langle \text{label } \phi_2 \rangle \,^\frown I_2{}^\frown$$
$$\ldots \,^\frown$$
$$\langle \text{label } \phi_n \rangle \,^\frown I_n)]\!] in =$$
$$outOf_I(\, \mathcal{M}_{I*}[\![I_0]\!] \, \rho_\iota \, \vartheta_1(\varnothing, in, \langle\rangle)\,)$$

10.5   A small example

As a small example of how Aida's continuation semantics works, consider the following Aida program:

$$example ==$$

$$\text{Aida}\langle \text{loadConst}(int_v \, 0), \text{output},$$
$$\text{goto } 1, \text{loadConst}(int_v \, 1), \text{output},$$
$$\text{label } 1, \text{loadConst}(int_v \, 2), \text{output}\rangle$$

Informally, this program outputs 0, jumps over the output of 1, and then outputs 2. This can be shown formally by calculating the meaning of the program with an empty input stream:

$$\mathcal{M}_A[\![example]\!]\langle\,\rangle$$

$$= outOf_I(\,\mathcal{M}_{I^*}[\![\langle\text{loadConst}(int_v\,0),\text{output},$$
$$\text{goto}\,1,\text{loadConst}(int_v\,1),\text{output}\rangle]\!]\,\rho_\iota\,\vartheta_1(\varnothing,\langle\,\rangle,\langle\,\rangle))$$

where $\vartheta_1 == \mathcal{M}_{I^*}[\![\langle\text{loadConst}(int_v\,2),\text{output}\rangle]\!]\,\rho_\iota(\text{id }State_I)$
and $\rho_\iota == \{1 \mapsto \vartheta_1\}$

Splitting the instruction list into two gives

$$= outOf_I(\,\mathcal{M}_{I^*}[\![\langle\text{loadConst}(int_v\,0)\rangle]\!]\,\widehat{}$$
$$\langle\text{output},\text{goto}\,1,\text{loadConst}(int_v\,1),\text{output}\rangle]\!]\,\rho_\iota\,\vartheta_1(\varnothing,\langle\,\rangle,\langle\,\rangle))$$

Using the definition of $\mathcal{M}_{I^*}[\![I_1\,\widehat{}\,I_2]\!]$ from section 10.4.2 gives

$$= outOf_I(\,\mathcal{M}_{I^*}[\![\langle\text{loadConst}(int_v\,0)\rangle]\!]\,\rho_\iota$$
$$(\mathcal{M}_{I^*}[\![\langle\text{output},\text{goto}\,1,\text{loadConst}(int_v\,1),\text{output}\rangle]\!]\,\rho_\iota\,\vartheta_1)(\varnothing,\langle\,\rangle,\langle\,\rangle))$$

Using the definition of $\mathcal{M}_{I^*}[\![\langle i\rangle]\!]$ from section 10.4.2 gives

$$= outOf_I(\,\mathcal{M}_I[\![\text{loadConst}(int_v\,0)]\!]\,\rho_\iota$$
$$(\mathcal{M}_{I^*}[\![\langle\text{output},\text{goto}\,1,\text{loadConst}(int_v\,1),\text{output}\rangle]\!]\,\rho_\iota\,\vartheta_1)(\varnothing,\langle\,\rangle,\langle\,\rangle))$$

The loadConst instruction loads its value into the accumulator, and proceeds with the current continuation:

$$= outOf_I(\,\mathcal{M}_{I^*}[\![\langle\text{output},\text{goto}\,1,\text{loadConst}(int_v\,1),\text{output}\rangle]\!]\,\rho_\iota\,\vartheta_1$$
$$(\{A \mapsto int_v\,0\},\langle\,\rangle,\langle\,\rangle))$$

Splitting the instruction sequence and using the definition of $\mathcal{M}_{I^*}[\![\_]\!]$ again, gives

$$= outOf_I(\,\mathcal{M}_I[\![\text{output}]\!]\,\rho_\iota$$
$$(\mathcal{M}_{I^*}[\![\langle\text{goto}\,1,\text{loadConst}(int_v\,1),\text{output}\rangle]\!]\,\rho_\iota\,\vartheta_1)(\{A \mapsto int_v\,0\},\langle\,\rangle,\langle\,\rangle))$$

The output instruction appends the value in the accumulator to the output stream, and proceeds with the current continuation:

$$= outOf_I(\,\mathcal{M}_{I^*}[\![\langle\text{goto}\,1,\text{loadConst}(int_v\,1),\text{output}\rangle]\!]\,\rho_\iota\,\vartheta_1$$
$$(\{A \mapsto int_v\,0\},\langle\,\rangle,\langle 0\rangle))$$

Splitting the instruction sequence and using the definition of $\mathcal{M}_{I^*}[\![\_]\!]$ again, gives

$$= outOf_I(\,\mathcal{M}_I[\![\text{goto}\,1]\!]\,\rho_\iota$$
$$(\mathcal{M}_{I^*}[\![\langle\text{loadConst}(int_v\,1),\text{output}\rangle]\!]\,\rho_\iota\,\vartheta_1)(\{A \mapsto int_v\,0\},\langle\,\rangle,\langle 0\rangle))$$

The meaning of the goto instruction is the meaning of the label (section 10.4.3), which is the continuation corresponding to the computation from the position of the label, not from the current position:

$$= \mathit{outOf_I}(\, \rho_\iota[\![\phi]\!](\{A \mapsto \mathit{int_v}\, 0\}, \langle\,\rangle, \langle 0\rangle)\,)$$

Looking up the label in the environment gives the corresponding continuation:

$$= \mathit{outOf_I}(\, \vartheta_1(\{A \mapsto \mathit{int_v}\, 0\}, \langle\,\rangle, \langle 0\rangle)\,)$$

Substituting for the continuation gives

$$= \mathit{outOf_I}(\, \mathcal{M}_{I*}[\![\langle \texttt{loadConst}(\mathit{int_v}\, 2), \texttt{output}\rangle]\!]\, \rho_\iota(\text{id }\mathit{State_I})$$
$$(\{A \mapsto \mathit{int_v}\, 0\}, \langle\,\rangle, \langle 0\rangle)\,)$$

Using the definition of $\mathcal{M}_{I*}[\![\_]\!]$ from section 10.4.2 multiple times gives

$$= \mathit{outOf_I}(\, \mathcal{M}_I[\![\texttt{loadConst}(\mathit{int_v}\, 2)]\!]\, \rho_\iota(\mathcal{M}_I[\![\texttt{output}]\!]\, \rho_\iota(\text{id }\mathit{State_I}))$$
$$(\{A \mapsto \mathit{int_v}\, 0\}, \langle\,\rangle, \langle 0\rangle)\,)$$

Loading the constant into the accumulator gives

$$= \mathit{outOf_I}(\, \mathcal{M}_I[\![\texttt{output}]\!]\, \rho_\iota(\text{id }\mathit{State_I})(\{A \mapsto \mathit{int_v}\, 2\}, \langle\,\rangle, \langle 0\rangle)\,)$$

Outputting the value in the accumulator gives

$$= \mathit{outOf_I}(\, (\text{id }\mathit{State_I})(\{A \mapsto \mathit{int_v}\, 2\}, \langle\,\rangle, \langle 0, 2\rangle)\,)$$

The identity continuation leaves the state unchanged, and hence the meaning of the *example* program is the output component of this state:

$$= \langle 0, 2\rangle$$
$\square$

This small example shows how continuation semantics enable jumps to be defined. As a larger example, the meaning of the Aida form of the *square* program is calculated later. But first, it has to be compiled. That is the subject of the next chapter.

Chapter 11

The Templates—Operational Semantics

This chapter gives an 'algorithmic' style of specification that defines the compiler: it defines what Aida statements are produced for each Tosca fragment. As an algorithm, it is rather overspecified in places. Aida labels are allocated sequentially, but whether the labels to implement a choice construct, for example, are allocated before or after any labels needed in its body constructs should make no difference to the correctness of the translation. However, a choice has to be made in the specification below. This freedom is an advantage: the particular choice made (after the body) makes the correctness proofs easier.

All the translations are from a Tosca language construct to a sequence of Aida instructions.

11.1 The translation environment

During translation, variable names are allocated memory locations, and labels are allocated to implement jumps in loops and choices.

Labels (which are modelled as numbers) are allocated sequentially, and never reused.

The translation environment is a mapping from variable names to distinct locations (that excludes the accumulator):

$$Env_O == NAME \rightarrowtail (Locn \setminus \{A\})$$

The location top is greater than any allocated memory location (including the accumulator), locations above this are used to store temporary variables (when evaluating nested expressions):

$$| \quad top : Locn$$

11.2   Declarations

Declarations do not translate to instructions, they just cause modifications to the translation environment:

$$\mathcal{O}_D\langle\!\langle\_\rangle\!\rangle : DECL \nrightarrow Env_O \nrightarrow Env_O$$

$$\mathcal{O}_{D*}\langle\!\langle\_\rangle\!\rangle : \text{seq } DECL \nrightarrow Env_O \nrightarrow Env_O$$

11.2.1   Multiple declarations

Translating an empty declaration list has no effect on the environment. Translating a list of a single declaration has the same effect as translating that declaration. Translating a declaration list composed of two sublists is done by translating the first sublist (and thereby changing the environment), then translating the second sublist in the new environment:

$$\mathcal{O}_{D*}\langle\!\langle\,\langle\,\rangle\,\rangle\!\rangle\,\rho_o = \rho_o$$

$$\mathcal{O}_{D*}\langle\!\langle\,\langle\delta\rangle\,\rangle\!\rangle\,\rho_o = \mathcal{O}_D\langle\!\langle\delta\rangle\!\rangle\,\rho_o$$

$$\mathcal{O}_{D*}\langle\!\langle\,\Delta_1 \,^\frown \Delta_2\,\rangle\!\rangle\,\rho_o = (\mathcal{O}_{D*}\langle\!\langle\Delta_2\rangle\!\rangle \circ \mathcal{O}_{D*}\langle\!\langle\Delta_1\rangle\!\rangle)\,\rho_o$$

11.2.2   Variable declaration

A variable declaration modifies the translation environment by mapping the variable to a previously unallocated location. The translation is

$$\exists\lambda : Locn \mid \lambda \notin (\{A\} \cup \text{ran}\,\rho_o) \bullet$$

$$\mathcal{O}_D\langle\!\langle\text{declVar}(\xi,\tau)\rangle\!\rangle\,\rho_o = \rho_o \oplus \{\xi \mapsto \lambda\}$$

11.3   Expressions

Translating expressions produces instructions, but does not alter the environment. The translation does need to know the environment, since expressions can reference variables. It also needs to know the location above which it can store temporary variables:

$$\mathcal{O}_E\langle\!\langle\_\rangle\!\rangle : EXPR \longrightarrow Env_O \longrightarrow Locn \longrightarrow \text{seq } INSTR$$

The resulting sequence of instructions has the effect of storing the value of the expression in the accumulator.

11.3.1 Constant

A constant is stored in the accumulator directly:

$$\mid \quad \mathcal{O}_E \langle\!\mid \text{const } \chi \mid\!\rangle \, \rho_o \, \lambda = \langle \texttt{loadConst } \chi \rangle$$

11.3.2 Named variable

The value of a variable is loaded into the accumulator:

$$\mid \quad \mathcal{O}_E \langle\!\mid \text{var } \xi \mid\!\rangle \, \rho_o \, \lambda = \langle \texttt{loadVar}(\rho_o[\![\xi]\!]) \rangle$$

11.3.3 Unary expression

For a unary expression, the body expression is translated (which results in the value of the body expression being stored in the accumulator) then the relevant unary operator is applied to this value:

$$
\begin{aligned}
&\mathcal{O}_E \langle\!\mid \text{unyExpr}(\psi, \epsilon) \mid\!\rangle \, \rho_o \, \lambda = \\
&\quad \mathcal{O}_E \langle\!\mid \epsilon \mid\!\rangle \, \rho_o \, \lambda \,\widehat{\ }\, \langle \texttt{unyOp } \psi \rangle
\end{aligned}
$$

11.3.4 Binary expressions

The second subexpression is translated first, and its result stored in a temporary location. The first subexpression is then translated (ensuring any of its sub-subexpressions are stored at higher temporary locations) leaving its result in the accumulator. The appropriate binary operator is then used to combine these two values:

$$
\begin{aligned}
&\mathcal{O}_E \langle\!\mid \text{binExpr}(\epsilon_1, \omega, \epsilon_2) \mid\!\rangle \, \rho_o \, \lambda = \\
&\quad \mathcal{O}_E \langle\!\mid \epsilon_2 \mid\!\rangle \, \rho_o \, \lambda \,\widehat{\ }\, \langle \texttt{store } \lambda \rangle \\
&\quad \widehat{\ }\, \mathcal{O}_E \langle\!\mid \epsilon_1 \mid\!\rangle \, \rho_o(\lambda + 1) \,\widehat{\ }\, \langle \texttt{binOp}(\omega, \lambda) \rangle
\end{aligned}
$$

11.4 Commands

Translating commands does not change the environment. The translation needs to know the next label available to implement loops and choices, and returns a suitably updated label along with the sequence of instructions:

$$
\begin{aligned}
&\mathcal{O}_C \langle\!\mid \_ \mid\!\rangle : CMD \twoheadrightarrow Env_O \longrightarrow Label \twoheadrightarrow (Label \times \text{seq } INSTR) \\
&\mathcal{O}_{C^*} \langle\!\mid \_ \mid\!\rangle : \text{seq } CMD \twoheadrightarrow Env_O \longrightarrow Label \twoheadrightarrow (Label \times \text{seq } INSTR)
\end{aligned}
$$

The two components of the result can be extracted using the functions

$$labelOf == first[Label, seq\ INSTR]$$
$$instrOf == second[Label, seq\ INSTR]$$

11.4.1   Multiple commands

Translating an empty command list has no effect on the label, and produces no instructions. Translating a list consisting of a single command has the same effect as translating that command. Translating a command list consisting of two sub-lists is done by translating the first sublist (which may produce instructions and change the label), then translating the second sublist with the new label. The two instruction lists are concatenated:

$$\mathcal{O}_{C^*}\langle\!\langle\,\rangle\rangle\!\rangle\, \rho_o\, \phi = (\phi, \langle\,\rangle)$$

$$\mathcal{O}_{C^*}\langle\!\langle\langle\gamma\rangle\rangle\!\rangle\, \rho_o\, \phi = \mathcal{O}_C\langle\!\langle\gamma\rangle\!\rangle\, \rho_o\, \phi$$

$$\exists\, \phi_1, \phi_2 : Label \mid$$
$$\qquad \phi_1 = labelOf(\mathcal{O}_{C^*}\langle\!\langle\Gamma_1\rangle\!\rangle\, \rho_o\, \phi)$$
$$\qquad \land\ \phi_2 = labelOf(\mathcal{O}_{C^*}\langle\!\langle\Gamma_2\rangle\!\rangle\, \rho_o\, \phi_1) \bullet$$
$$\quad \mathcal{O}_{C^*}\langle\!\langle\Gamma_1 \,^\frown\, \Gamma_2\rangle\!\rangle\, \rho_o\, \phi =$$
$$\qquad (\phi_2,$$
$$\qquad\qquad instrOf(\mathcal{O}_{C^*}\langle\!\langle\Gamma_1\rangle\!\rangle\, \rho_o\, \phi)$$
$$\qquad\qquad {}^\frown instrOf(\mathcal{O}_{C^*}\langle\!\langle\Gamma_2\rangle\!\rangle\, \rho_o\, \phi_1))$$

11.4.2   Block

Translating a block command is the same as translating the list of body commands. The translation is

$$\mathcal{O}_C\langle\!\langle\, block\ \Gamma\rangle\!\rangle\, \rho_o\, \phi = \mathcal{O}_{C^*}\langle\!\langle\Gamma\rangle\!\rangle\, \rho_o\, \phi$$

11.4.3   Skip

A skip statement does not change the next label, and translates to no instructions:

$$\mathcal{O}_C\langle\!\langle\, skip\rangle\!\rangle\, \rho_o\, \phi = (\phi, \langle\,\rangle)$$

11.4.4   Assignment

The expression is translated. This leaves its value in the accumulator, from where it is stored in the relevant name's location. The next label is unchanged:

$$\mathcal{O}_C (\!| \, \text{assign}(\xi, \epsilon) \, |\!) \, \rho_o \, \phi =$$
$$(\phi, \mathcal{O}_E (\!| \, \epsilon \, |\!) \, \rho_o \ top \ \widehat{\ } \ \langle \text{store}(\rho_o [\![\xi]\!]) \rangle)$$

11.4.5 Choice

Two labels are needed to implement a choice construct, for jumping to the else part, and to the end of the choice. The final 'next label' is modified by any labels allocated on translating the two subcommands, plus these two labels. So, if before the choice the next label is m, then the *then* subcommand is translated with this value for the next label. If translating it results in the allocation of j labels the resulting value of the next label, with which the *else* subcommand is translated, is $\phi_1 = m + j$. If translating the *then* subcommand results in l more labels, after translating it the next label is $\phi_2 = m + j + l$. The final value for next label also has the two labels used for implementing the choice construct itself: $\phi_3 = m + j + l + 2$.

The translation is

$$\exists \, \phi_1, \phi_2 : Label \ |$$
$$\phi_1 = labelOf(\mathcal{O}_C (\!| \, \gamma_1 \, |\!) \, \rho_o \, \phi)$$
$$\wedge \ \phi_2 = labelOf(\mathcal{O}_C (\!| \, \gamma_2 \, |\!) \, \rho_o \, \phi_1) \ \bullet$$
$$\mathcal{O}_C (\!| \, \text{choice}(\epsilon, \gamma_1, \gamma_2) \, |\!) \, \rho_o \, \phi =$$
$$(2 + \phi_2,$$
$$\mathcal{O}_E (\!| \, \epsilon \, |\!) \, \rho_o \ top$$
$$\widehat{\ } \langle \text{jump} \, \phi_2 \rangle$$
$$\widehat{\ } \ instrOf(\mathcal{O}_C (\!| \, \gamma_1 \, |\!) \, \rho_o \, \phi)$$
$$\widehat{\ } \langle \text{goto}(1 + \phi_2), \text{label} \, \phi_2 \rangle$$
$$\widehat{\ } \ instrOf(\mathcal{O}_C (\!| \, \gamma_2 \, |\!) \, \rho_o \, \phi_1)$$
$$\widehat{\ } \langle \text{label}(1 + \phi_2) \rangle)$$

11.4.6 Loop

Two labels are needed to implement a loop construct, for jumping back to the beginning, and to the end of the loop. The final 'next label' value is modified by any labels allocated on translating the body command, plus these two labels. So, if before the loop the next label is ϕ_m, then the body command is translated with this label. If translating the body results in the allocation of j labels the resulting value of the next label is $\phi_1 = m + j$. The final result also has the two labels used for implementing the loop construct itself: $\phi_2 = m + j + 2$.

The translation is

$$\exists\,\phi_1 : Label \mid \phi_1 = labelOf(\mathcal{O}_C\langle\!\langle\gamma\rangle\!\rangle\,\rho_o\,\phi)\ \bullet$$

$$\mathcal{O}_C\langle\!\langle\,\mathsf{loop}(\epsilon,\gamma)\,\rangle\!\rangle\,\rho_o\,\phi =$$
$$(2 + \phi_1,$$
$$\langle\mathsf{label}\ \phi_1\rangle$$
$$\raise0pt\hbox{$^\frown$}\mathcal{O}_E\langle\!\langle\,\epsilon\,\rangle\!\rangle\,\rho_o\ \ top$$
$$\raise0pt\hbox{$^\frown$}\langle\mathsf{jump}(1 + \phi_1)\rangle$$
$$\raise0pt\hbox{$^\frown$}\ instrOf(\mathcal{O}_C\langle\!\langle\gamma\rangle\!\rangle\,\rho_o\,\phi)$$
$$\raise0pt\hbox{$^\frown$}\langle\mathsf{goto}\ \phi_1, \mathsf{label}(1 + \phi_1)\rangle\,)$$

11.4.7   Input

A Tosca input is translated as an Aida input to the accumulator, followed by a store at the relevant name's location. It does not change the next label:

$$\mathcal{O}_C\langle\!\langle\,\mathsf{input}\ \xi\,\rangle\!\rangle\,\rho_o\,\phi =$$
$$(\phi, \langle\mathsf{input}, \mathsf{store}(\rho_o[\![\xi]\!])\rangle)$$

11.4.8   Output

A Tosca output is translated by translating the expression (leaving the result in the accumulator), followed by an Aida output from the accumulator. It does not change the next label:

$$\mathcal{O}_C\langle\!\langle\,\mathsf{output}\ \epsilon\,\rangle\!\rangle\,\rho_o\,\phi =$$
$$(\phi, \mathcal{O}_E\langle\!\langle\,\epsilon\,\rangle\!\rangle\,\rho_o\ \ top\ \raise0pt\hbox{$^\frown$}\ \langle\mathsf{output}\rangle)$$

11.4.9   A program

A program is translated by translating the declarations in the initially empty environment, and then translating the body command in the declarations' environment:

$$\mathcal{O}_P\langle\!\langle\,\_\,\rangle\!\rangle : PROG \twoheadrightarrow AIDA\_PROG$$

$$\exists\,\rho_o : Env_O \mid \rho_o = \mathcal{O}_{D^\star}\langle\!\langle\Delta\rangle\!\rangle\varnothing\ \bullet$$

$$A < min(\mathrm{ran}\,\rho_o)$$
$$\wedge\ top > max(\mathrm{ran}\,\rho_o)$$
$$\wedge\ \mathcal{O}_P\langle\!\langle\,\mathsf{Tosca}(\Delta,\gamma)\,\rangle\!\rangle = \mathsf{Aida}(instrOf(\mathcal{O}_C\langle\!\langle\gamma\rangle\!\rangle\,\rho_o\,0))$$

A convenient choice for the location of the accumulator is to be less than any allocated location, where all such locations are given by the range of the translation environment function, $\mathrm{ran}\,\rho_o$. This choice allows higher location values to be used as temporary locations with impunity. The location *top* is defined to be greater than any allocated memory location (and, hence, necessarily higher than the accumulator).

Chapter 12

The 'Square' Example, Compiled

12.1 Compiling the example

Translating the example *square* program (Chapter 5) from the high level language Tosca into the low level language Aida (that is, compiling it) gives

$$\mathcal{O}_P \langle\!| \, square \, |\!\rangle$$
$$= \mathcal{O}_P \langle\!| \, \mathsf{Tosca}(\Delta_{all}, \gamma_{body}) \, |\!\rangle$$

First, we need to translate the declarations, in an initially empty translation environment, to give the translation environment for commands:

$$\rho_o$$
$$= \mathcal{O}_{D*} \langle\!| \, \Delta_{all} \, |\!\rangle \varnothing$$
$$= \mathcal{O}_{D*} \langle\!| \, \langle \mathsf{declVar}(n, \mathsf{integer}), \mathsf{declVar}(sq, \mathsf{integer}),$$
$$\mathsf{declVar}(limit, \mathsf{integer}) \rangle \, |\!\rangle \varnothing$$
$$= \mathcal{O}_D \langle\!| \, \mathsf{declVar}(limit, \mathsf{integer}) \, |\!\rangle$$
$$\mathcal{O}_D \langle\!| \, \mathsf{declVar}(sq, \mathsf{integer}) \, |\!\rangle$$
$$\mathcal{O}_D \langle\!| \, \mathsf{declVar}(n, \mathsf{integer}) \, |\!\rangle \varnothing$$

Let's allocate memory locations sequentially, starting at zero, and choose the location of the accumulator to be -1. (The numbers representing memory locations are written as $0_\lambda, 1_\lambda, \ldots$, and those representing labels as $0_\phi, 1_\phi, \ldots$, rather than both as $0, 1, \ldots$, so that they may more easily be distinguished in this example.)

$$\rho_o = \{ n \mapsto 0_\lambda, \, sq \mapsto 1_\lambda, \, limit \mapsto 2_\lambda \}$$

Now we can translate the body command in this environment. Setting *top* equal to 3_λ (which is greater than the accumulator and all the allocated locations):

$\mathcal{O}_P (\!| \, square \, |\!)$

$= \mathtt{Aida}(\, instrOf(\mathcal{O}_C (\!| \, \gamma_{body} \, |\!) \, \rho_o \, 0_\phi))$

$= \mathtt{Aida}(\, instrOf(\mathcal{O}_{C*} (\!| \, \langle \mathsf{assign}(n, \mathsf{const}\ int_v\ 1), \mathsf{assign}(sq, \mathsf{const}\ int_v\ 1),$
    $\mathsf{input}\ limit, \mathsf{output}(\mathsf{var}\ sq),$
    $\mathsf{loop}(\mathsf{binExpr}(\mathsf{var}\ n, \mathsf{less}, \mathsf{var}\ limit), \gamma_{loop}) \rangle \, |\!) \, \rho_o \, 0_\phi))$

Translating the first assignment gives

$\mathcal{O}_C (\!| \, \mathsf{assign}(n, \mathsf{const}\ int_v\ 1) \, |\!) \, \rho_o \, 0_\phi$

$\quad = (0_\phi, \mathcal{O}_E (\!| \, \mathsf{const}\ int_v\ 1 \, |\!) \, \rho_o \, 3_\lambda \ \widehat{\ }\ \langle \mathsf{store}\ \rho_o[\![n]\!] \rangle)$

$\quad = (0_\phi, \langle \mathtt{loadConst}\ int_v\ 1, \mathtt{store}\ 0_\lambda \rangle)$

This has not changed the next label value, so the translation of the second assignment is

$\mathcal{O}_C (\!| \, \mathsf{assign}(sq, \mathsf{const}\ int_v\ 1) \, |\!) \, \rho_o \, 0_\phi$

$\quad = (0_\phi, \langle \mathtt{loadConst}\ int_v\ 1, \mathtt{store}\ 1_\lambda \rangle)$

Again, this has not changed the next label value, and the translation of the input proceeds similarly:

$\mathcal{O}_C (\!| \, \mathsf{input}\ limit \, |\!) \, \rho_o \, 0_\phi$

$\quad = (0_\phi, \mathsf{input}\ \widehat{\ }\ \langle \mathsf{store}\ \rho_o[\![limit]\!] \rangle)$

$\quad = (0_\phi, \langle \mathtt{input}, \mathtt{store}\ 2_\lambda \rangle)$

The next label value is still 0_ϕ. Translating the output command gives

$\mathcal{O}_C (\!| \, \mathsf{output}(\mathsf{var}\ sq) \, |\!) \, \rho_o \, 0_\phi$

$\quad = (0_\phi, \mathcal{O}_E (\!| \, \mathsf{var}\ sq \, |\!) \, \rho_o \, 3_\lambda \ \widehat{\ }\ \langle \mathsf{output} \rangle)$

$\quad = (0_\phi, \langle \mathtt{loadVar}\ \rho_o[\![sq]\!], \mathtt{output} \rangle)$

$\quad = (0_\phi, \langle \mathtt{loadVar}\ 1_\lambda, \mathtt{output} \rangle)$

Putting these translations together gives

$\mathcal{O}_P (\!| \, square \, |\!)$

$= \mathtt{Aida}(\, \langle \mathtt{loadConst}\ int_v\ 1, \mathtt{store}\ 0_\lambda,$
    $\mathtt{loadConst}\ int_v\ 1, \mathtt{store}\ 1_\lambda,$
    $\mathtt{input}, \mathtt{store}\ 2_\lambda,$
    $\mathtt{loadVar}\ 1_\lambda, \mathtt{output} \rangle$
    $\widehat{\ }\ instrOf(\mathcal{O}_C (\!| \, \mathsf{loop}(\mathsf{binExpr}(\mathsf{var}\ n, \mathsf{less}, \mathsf{var}\ limit), \gamma_{loop}) \, |\!) \, \rho_o \, 0_\phi))$

The translation of the loop expression is

$$\mathcal{O}_E \langle\!\langle \text{binExpr}(\text{var } n, \text{less}, \text{var } limit) \rangle\!\rangle \, \rho_o \, 3_\lambda$$
$$= \mathcal{O}_E \langle\!\langle \text{var } limit \rangle\!\rangle \, \rho_o \, 3_\lambda \,\,\widehat{}\,\, \langle \text{store } 3_\lambda \rangle$$
$$\quad \widehat{}\, \mathcal{O}_E \langle\!\langle \text{var } n \rangle\!\rangle \, \rho_o \, 4_\lambda \,\,\widehat{}\,\, \langle \text{binOp}(\text{less}, 3_\lambda) \rangle$$
$$= \langle \text{loadVar } 2_\lambda, \text{store } 3_\lambda, \text{loadVar } 0_\lambda, \text{binOp}(\text{less}, 3_\lambda) \rangle$$

The translation of the loop body is performed with the current value of the next label, 0_ϕ. So

$$\mathcal{O}_C \langle\!\langle \gamma_{loop} \rangle\!\rangle \, \rho_o \, 0_\phi$$
$$= \mathcal{O}_{C*} \langle\!\langle \langle \text{assign}(sq,$$
$$\quad\quad \text{binExpr}(\text{binExpr}(\text{var } sq, \text{plus}, \text{const } int_v \, 1),$$
$$\quad\quad\quad \text{plus}, \text{binExpr}(\text{var } n, \text{plus}, \text{var } n)))$$
$$\quad \text{assign}(n, \text{binExpr}(\text{var } n, \text{plus}, \text{const } int_v \, 1)),$$
$$\quad \text{output}(\text{var } sq) \rangle \rangle\!\rangle \, \rho_o \, 0_\phi$$

Translating the first assignment, that to sq, gives

$$\mathcal{O}_C \langle\!\langle \text{assign}(sq,$$
$$\quad \text{binExpr}(\text{binExpr}(\text{var } sq, \text{plus}, \text{const } int_v \, 1),$$
$$\quad\quad \text{plus}, \text{binExpr}(\text{var } n, \text{plus}, \text{var } n))) \rangle\!\rangle \, \rho_o \, 0_\phi$$
$$= (\, 0_\phi,$$
$$\quad \mathcal{O}_E \langle\!\langle \text{binExpr}(\text{binExpr}(\text{var } sq, \text{plus}, \text{const } int_v \, 1),$$
$$\quad\quad \text{plus}, \text{binExpr}(\text{var } n, \text{plus}, \text{var } n)) \rangle\!\rangle \, \rho_o \, 3_\lambda$$
$$\quad \widehat{}\, \langle \text{store } \rho_o[\![sq]\!] \rangle \,)$$
$$= (\, 0_\phi,$$
$$\quad \mathcal{O}_E \langle\!\langle \text{binExpr}(\text{var } sq, \text{plus}, \text{const } int_v \, 1) \rangle\!\rangle \, \rho_o \, 3_\lambda$$
$$\quad \widehat{}\, \langle \text{store } 3_\lambda \rangle$$
$$\quad \widehat{}\, \mathcal{O}_E \langle\!\langle \text{binExpr}(\text{var } n, \text{plus}, \text{var } n) \rangle\!\rangle \, \rho_o \, 4_\lambda$$
$$\quad \widehat{}\, \langle \text{binOp}(\text{plus}, 3_\lambda), \text{store } 1_\lambda \rangle \,)$$
$$= (\, 0_\phi,$$
$$\quad \mathcal{O}_E \langle\!\langle \text{var } sq \rangle\!\rangle \, \rho_o \, 3_\lambda \,\,\widehat{}\,\, \langle \text{store } 3_\lambda \rangle$$
$$\quad \mathcal{O}_E \langle\!\langle \text{const } int_v \, 1 \rangle\!\rangle \, \rho_o \, 4_\lambda$$
$$\quad \widehat{}\, \langle \text{binOp}(\text{plus}, 3_\lambda), \text{store } 3_\lambda \rangle$$
$$\quad \widehat{}\, \mathcal{O}_E \langle\!\langle \text{var } n \rangle\!\rangle \, \rho_o \, 4_\lambda \,\,\widehat{}\,\, \langle \text{store } 4_\lambda \rangle \widehat{}$$
$$\quad \mathcal{O}_E \langle\!\langle \text{var } n \rangle\!\rangle \, \rho_o \, 5_\lambda$$
$$\quad \widehat{}\, \langle \text{binOp}(\text{plus}, 4_\lambda), \text{binOp}(\text{plus}, 3_\lambda), \text{store } 1_\lambda \rangle \,)$$
$$= (\, 0_\phi,$$
$$\quad \langle \text{loadVar } 1_\lambda, \text{store } 3_\lambda,$$
$$\quad \text{loadConst } int_v \, 1,$$
$$\quad \text{binOp}(\text{plus}, 3_\lambda), \text{store } 3_\lambda,$$
$$\quad \text{loadVar } 0_\lambda, \text{store } 4_\lambda,$$
$$\quad \text{loadVar } 0_\lambda,$$
$$\quad \text{binOp}(\text{plus}, 4_\lambda), \text{binOp}(\text{plus}, 3_\lambda), \text{store } 1_\lambda \rangle \,)$$

Translating the second assignment, to n, gives

$$\mathcal{O}_C \langle\!| \mathsf{assign}(n, \mathsf{binExpr}(\mathsf{var}\ n, \mathsf{plus}, \mathsf{const}\ int_v\ 1)) |\!\rangle 0_\phi 3_\lambda$$

$$= (\,0_\phi, \mathcal{O}_E \langle\!| \mathsf{binExpr}(\mathsf{var}\ n, \mathsf{plus}, \mathsf{const}\ int_v\ 1)|\!\rangle \rho_o\, 3_\lambda \,\widehat{\ }\,\langle \mathsf{store}\ \rho_o[\![n]\!]\rangle\,)$$

$$= (\,0_\phi,$$
$$\qquad \mathcal{O}_E \langle\!| \mathsf{var}\ n |\!\rangle \rho_o\, 3_\lambda \,\widehat{\ }\,\langle \mathsf{store}\ 3_\lambda\rangle$$
$$\qquad \widehat{\ }\,\mathcal{O}_E \langle\!| \mathsf{const}\ int_v\ 1 |\!\rangle \rho_o\, 4_\lambda \,\widehat{\ }\,\langle \mathsf{binOp}(plus, 3_\lambda),$$
$$\qquad \mathsf{store}\ 0_\lambda\rangle\,)$$

$$= (\,0_\phi,$$
$$\qquad \langle \mathsf{loadVar}\ 0_\lambda, \mathsf{store}\ 3_\lambda,$$
$$\qquad \mathsf{loadConst}\ int_v\ 1, \mathsf{binOp}(plus, 3_\lambda),$$
$$\qquad \mathsf{store}\ 0_\lambda\rangle\,)$$

Translating the output command:

$$\mathcal{O}_C \langle\!| \mathsf{output}(\mathsf{var}\ sq) |\!\rangle \rho_o\, 0_\phi$$
$$\qquad = (0_\phi, \langle \mathsf{loadVar}\ 1_\lambda, \mathsf{output}\rangle)$$

Hence, the translation of the complete loop body command is these three sequences of instructions concatenated. The next label value is still 0. The complete compiled version is

$$\mathcal{O}_P \langle\!| \,square\, |\!\rangle$$
$$= \mathsf{Aida}(\ \langle \mathsf{loadConst}\ int_v\ 1, \mathsf{store}\ 0_\lambda,$$
$$\qquad\qquad \mathsf{loadConst}\ int_v\ 1, \mathsf{store}\ 1_\lambda,$$
$$\qquad\qquad \mathsf{input}, \mathsf{store}\ 2_\lambda,$$
$$\qquad\qquad \mathsf{loadVar}\ 1_\lambda, \mathsf{output},$$
$$\qquad\quad \mathsf{label}\ 0_\phi,$$
$$\qquad\qquad \mathsf{loadVar}\ 2_\lambda, \mathsf{store}\ 3_\lambda,$$
$$\qquad\qquad \mathsf{loadVar}\ 0_\lambda, \mathsf{binOp}(\mathsf{less}, 3_\lambda),$$
$$\qquad\qquad \mathsf{jump}\ 1_\phi,$$
$$\qquad\qquad \mathsf{loadVar}\ 1_\lambda, \mathsf{store}\ 3_\lambda,$$
$$\qquad\qquad \mathsf{loadConst}\ int_v\ 1, \mathsf{binOp}(\mathsf{plus}, 3_\lambda),$$
$$\qquad\qquad \mathsf{store}\ 3_\lambda,$$
$$\qquad\qquad \mathsf{loadVar}\ 0_\lambda, \mathsf{store}\ 4_\lambda,$$
$$\qquad\qquad \mathsf{loadVar}\ 0_\lambda, \mathsf{binOp}(\mathsf{plus}, 4_\lambda),$$
$$\qquad\qquad \mathsf{binOp}(\mathsf{plus}, 3_\lambda),$$
$$\qquad\qquad \mathsf{store}\ 1_\lambda,$$
$$\qquad\qquad \mathsf{loadVar}\ 0_\lambda, \mathsf{store}\ 3_\lambda,$$
$$\qquad\qquad \mathsf{loadConst}\ int_v\ 1, \mathsf{binOp}(plus, 3_\lambda),$$
$$\qquad\qquad \mathsf{store}\ 0_\lambda,$$
$$\qquad\qquad \mathsf{loadVar}\ 1_\lambda, \mathsf{output},$$
$$\qquad\qquad \mathsf{goto}\ 0_\phi,$$
$$\qquad\quad \mathsf{label}\ 1_\phi\rangle\,)$$

□

12.2   The meaning after compilation

In this section, the meaning of the Aida version of the *square* program is calculated, for an input of 3. Tracing through this computation demonstrates how the
structure of the Aida program mirrors that of the original Tosca program. This
is the sort of close correspondence required for compiled code in high integrity
applications, that enables it to be validated against the source code.

Naming the sequence of instructions corresponding to the body of the loop as

$$I_{body} ==$$
$$\langle \text{loadVar } 1_\lambda, \text{store } 3_\lambda,$$
$$\text{loadConst } int_v \, 1, \text{binOp(plus}, 3_\lambda),$$
$$\text{store } 3_\lambda,$$
$$\text{loadVar } 0_\lambda, \text{store } 4_\lambda,$$
$$\text{loadVar } 0_\lambda, \text{binOp(plus}, 4_\lambda),$$
$$\text{binOp(plus}, 3_\lambda),$$
$$\text{store } 1_\lambda,$$
$$\text{loadVar } 0_\lambda, \text{store } 3_\lambda,$$
$$\text{loadConst } int_v \, 1, \text{binOp(plus}, 3_\lambda),$$
$$\text{store } 0_\lambda,$$
$$\text{loadVar } 1_\lambda, \text{output}\rangle$$

gives the meaning of the whole program as

$$result ==$$
$$outOf_I(\, \mathcal{M}_I[\![\text{Aida}(\langle\text{loadConst } int_v \, 1, \text{store } 0_\lambda,$$
$$\text{loadConst } int_v \, 1, \text{store } 1_\lambda,$$
$$\text{input}, \text{store } 2_\lambda,$$
$$\text{loadVar } 1_\lambda, \text{output},$$
$$\text{label } 0_\phi,$$
$$\text{loadVar } 2_\lambda, \text{store } 3_\lambda,$$
$$\text{loadVar } 0_\lambda, \text{binOp(less}, 3_\lambda),$$
$$\text{jump } 1_\phi\rangle$$
$$\frown I_{body}$$
$$\frown\langle\text{goto } 0_\phi,$$
$$\text{label } 1_\phi\rangle)]\!](\varnothing, \langle 3\rangle, \langle\,\rangle)\,)$$

To calculate the meaning of *result* we need to define the various components needed
for calculating the meaning of an Aida construct. This includes the environment,
mapping the two labels to their continuations

$$\rho_\iota == \{0_\phi \mapsto \vartheta_0, 1_\phi \mapsto \vartheta_1\}$$

and the two continuations representing the computations after the labels

$$\vartheta_0 ==$$
$$\mathcal{M}_{I*}[\![\langle \texttt{loadVar}\,2_\lambda, \texttt{store}\,3_\lambda, \texttt{loadVar}\,0_\lambda, \texttt{binOp}(\texttt{less},3_\lambda), \texttt{jump}\,1_\phi\rangle$$
$$\widehat{} I_{body} \,\widehat{}\, \langle \texttt{goto}\,0_\phi\rangle]\!]\,\rho_\iota\,\vartheta_1$$

$$\vartheta_1 == \mathcal{M}_{I*}[\![\langle\,\rangle]\!]\,\rho_\iota(\text{id}\,State_I)$$

Evaluating the `Aida` construct gives

result

$$= outOf_I(\,\mathcal{M}_{I*}[\![\langle \texttt{loadConst}\,int_v\,1, \texttt{store}\,0_\lambda, \texttt{loadConst}\,int_v\,1, \texttt{store}\,1_\lambda,$$
$$\texttt{input}, \texttt{store}\,2_\lambda, \texttt{loadVar}\,1_\lambda, \texttt{output}\rangle]\!]\,\rho_\iota\,\vartheta_0(\varnothing, \langle 3\rangle, \langle\,\rangle)\,)$$

Separating out the first instruction of the list gives

$$= outOf_I(\,\mathcal{M}_I[\![\texttt{loadConst}\,int_v\,1]\!]\,\rho_\iota(\mathcal{M}_{I*}[\![\langle \texttt{store}\,0_\lambda,$$
$$\texttt{loadConst}\,int_v\,1, \texttt{store}\,1_\lambda,$$
$$\texttt{input}, \texttt{store}\,2_\lambda, \texttt{loadVar}\,1_\lambda, \texttt{output}\rangle]\!]\,\rho_\iota\,\vartheta_0)(\varnothing, \langle 3\rangle, \langle\,\rangle)\,)$$

Evaluating this `loadConst` instruction gives

$$= outOf_I(\,\mathcal{M}_{I*}[\![\langle \texttt{store}\,0_\lambda, \texttt{loadConst}\,int_v\,1, \texttt{store}\,1_\lambda,$$
$$\texttt{input}, \texttt{store}\,2_\lambda, \texttt{loadVar}\,1_\lambda, \texttt{output}\rangle]\!]\,\rho_\iota\,\vartheta_0(\{A \mapsto int_v\,1\}, \langle 3\rangle, \langle\,\rangle)\,)$$

Proceeding similarly with the rest of the instructions leads to

$$= outOf_I(\,\vartheta_0(\{A \mapsto int_v\,1, 0_\lambda \mapsto int_v\,1, 1_\lambda \mapsto int_v\,1, 2_\lambda \mapsto int_v\,3\}, \langle\,\rangle, \langle 1\rangle)\,)$$

Substituting for ϑ_0 gives

$$= outOf_I(\,\mathcal{M}_{I*}[\![\langle \texttt{loadVar}\,2_\lambda, \texttt{store}\,3_\lambda, \texttt{loadVar}\,0_\lambda, \texttt{binOp}(\texttt{less},3_\lambda), \texttt{jump}\,1_\phi\rangle$$
$$\widehat{} I_{body} \,\widehat{}\, \langle \texttt{goto}\,0_\phi\rangle]\!]\,\rho_\iota\,\vartheta_1(\{A \mapsto int_v\,1,$$
$$0_\lambda \mapsto int_v\,1, 1_\lambda \mapsto int_v\,1, 2_\lambda \mapsto int_v\,3\}, \langle\,\rangle, \langle 1\rangle)\,)$$

Evaluating the first four instructions (up to the `jump`) gives

$$= outOf_I(\,\mathcal{M}_{I*}[\![\langle \texttt{jump}\,1_\phi\rangle \,\widehat{}\, I_{body} \,\widehat{}\, \langle \texttt{goto}\,0_\phi\rangle]\!]\,\rho_\iota\,\vartheta_1(\{A \mapsto bool_v\,\mathsf{T},$$
$$0_\lambda \mapsto int_v\,1, 1_\lambda \mapsto int_v\,1, 2_\lambda \mapsto int_v\,3, 3_\lambda \mapsto int_v\,3\},$$
$$\langle\,\rangle, \langle 1\rangle)\,)$$

The value in the accumulator is T (corresponding to the test on the Tosca while loop being T), so the `jump` does nothing: the instructions corresponding to the body of the loop are executed. Evaluating the rest of the instructions up to the `goto` (corresponding to the end of the loop) gives

$$= outOf_I(\,\mathcal{M}_I[\![\texttt{goto}\,0_\phi]\!]\,\rho_\iota\,\vartheta_1(\{A \mapsto int_v\,4,$$
$$0_\lambda \mapsto int_v\,2, 1_\lambda \mapsto int_v\,4, 2_\lambda \mapsto int_v\,3,$$
$$3_\lambda \mapsto int_v\,1, 4_\lambda \mapsto int_v\,1\}, \langle\,\rangle, \langle 1, 4\rangle)\,)$$

The goto means the following computation is performed with continuation ϑ_0 (corresponding to jumping back to the beginning of the loop):

$$= outOf_I(\ \vartheta_0(\{A \mapsto int_v\ 4, 0_\lambda \mapsto int_v\ 2, 1_\lambda \mapsto int_v\ 4, 2_\lambda \mapsto int_v\ 3,$$
$$3_\lambda \mapsto int_v\ 1, 4_\lambda \mapsto int_v\ 1\}, \langle\ \rangle, \langle 1, 4 \rangle)\ )$$

Substituting for ϑ_0 leaves us back at the beginning of the loop, but with a different state:

$$= outOf_I(\ \mathcal{M}_{I^\bullet}[\![\langle \texttt{loadVar}\ 2_\lambda, \texttt{store}\ 3_\lambda, \texttt{loadVar}\ 0_\lambda, \texttt{binOp}(\texttt{less}, 3_\lambda), \texttt{jump}\ 1_\phi \rangle$$
$$\widehat{}\ I_{body}\ \widehat{}\ \langle \texttt{goto}\ 0_\phi \rangle]\!]\ \rho_\iota\ \vartheta_1(\{A \mapsto int_v\ 4,$$
$$0_\lambda \mapsto int_v\ 2, 1_\lambda \mapsto int_v\ 4, 2_\lambda \mapsto int_v\ 3,$$
$$3_\lambda \mapsto int_v\ 1, 4_\lambda \mapsto int_v\ 1\}, \langle\ \rangle, \langle 1, 4 \rangle)\ )$$

Evaluating the first four instructions (up to the jump) again, gives

$$= outOf_I(\ \mathcal{M}_{I^\bullet}[\![\langle \texttt{jump}\ 1_\phi \rangle\ \widehat{}\ I_{body}\ \widehat{}\ \langle \texttt{goto}\ 0_\phi \rangle]\!]\ \rho_\iota\ \vartheta_1(\{A \mapsto bool_v\ \mathsf{T},$$
$$0_\lambda \mapsto int_v\ 2, 1_\lambda \mapsto int_v\ 4, 2_\lambda \mapsto int_v\ 3,$$
$$3_\lambda \mapsto int_v\ 3, 4_\lambda \mapsto int_v\ 1\}, \langle\ \rangle, \langle 1, 4 \rangle)\ )$$

The value in the accumulator is still T, so again the jump does nothing. Evaluating the rest of the instructions up to the goto gives

$$= outOf_I(\ \mathcal{M}_I[\![\texttt{goto}\ 0_\phi]\!]\ \rho_\iota\ \vartheta_1(\{A \mapsto int_v\ 9,$$
$$0_\lambda \mapsto int_v\ 3, 1_\lambda \mapsto int_v\ 9, 2_\lambda \mapsto int_v\ 3,$$
$$3_\lambda \mapsto int_v\ 2, 4_\lambda \mapsto int_v\ 2\}, \langle\ \rangle, \langle 1, 4, 9 \rangle)\ )$$

Again, the goto means the following computation is performed with continuation ϑ_0. Executing the first four commands, up to the jump, results in

$$= outOf_I(\ \mathcal{M}_{I^\bullet}[\![\langle \texttt{jump}\ 1_\phi \rangle\ \widehat{}\ I_{body}\ \widehat{}\ \langle \texttt{goto}\ 0_\phi \rangle]\!]\ \rho_\iota\ \vartheta_1(\{A \mapsto bool_v\ \mathsf{F},$$
$$0_\lambda \mapsto int_v\ 3, 1_\lambda \mapsto int_v\ 9, 2_\lambda \mapsto int_v\ 3,$$
$$3_\lambda \mapsto int_v\ 3, 4_\lambda \mapsto int_v\ 2\}, \langle\ \rangle, \langle 1, 4, 9 \rangle)\ )$$

This time the value in the accumulator is F (we have finished looping), so the jump behaves like a goto to label 1, corresponding to the end of the loop. So we have

$$= outOf_I(\ \vartheta_1(\{A \mapsto bool_v\ \mathsf{F}, 0_\lambda \mapsto int_v\ 3, 1_\lambda \mapsto int_v\ 9, 2_\lambda \mapsto int_v\ 3,$$
$$3_\lambda \mapsto int_v\ 3, 4_\lambda \mapsto int_v\ 2\}, \langle\ \rangle, \langle 1, 4, 9 \rangle)\ )$$

Substituting for ϑ_1 gives

$$= outOf_I(\ \mathcal{M}_{I^\bullet}[\![\langle\ \rangle]\!]\ \rho_\iota(\text{id}\ State_I)(\{A \mapsto bool_v\ \mathsf{F},$$
$$0_\lambda \mapsto int_v\ 3, 1_\lambda \mapsto int_v\ 9, 2_\lambda \mapsto int_v\ 3,$$
$$3_\lambda \mapsto int_v\ 3, 4_\lambda \mapsto int_v\ 2\}, \langle\ \rangle, \langle 1, 4, 9 \rangle)\ )$$

$$= outOf_I(\ \{A \mapsto bool_v\ \mathsf{F}, 0_\lambda \mapsto int_v\ 3, 1_\lambda \mapsto int_v\ 9, 2_\lambda \mapsto int_v\ 3,$$
$$3_\lambda \mapsto int_v\ 3, 4_\lambda \mapsto int_v\ 2\}, \langle\ \rangle, \langle 1, 4, 9 \rangle\ )$$

$$= \langle 1, 4, 9 \rangle$$

$\square$

So we see that the Aida meaning of the translation of *square* is the same as the Tosca meaning of *square*, for an input of $\langle 3 \rangle$. Proving that the corresponding meanings are *always* the same, for *any* Tosca program, is the topic of the next chapter.

Chapter 13

The Proofs—Calculating the Meaning of the Templates

13.1 Introduction

So far, the translation from Tosca to Aida has been purely syntactic. In this chapter, the semantics of both languages are used to prove that this translation is in fact correct.

What constitutes a correct translation? At the most abstract level, an Aida program is a correct translation of a Tosca program if the Aida meaning of the translation is the same as the Tosca meaning of the original. So the required correctness proof is

$$\vdash \mathcal{M}_P[\![\mathsf{Tosca}(\Delta, \gamma)]\!] = \mathcal{M}_A[\![\mathcal{O}_P(\!|\mathsf{Tosca}(\Delta, \gamma)|\!)]\!]$$

In order to be able to manage the sheer size of this correctness proof, it is decomposed into a lot of simpler smaller proofs, one proof for each language construct. The collection of these subproofs constitutes the complete proof.

13.2 Retrieve functions

Tosca constructs can modify the Tosca environment and state. Each individual translation of each Tosca construct is deemed correct if the resulting sequence of Aida instructions modifies the corresponding Aida state in the appropriate way.

What is the corresponding state? The Aida state is 'bigger' than the Tosca one: as well as locations to store values of variables, it also has memory locations for an accumulator (used to hold the values of expressions), and ones for storing temporary variables during complex expression evaluation. The translation environment holds information (the mapping from variable names to locations), and needs to be considered, too.

Let's define two retrieve functions (so called, because they 'retrieve' the relevant Tosca state and environment from an Aida state and translation environment).

13.2.1 Retrieve the environment

The environment retrieve function is defined to be

$$
\begin{array}{|l}
\Re_E : Env_O \longrightarrow Env \\
\hline
\forall \rho_o : Env_O \bullet \Re_E \, \rho_o = \rho_o
\end{array}
$$

The Tosca environment corresponding to a translation environment refers to the same variables, and maps them to the same locations.

13.2.2 Retrieve the state

The state retrieve function is defined to be

$$
\begin{array}{|l}
\Re_S : Env_O \longrightarrow State_I \longrightarrow State \\
\hline
\forall \rho_o : Env_O;\ \varsigma_\iota : Store_I;\ in : Input;\ out : Output \bullet \\
\quad \Re_S \, \rho_o(\varsigma_\iota, in, out) = ((\operatorname{ran} \rho_o) \lhd \varsigma_\iota, in, out)
\end{array}
$$

The Tosca state retrieved from an Aida state is that part of the Aida state containing the values of named variables, which are found from the translation environment. Hence, it excludes Aida's accumulator and temporary locations.

It is also useful to have a function that restricts the Aida state to a state containing just those locations corresponding to the accumulator, Tosca locations, and the temporary locations from *top* up to, but not including, some value, whilst ignoring the temporary locations at and above that value. This function has the effect of restricting the state to those values currently being considered, and ignoring values of temporary variables, left over from previous nested expression evaluations:

$$
\begin{array}{|l}
restrict : Env_O \times Locn \times State_I \longrightarrow State_I \\
\hline
\forall \rho_o : Env_O;\ \lambda : Locn;\ \varsigma_\iota : Store_I;\ in : Input;\ out : Output \bullet \\
\quad restrict(\rho_o, \lambda, (\varsigma_\iota, in, out)) = \\
\qquad ((\{A\} \cup \operatorname{ran} \rho_o \cup (top \mathbin{..} \lambda - 1)) \lhd \varsigma_\iota, in, out\,)
\end{array}
$$

The following lemmas about *restrict* are useful later.

Lemma r1. Restricting a state to a memory value, then restricting it to a smaller value, has the same effect as a single restriction to the smaller value:

$$
n : \mathsf{N} \vdash restrict(\rho_o, \lambda, restrict(\rho_o, \lambda + n, \sigma_\iota)) = restrict(\rho_o, \lambda, \sigma_\iota)
$$

In this and all the following proofs, each line of the proof is annotated by an explanation of the definition, law or lemma used in deriving that line from the previous one. Definitions corresponding to Tosca, Aida, or template specifications are also labelled by the relevant section number where they can be found. Laws correspond to standard laws about Z operators, as given in [Spivey 1992].

Proof:

$$restrict(\rho_o, \lambda, restrict(\rho_o, \lambda + n, (\varsigma_\iota, in, out)))$$

$$= restrict(\rho_o, \lambda,$$
$$\quad ((\{A\} \cup ran\, \rho_o \cup(top\,..\,\lambda + n - 1)) \lhd \varsigma_\iota, in, out))$$

$$= ((\{A\} \cup ran\, \rho_o \cup(top\,..\,\lambda - 1)) \lhd$$
$$\quad ((\{A\} \cup ran\, \rho_o \cup(top\,..\,\lambda + n - 1)) \lhd \varsigma_\iota), in, out)$$

$$= ((((\{A\} \cup ran\, \rho_o \cup(top\,..\,\lambda - 1)) \cap$$
$$\quad (\{A\} \cup ran\, \rho_o \cup(top\,..\,\lambda + n - 1))) \lhd \varsigma_\iota, in, out)$$

$$= ((\{A\} \cup ran\, \rho_o \cup(top\,..\,\lambda - 1)) \lhd \varsigma_\iota, in, out)$$

$$= restrict(\rho_o, \lambda, (\varsigma_\iota, in, out))$$

□

Lemma r2. Retrieving a restricted state has the same result as retrieving the unrestricted state:

$$\vdash \Re_S \rho_o(restrict(\rho_o, \lambda, \sigma_\iota)) = \Re_S \rho_o \sigma_\iota$$

Proof:

$$\Re_S \rho_o(restrict(\rho_o, \lambda, (\varsigma_\iota, in, out)))$$

$= \Re_S \rho_o((\{A\} \cup ran\, \rho_o \cup(top\,..\,\lambda - 1)) \lhd \varsigma_\iota, in, out)$	[defn *restrict*]
$= (ran\, \rho_o \lhd((\{A\} \cup ran\, \rho_o \cup(top\,..\,\lambda - 1)) \lhd \varsigma_\iota), in, out)$	[defn $\Re_S$]
$= (ran\, \rho_o \cap(\{A\} \cup ran\, \rho_o \cup(top\,..\,\lambda - 1)) \lhd \varsigma_\iota, in, out)$	[law $\lhd$]
$= (ran\, \rho_o \lhd \varsigma_\iota, in, out)$	[law $\cap, \cup$]
$= \Re_S \rho_o(\varsigma_\iota, in, out)$	[defn $\Re_S$]

□

13.3 Correctness conditions

The correctness arguments have the following structure.

1. An initial hypothesis. The initial Tosca state and environment are related by the retrieve functions to the initial Aida state and translation environment

$$Init_S \;==\; \sigma = \Re_S\,\rho_o\,\sigma_\iota$$
$$Init_E \;==\; \rho = \Re_E\,\rho_o$$

2. A final Tosca state and environment. These are calculated by applying the relevant meaning function to the before state and environment.

3. A final translation environment. This is found by translating the Tosca construct.

4. A final Aida state. This is calculated from the meaning of the sequence of Aida instructions produced by the translation.

5. A proof. The final Tosca state and environment are equal to the retrieved final state and environment.

In summary, if you start in an Aida state, first retrieve the Tosca state, then perform the Tosca operation, you should end up in the same place as you would if you first performed the translated Aida instructions, then retrieved the Tosca state. These two equivalent paths can be summarized in a generic 'correctness diagram' (Figure 13.1).

The initial Tosca state (unprimed) is the name given to the retrieved Aida state. The final states (those primed) are names given to the quantities as transformed by the appropriate Tosca, Aida, or translation meaning functions. So three of the relationships are determined by the retrieve functions, Tosca's semantics, the operational semantics, and Aida's semantics. That the fourth relationship holds is what must be proved.

13.4 Proof by structural induction

Let's say that some property needs to be proved for a general Tosca command. A command can be one of several kinds—a block, a skip, and so on—as given by the structure of the syntax for commands (section 4.7). If the property holds for each particular sort of command, then it holds for any command in general. So a proof for a general command consists of a separate proof for each branch in its free type syntax definition.

Now consider a particular branch in the syntax definition. If it is a 'base case' branch (skip in the case of commands) then the property must be proved for that

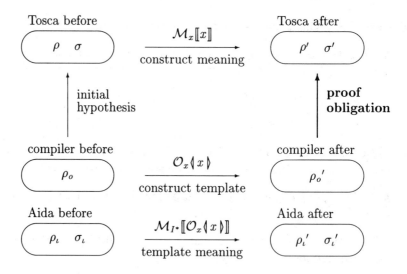

Figure 13.1 A generic correctness diagram

case. In the recursive branches the construct is built from various subcomponents. For example, a choice command has three subcomponents: an expression and two commands. To prove a property of a choice command, it is sufficient to assume that the relevant property holds for its subcomponents, and then just prove that the way they have been combined to form the *choice* is correct. This assumption is called the *induction hypothesis*, which assumes the relevant properties for the components when attempting to prove a property of the composite construct. This assumption works because it mirrors the recursive structure of the language definition; all recursive constructs are ultimately built from primitive 'base case' constructs (skip for commands, const and var for expressions) and so the chain of assumptions bottoms-out at some point.

13.5   Declarations

13.5.1   Correctness condition

Evaluating a Tosca declaration changes the environment, but not the state. Translating a Tosca declaration changes the translation environment; it translates to no Aida instructions, so has no effect on the Aida state or environment. The correctness diagram for declarations is shown in Figure 13.2.

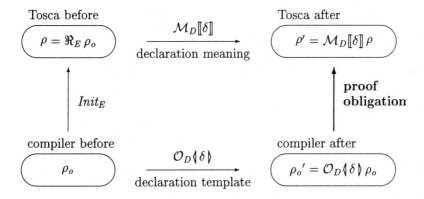

Figure 13.2 The correctness diagram for declarations

The translation is correct if the final Tosca environment corresponds to the final translation environment. The correctness condition is

$$Init_E;\ \rho' = \mathcal{M}_D[\![\delta]\!]\,\rho\,;\ \rho_o' = \mathcal{O}_D(\!\langle\delta\rangle\!)\,\rho_o$$
$$\vdash \rho' = \Re_E\,\rho_o'$$

The correctness condition for multiple declarations is analogous:

$$Init_E;\ \rho' = \mathcal{M}_{D*}[\![\Delta]\!]\,\rho\,;\ \rho_o' = \mathcal{O}_{D*}(\!\langle\Delta\rangle\!)\,\rho_o$$
$$\vdash \rho' = \Re_E\,\rho_o'$$

13.5.2 Variable declaration

The specification of the memory location allocation in the dynamic semantics and in the translation have deliberately been left loose. Hence, the locations can be chosen so as to simplify the proofs. Let's assume that the *same* locations are allocated in the Tosca dynamic semantics as in translation.

Here $\delta = \mathsf{declVar}(\xi, \tau)$. So

$$\rho_o'$$
$$= \mathcal{O}_D(\!\langle\mathsf{declVar}(\xi, \tau)\rangle\!)\,\rho_o \qquad\qquad [\text{defn } \rho_o']$$
$$= \rho_o \oplus \{\xi \mapsto \lambda\} \qquad\qquad [\text{template } 11.2.2]$$
$$= \rho \oplus \{\xi \mapsto \lambda\} \qquad\qquad [Init_E]$$
$$= \mathcal{M}_D[\![\mathsf{declVar}(\xi, \lambda)]\!]\,\rho \qquad\qquad [\text{Tosca } 8.2.1.4]$$
$$= \rho' \qquad\qquad [\text{defn } \rho']$$

$\square$

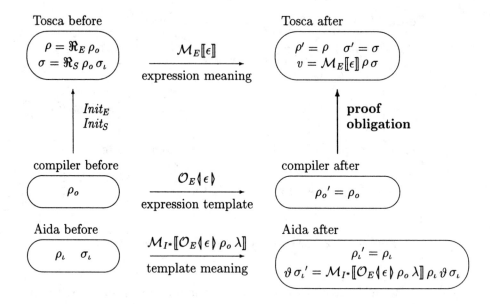

Figure 13.3 The correctness diagram for expressions

13.5.3   Multiple declarations

The definition of the translation for multiple declarations follows the form of the definition of the meaning of multiple declarations. Given the correctness of the single declaration translation, the multiple declaration correctness follows directly.

13.6   Expressions

13.6.1   Correctness condition

Evaluating a Tosca expression produces a value, and changes neither the environment nor the state (except possibly for some temporary variables). The translation is correct if doing the translation and evaluating the translated fragments leaves the states and environments corresponding, while storing the associated value in the accumulator. The correctness diagram for expressions is shown in Figure 13.3.

Expression evaluation does not change the environment. After evaluation, the result of an expression should be stored in the accumulator. None of the values stored in those Aida locations corresponding to Tosca locations should be changed, neither should those in temporary locations below the current 'next location' value. Ones stored at and above this value may be changed during evaluation, since they may be intermediate results, no longer needed. The correctness condition is

$Init_E$; $Init_S$;
$\rho_o{}' = \rho_o$; $\rho_\iota{}' = \rho_\iota$; $\vartheta\,\sigma_\iota{}' = \mathcal{M}_{I*}[\![\mathcal{O}_E (\!\epsilon\!)\, \rho_o\,\lambda]\!]\,\rho_\iota\,\vartheta\,\sigma_\iota$;
$\sigma' = \sigma$; $\rho' = \rho$;
$v = \mathcal{M}_E[\![\epsilon]\!]\,\rho\,\sigma$

$\qquad \vdash restrict(\rho_o{}', \lambda, \vartheta\,\sigma_\iota{}') = restrict(\rho_o, \lambda, \vartheta(\sigma_\iota \boxplus \{A \mapsto v\}))$

For the two base cases (constant and variable) it is possible to prove the stronger condition

$\qquad \ldots \vdash \vartheta\,\sigma_\iota{}' = \vartheta(\sigma_\iota \boxplus \{A \mapsto v\})$

because neither of these change any temporary locations.

13.6.2 Induction hypothesis

Where subexpressions occur in an expression, they are assumed to have been translated correctly, leaving the correct value in the accumulator and not affecting any of the temporary locations *below* λ:

$restrict(\rho_o, \lambda_h, \mathcal{M}_{I*}[\![\mathcal{O}_E (\!\epsilon\!)], \rho_o, \lambda_h]\!]\,\rho_\iota\,\vartheta_h\,\sigma_\iota$
$\quad = restrict(\rho_o, \lambda_h, \vartheta_h(\sigma_\iota \boxplus \{A \mapsto \mathcal{M}_E[\![\epsilon]\!]\,\rho\,\sigma\}))$

13.6.3 Constant

Here $\epsilon = $ const χ. This is a base case, so there is no need for the induction hypothesis. So

$\vartheta\,\sigma_\iota{}'$

$\quad = \mathcal{M}_{I*}[\![\mathcal{O}_E (\!$ const $\chi\!)\, \rho_o\,\lambda]\!]\,\rho_\iota\,\vartheta\,\sigma_\iota \qquad\qquad$ [defn $\sigma_\iota{}'$]

$\quad = \mathcal{M}_I[\![\text{loadConst}\ \chi]\!]\,\rho_\iota\,\vartheta\,\sigma_\iota \qquad\qquad$ [template 11.3.1]

$\quad = \vartheta(\sigma_\iota \boxplus \{A \mapsto \chi\}) \qquad\qquad$ [Aida 10.4.5]

$\quad = \vartheta(\sigma_\iota \boxplus \{A \mapsto \mathcal{M}_E[\![\text{const}\ \chi]\!]\,\rho\,\sigma\}) \qquad\qquad$ [Tosca 8.4.2.4]

$\quad = \vartheta(\sigma_\iota \boxplus \{A \mapsto v\}) \qquad\qquad$ [defn v]

$\square$

13.6.4   Named variable

Here $\epsilon = \text{var } \xi$. This is a base case, so there is no need for the induction hypothesis. So

$$\vartheta\, \sigma_\iota{}'$$

$$= \mathcal{M}_{I*}[\![\mathcal{O}_E\{\!\text{var } \xi\}\, \rho_o\, \lambda]\!]\, \rho_\iota\, \vartheta\, \sigma_\iota \qquad\qquad [\text{defn } \sigma_\iota{}']$$

$$= \mathcal{M}_I[\![\texttt{loadVar}\, \rho_o[\![\xi]\!]]\!]\, \rho_\iota\, \vartheta\, \sigma_\iota \qquad\qquad [\text{template } 11.3.2]$$

$$= \vartheta(\sigma_\iota \boxplus \{A \mapsto \mathit{storeOf}_I\, \sigma_\iota\, \rho_o[\![\xi]\!]\}) \qquad\qquad [\text{Aida } 10.4.6]$$

$$= \vartheta(\sigma_\iota \boxplus \{A \mapsto \mathit{storeOf}\, \sigma\, \rho[\![\xi]\!]\}) \qquad\qquad [\text{defn } \sigma, \rho]$$

$$= \vartheta(\sigma_\iota \boxplus \{A \mapsto \mathcal{M}_E[\![\text{var } \xi]\!]\, \rho\, \sigma\}) \qquad\qquad [\text{Tosca } 8.4.3.4]$$

$$= \vartheta(\sigma_\iota \boxplus \{A \mapsto v\}) \qquad\qquad [\text{defn } v]$$

□

13.6.5   Unary expression

Here $\epsilon = \text{unyExpr}(\psi, \epsilon)$. The induction hypothesis is assumed for the subexpression. So

$$\mathit{restrict}(\rho_o, \lambda, \vartheta\, \sigma_\iota{}')$$

$$= \mathit{restrict}(\rho_o, \lambda, \mathcal{M}_{I*}[\![\mathcal{O}_E\{\!\text{unyExpr}(\psi, \epsilon)\}\, \rho_o\, \lambda]\!]\, \rho_\iota\, \vartheta\, \sigma_\iota) \qquad [\text{defn } \sigma_\iota{}']$$

$$= \mathit{restrict}(\rho_o, \lambda, \qquad\qquad\qquad\qquad\qquad\qquad [\text{template } 11.3.3]$$
$$\mathcal{M}_{I*}[\![\mathcal{O}_E\{\!\epsilon\}\, \rho_o\, \lambda^\frown\langle\texttt{unyOp } \psi\rangle]\!]\, \rho_\iota\, \vartheta\, \sigma_\iota)$$

$$= \mathit{restrict}(\rho_o, \lambda, \qquad\qquad\qquad\qquad\qquad\qquad [\text{Aida } 10.4.2]$$
$$\mathcal{M}_{I*}[\![\mathcal{O}_E\{\!\epsilon\}\, \rho_o\, \lambda]\!]\, \rho_\iota(\mathcal{M}_I[\![\texttt{unyOp } \psi]\!]\, \rho_\iota\, \vartheta)\, \sigma_\iota)$$

$$= \mathit{restrict}(\rho_o, \lambda, \qquad\qquad\qquad\qquad\qquad\qquad [\text{induction hyp.}]$$
$$\mathcal{M}_I[\![\texttt{unyOp } \psi]\!]\, \rho_\iota\, \vartheta(\sigma_\iota \boxplus \{A \mapsto \mathcal{M}_E[\![\epsilon]\!]\, \rho\, \sigma\}))$$

$$= \mathit{restrict}(\rho_o, \lambda, \vartheta(\sigma_\iota \boxplus \{A \mapsto \mathcal{M}_U[\![\psi]\!]\mathcal{M}_E[\![\epsilon]\!]\, \rho\, \sigma\})) \qquad [\text{Aida } 10.4.8]$$

$$= \mathit{restrict}(\rho_o, \lambda, \vartheta(\sigma_\iota \boxplus \{A \mapsto \mathcal{M}_E[\![\text{unyExpr}(\psi, \epsilon)]\!]\, \rho\, \sigma\})) \quad [\text{Tosca } 8.4.4.4]$$

$$= \mathit{restrict}(\rho_o, \lambda, \vartheta(\sigma_\iota \boxplus \{A \mapsto v\}) \qquad\qquad\qquad [\text{defn } v]$$

□

13.6.6 Binary expression

Here $\epsilon = \mathsf{binExpr}(\epsilon_1, \omega, \epsilon_2)$. The induction hypothesis is assumed twice, once for each subexpression, with different values of λ_h. So

$$restrict(\rho_o, \lambda, \vartheta\, \sigma_\iota')$$

$$= restrict(\rho_o, \lambda, \mathcal{M}_{I*}[\![\mathcal{O}_E \langle\!|\, \mathsf{binExpr}(\epsilon_1, \omega, \epsilon_2) \,|\!\rangle\, \rho_o\, \lambda]\!]\, \rho_\iota\, \vartheta\, \sigma_\iota) \qquad [\text{defn } \sigma_\iota']$$

$$= restrict(\rho_o, \lambda, \qquad\qquad\qquad\qquad\qquad\qquad [\text{template } 11.3.4]$$
$$\mathcal{M}_{I*}[\![\mathcal{O}_E \langle\!|\, \epsilon_2 \,|\!\rangle\, \rho_o\, \lambda\, \hat{} \langle \mathtt{store}\, \lambda \rangle\, \hat{}\, \mathcal{O}_E \langle\!|\, \epsilon_1 \,|\!\rangle\, \rho_o(\lambda + 1)$$
$$\hat{} \langle \mathtt{binOp}(\omega, \lambda) \rangle]\!]\, \rho_\iota\, \vartheta\, \sigma_\iota)$$

$$= restrict(\rho_o, \lambda, \qquad\qquad\qquad\qquad\qquad\qquad\qquad [\text{Aida } 10.4.2]$$
$$\mathcal{M}_{I*}[\![\mathcal{O}_E \langle\!|\, \epsilon_2 \,|\!\rangle\, \rho_o\, \lambda]\!]\, \rho_\iota(\mathcal{M}_{I*}[\![\langle \mathtt{store}\, \lambda \rangle\, \hat{}\, \mathcal{O}_E \langle\!|\, \epsilon_1 \,|\!\rangle\, \rho_o(\lambda + 1)$$
$$\hat{} \langle \mathtt{binOp}(\omega, \lambda) \rangle]\!]\, \rho_\iota\, \vartheta)\, \sigma_\iota)$$

$$= restrict(\rho_o, \lambda, \mathcal{M}_{I*}[\![\langle \mathtt{store}\, \lambda \rangle\, \hat{}\, \mathcal{O}_E \langle\!|\, \epsilon_1 \,|\!\rangle\, \rho_o(\lambda + 1) \qquad [\text{induction hyp.}]$$
$$\hat{} \langle \mathtt{binOp}(\omega, \lambda) \rangle]\!]\, \rho_\iota\, \vartheta(\sigma_\iota \boxplus \{A \mapsto \mathcal{M}_E[\![\epsilon_2]\!]\, \rho\, \sigma\}))$$

$$= restrict(\rho_o, \lambda, \qquad\qquad\qquad\qquad\qquad\qquad\qquad [\text{Aida } 10.4.7]$$
$$\mathcal{M}_{I*}[\![\mathcal{O}_E \langle\!|\, \epsilon_1 \,|\!\rangle\, \rho_o(\lambda + 1)]\!]\, \rho_\iota(\mathcal{M}_I[\![\mathtt{binOp}(\omega, \lambda)]\!]\, \rho_\iota\, \vartheta)$$
$$(\sigma_\iota \boxplus \{A \mapsto \mathcal{M}_E[\![\epsilon_2]\!]\, \rho\, \sigma, \lambda \mapsto \mathcal{M}_E[\![\epsilon_2]\!]\, \rho\, \sigma\}))$$

$$= restrict(\rho_o, \lambda, restrict(\rho_o, \lambda + 1, \qquad\qquad\qquad\qquad [\text{lemma } \mathbf{r1}]$$
$$\mathcal{M}_{I*}[\![\mathcal{O}_E \langle\!|\, \epsilon_1 \,|\!\rangle\, \rho_o(\lambda + 1)]\!]\, \rho_\iota(\mathcal{M}_I[\![\mathtt{binOp}(\omega, \lambda)]\!]\, \rho_\iota\, \vartheta)$$
$$(\sigma_\iota \boxplus \{A \mapsto \mathcal{M}_E[\![\epsilon_2]\!]\, \rho\, \sigma, \lambda \mapsto \mathcal{M}_E[\![\epsilon_2]\!]\, \rho\, \sigma\})))$$

$$= restrict(\rho_o, \lambda, restrict(\rho_o, \lambda + 1, \qquad\qquad\qquad\qquad [\text{induction hyp.}]$$
$$\mathcal{M}_I[\![\mathtt{binOp}(\omega, \lambda)]\!]\, \rho_\iota\, \vartheta$$
$$(\sigma_\iota \boxplus \{A \mapsto \mathcal{M}_E[\![\epsilon_1]\!]\, \rho\, \sigma, \lambda \mapsto \mathcal{M}_E[\![\epsilon_2]\!]\, \rho\, \sigma\})))$$

$$= restrict(\rho_o, \lambda, restrict(\rho_o, \lambda + 1, \qquad\qquad\qquad\qquad [\text{Tosca } 10.4.9]$$
$$\vartheta(\sigma_\iota \boxplus \{A \mapsto \mathcal{M}_B[\![\omega]\!](\mathcal{M}_E[\![\epsilon_1]\!]\, \rho\, \sigma, \mathcal{M}_E[\![\epsilon_2]\!]\, \rho\, \sigma),$$
$$\lambda \mapsto \mathcal{M}_E[\![\epsilon_2]\!]\, \rho\, \sigma\})))$$

$$= restrict(\rho_o, \lambda, \qquad\qquad\qquad\qquad\qquad\qquad\qquad [\text{lemma } \mathbf{r1}]$$
$$\vartheta(\sigma_\iota \boxplus \{A \mapsto \mathcal{M}_B[\![\omega]\!](\mathcal{M}_E[\![\epsilon_1]\!]\, \rho\, \sigma, \mathcal{M}_E[\![\epsilon_2]\!]\, \rho\, \sigma)\}))$$

$$= restrict(\rho_o, \lambda, \qquad\qquad\qquad\qquad\qquad\qquad\qquad [\text{Tosca } 8.4.5.4]$$
$$\vartheta(\sigma_\iota \boxplus \{A \mapsto \mathcal{M}_E[\![\mathsf{binExpr}(\epsilon_1, \omega, \epsilon_2)]\!]\, \rho\, \sigma\}))$$

$$= restrict(\rho_o, \lambda, \vartheta(\sigma_\iota \boxplus \{A \mapsto v\})) \qquad\qquad\qquad [\text{defn } v]$$

$\square$

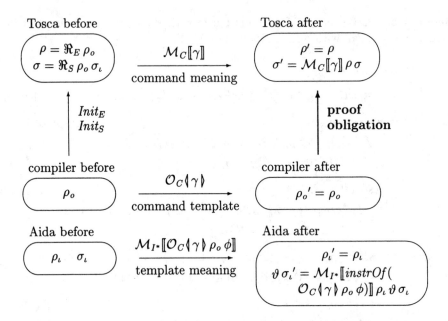

Figure 13.4 The correctness diagram for commands

13.7   Commands

13.7.1   Correctness condition

Evaluating a Tosca command can change the state, but not the environment. The translation is correct if doing the translation and evaluating the translated fragments make a corresponding change to the translation environment and Aida environment and state. The correctness diagram for commands is shown in Figure 13.4.

The correctness condition is

$Init_E$; $Init_S$;
$\rho' = \rho$; $\sigma' = \mathcal{M}_C[\![\gamma]\!] \rho \sigma$;
$\rho_o' = \rho_o$;
$\rho_\iota' = \rho_\iota$;
$\vartheta \sigma_\iota' = \mathcal{M}_{I*}[\![instrOf(\mathcal{O}_C\langle\gamma\rangle \rho_o \phi)]\!] \rho_\iota \vartheta \sigma_\iota$

$\qquad \vdash \sigma' = \Re_S \rho_o \sigma_\iota'$

The correctness condition for multiple commands is analogous:

$Init_E$; $Init_S$;
$\rho' = \rho$; $\sigma' = \mathcal{M}_{C^*}[\![\Gamma]\!]\,\rho\,\sigma$;
$\rho_o{}' = \rho_o$;
$\rho_\iota{}' = \rho_\iota$;
$\vartheta\,\sigma_\iota{}' = \mathcal{M}_{I^*}[\![instrOf(\mathcal{O}_{C^*}\langle\!|\,\Gamma\,|\!\rangle\,\rho_o\,\phi)]\!]\,\rho_\iota\,\vartheta\,\sigma_\iota$
$\qquad\vdash \sigma' = \Re_S\,\rho_o\,\sigma_\iota{}'$

Notice that, in order to prove $f(\sigma_{\iota 1}) = f(\sigma_{\iota 2})$, it is sufficient to prove $f(\vartheta\,\sigma_{\iota 1}) = f(\vartheta\,\sigma_{\iota 2})$ for arbitrary ϑ.

13.7.2 Induction hypothesis

The induction hypothesis for commands is that any subcommands are translated correctly:

$\Re_S\,\rho_o\,\sigma_\iota{}' = \mathcal{M}_C[\![\gamma]\!]\,\rho\,\sigma$
$\qquad$ where $\vartheta_h\,\sigma_\iota{}' == \mathcal{M}_{I^*}[\![instrOf(\mathcal{O}_C\langle\!|\,\gamma\,|\!\rangle\,\rho_o\,\phi)]\!]\,\rho_\iota\,\vartheta_h\,\sigma_\iota$

13.7.3 Block

The correctness of the **block** instruction follows directly from the correctness of the multiple command translation.

13.7.4 Skip

Here $\gamma = $ **skip**. This is a base case, so there is no need for the induction hypothesis.
$\quad$ Lemma:

$\vartheta\,\sigma_\iota{}'$
$\quad = \mathcal{M}_{I^*}[\![instrOf(\mathcal{O}_C\langle\!|\,\textbf{skip}\,|\!\rangle\,\rho_o\,\phi)]\!]\,\rho_\iota\,\vartheta\,\sigma_\iota$ $\hfill$ [defn $\sigma_\iota{}'$]
$\quad = \mathcal{M}_{I^*}[\![\langle\,\rangle]\!]\,\rho_\iota\,\vartheta\,\sigma_\iota$ $\hfill$ [template 11.4.3]
$\quad = \vartheta\,\sigma_\iota$ $\hfill$ [Aida 10.4.2]
$\quad\square$

So

$\Re_S\,\rho_o\,\sigma_\iota{}'$
$\quad = \Re_S\,\rho_o\,\sigma_\iota$ $\hfill$ [lemma]
$\quad = \sigma$ $\hfill$ [defn σ]
$\quad = \mathcal{M}_C[\![\textbf{skip}]\!]\,\rho\,\sigma$ $\hfill$ [Tosca 8.5.4.4]
$\quad = \sigma'$ $\hfill$ [defn σ']
$\quad\square$

13.7.5   Assignment

Here $\gamma = \mathsf{assign}(\xi, \epsilon)$. The expression induction hypothesis is assumed for the expression component.

Lemma:

$$restrict(\rho_o, top, \vartheta\,\sigma_\iota')$$

$$= restrict(\rho_o, top, \hspace{4cm} [\text{defn } \sigma_\iota']$$
$$\mathcal{M}_{I*}[\![instrOf(\mathcal{O}_C \langle\!\langle \mathsf{assign}(\xi, \epsilon)\rangle\!\rangle\, \rho_o\, \phi)]\!]\,\rho_\iota\,\vartheta\,\sigma_\iota)$$

$$= restrict(\rho_o, top, \hspace{4cm} [\text{template 11.4.4}]$$
$$\mathcal{M}_{I*}[\![\mathcal{O}_E\langle\!\langle \epsilon\rangle\!\rangle\,\rho_o\, top\,\,^\frown\,\langle \mathsf{store}\,\rho_o[\![\xi]\!]\rangle]\!]\,\rho_\iota\,\vartheta\,\sigma_\iota)$$

$$= restrict(\rho_o, top, \hspace{4cm} [\text{Aida 10.4.2}]$$
$$\mathcal{M}_{I*}[\![\mathcal{O}_E\langle\!\langle \epsilon\rangle\!\rangle\,\rho_o\, top]\!]\,\rho_\iota(\mathcal{M}_I[\![\mathsf{store}\,\rho_o[\![\xi]\!]]\!]\,\rho_\iota\,\vartheta)\,\sigma_\iota)$$

$$= restrict(\rho_o, top, \hspace{4cm} [\text{induction hyp.}]$$
$$\mathcal{M}_I[\![\mathsf{store}\,\rho_o[\![\xi]\!]]\!]\,\rho_\iota\,\vartheta(\sigma_\iota\,\boxplus\{A \mapsto \mathcal{M}_E[\![\epsilon]\!]\,\rho\,\sigma\}))$$

$$= restrict(\rho_o, top, \hspace{4cm} [\text{Aida 10.4.7}]$$
$$\vartheta(\sigma_\iota\,\boxplus\{A \mapsto \mathcal{M}_E[\![\epsilon]\!]\,\rho\,\sigma, \rho_o[\![\xi]\!] \mapsto \mathcal{M}_E[\![\epsilon]\!]\,\rho\,\sigma\}))$$

$\square$

So

$$\Re_S\,\rho_o\,\sigma_\iota'$$

$$= \Re_S\,\rho_o\,restrict(\rho_o, top, \sigma_\iota') \hspace{3cm} [\text{lemma } \mathbf{r2}]$$

$$= \Re_S\,\rho_o\,restrict(\rho_o, top, \hspace{3cm} [\text{lemma}]$$
$$\sigma_\iota\,\boxplus\{A \mapsto \mathcal{M}_E[\![\epsilon]\!]\,\rho\,\sigma, \rho_o[\![\xi]\!] \mapsto \mathcal{M}_E[\![\epsilon]\!]\,\rho\,\sigma\})$$

$$= \Re_S\,\rho_o(\sigma_\iota\,\boxplus\{\rho_o[\![\xi]\!] \mapsto \mathcal{M}_E[\![\epsilon]\!]\,\rho\,\sigma\}) \hspace{2cm} [\text{defn } restrict]$$

$$= \sigma\,\boxplus\{\rho_o[\![\xi]\!] \mapsto \mathcal{M}_E[\![\epsilon]\!]\,\rho\,\sigma\} \hspace{2.5cm} [\text{defn } \Re_S, \sigma]$$

$$= \sigma\,\boxplus\{\rho[\![\xi]\!] \mapsto \mathcal{M}_E[\![\epsilon]\!]\,\rho\,\sigma\} \hspace{2.7cm} [\text{defn } \rho]$$

$$= \mathcal{M}_C[\![\mathsf{assign}(\xi, \epsilon)]\!]\,\rho\,\sigma \hspace{3cm} [\text{Tosca 8.5.5.4}]$$

$$= \sigma' \hspace{6cm} [\text{defn } \sigma']$$

$\square$

13.7.6   Choice

Here $\gamma = \mathsf{choice}(\epsilon, \gamma_1, \gamma_2)$. The expression induction hypothesis is assumed for the expression component, and the command induction hypothesis is assumed twice, once for each branch subcommand.

Lemma:

$restrict(\rho_o, top, \vartheta\, \sigma_\iota')$

$\qquad = restrict(\,\rho_o, top, \hfill \text{[defn } \sigma_\iota'\text{]}$
$\qquad\qquad \mathcal{M}_{I*}[\![instrOf(\mathcal{O}_C\langle\!|\,\mathsf{choice}(\epsilon, \gamma_1, \gamma_2)\,|\!\rangle\,\rho_o\,\phi)]\!]\,\rho_\iota\,\vartheta\,\sigma_\iota\,)$

$\qquad = restrict(\,\rho_o, top, \hfill \text{[template 11.4.5]}$
$\qquad\qquad \mathcal{M}_{I*}[\![\mathcal{O}_E\langle\!|\,\epsilon\,|\!\rangle\,\rho_o\,top \,^\frown\, \langle\mathtt{jump}\,\phi_2\rangle \,^\frown\, instrOf(\mathcal{O}_C\langle\!|\,\gamma_1\,|\!\rangle\,\rho_o\,\phi)$
$\qquad\qquad\quad {}^\frown\langle\mathtt{goto}(1+\phi_2), \mathtt{label}\,\phi_2\rangle \,^\frown\, instrOf(\mathcal{O}_C\langle\!|\,\gamma_2\,|\!\rangle\,\rho_o\,\phi_1)$
$\qquad\qquad\quad {}^\frown\langle\mathtt{label}(1+\phi_2)\rangle]\!]\,\rho_\iota\,\vartheta\,\sigma_\iota\,)$

$\qquad = restrict(\,\rho_o, top, \mathcal{M}_{I*}[\![\mathcal{O}_E\langle\!|\,\epsilon\,|\!\rangle\,\rho_o\,top]\!]\,\rho_\iota \hfill \text{[Aida 10.4.2]}$
$\qquad\qquad (\mathcal{M}_{I*}[\![\langle\mathtt{jump}\,\phi_2\rangle \,^\frown\, instrOf(\mathcal{O}_C\langle\!|\,\gamma_1\,|\!\rangle\,\rho_o\,\phi)$
$\qquad\qquad\quad {}^\frown\langle\mathtt{goto}(1+\phi_2), \mathtt{label}\,\phi_2\rangle \,^\frown\, instrOf(\mathcal{O}_C\langle\!|\,\gamma_2\,|\!\rangle\,\rho_o\,\phi_1)$
$\qquad\qquad\quad {}^\frown\langle\mathtt{label}(1+\phi_2)\rangle]\!]\,\rho_\iota\,\vartheta)\,\sigma_\iota\,)$

$\qquad = restrict(\,\rho_o, top, \hfill \text{[induction hyp.]}$
$\qquad\qquad \mathcal{M}_{I*}[\![\langle\mathtt{jump}\,\phi_2\rangle \,^\frown\, instrOf(\mathcal{O}_C\langle\!|\,\gamma_1\,|\!\rangle\,\rho_o\,\phi) \,^\frown\, \langle\mathtt{goto}(1+\phi_2), \mathtt{label}\,\phi_2\rangle$
$\qquad\qquad\quad {}^\frown\, instrOf(\mathcal{O}_C\langle\!|\,\gamma_2\,|\!\rangle\,\rho_o\,\phi_1) \,^\frown\, \langle\mathtt{label}(1+\phi_2)\rangle]\!]\,\rho_\iota\,\vartheta\,\sigma_{\iota A}\,)$
$\qquad\qquad \text{where } \sigma_{\iota A} == \sigma_\iota \boxplus \{A \mapsto \mathcal{M}_E[\![\epsilon]\!]\,\rho\,\sigma\}$

$\qquad = restrict(\,\rho_o, top, \hfill \text{[Aida 10.4.4]}$
$\qquad\qquad \textbf{if } \mathcal{M}_E[\![\epsilon]\!]\,\rho\,\sigma = bool_v\,\mathsf{F}$
$\qquad\qquad \textbf{then } \rho_\iota[\![\phi_2]\!]\,\sigma_{\iota A}$
$\qquad\qquad \textbf{else } \mathcal{M}_{I*}[\![instrOf(\mathcal{O}_C\langle\!|\,\gamma_1\,|\!\rangle\,\rho_o\,\phi) \,^\frown\, \langle\mathtt{goto}(1+\phi_2), \mathtt{label}\,\phi_2\rangle$
$\qquad\qquad\qquad {}^\frown\, instrOf(\mathcal{O}_C\langle\!|\,\gamma_2\,|\!\rangle\,\rho_o\,\phi_1) \,^\frown\, \langle\mathtt{label}(1+\phi_2)\rangle]\!]\,\rho_\iota\,\vartheta\,\sigma_{\iota A}\,)$

$\qquad = restrict(\,\rho_o, top, \hfill \text{[Aida 10.4.12]}$
$\qquad\qquad \textbf{if } \mathcal{M}_E[\![\epsilon]\!]\,\rho\,\sigma = bool_v\,\mathsf{T}$
$\qquad\qquad \textbf{then } \mathcal{M}_{I*}[\![instrOf(\mathcal{O}_C\langle\!|\,\gamma_1\,|\!\rangle\,\rho_o\,\phi)]\!]\,\rho_\iota(\mathcal{M}_{I*}[\![\langle\mathtt{goto}(1+\phi_2), \mathtt{label}\,\phi_2\rangle$
$\qquad\qquad\qquad {}^\frown\, instrOf(\mathcal{O}_C\langle\!|\,\gamma_2\,|\!\rangle\,\rho_o\,\phi_1) \,^\frown\, \langle\mathtt{label}(1+\phi_2)\rangle]\!]\,\rho_\iota\,\vartheta)\,\sigma_{\iota A}$
$\qquad\qquad \textbf{else } \mathcal{M}_{I*}[\![instrOf(\mathcal{O}_C\langle\!|\,\gamma_2\,|\!\rangle\,\rho_o\,\phi_1)]\!]\,\rho_\iota$
$\qquad\qquad\qquad (\mathcal{M}_{I*}[\![\langle\mathtt{label}(1+\phi_2)\rangle]\!]\,\rho_\iota\,\vartheta)\,\sigma_{\iota A}\,)$

$$= restrict(\rho_o, top, \qquad\qquad \text{[induction hyp.]}$$

$\quad$ **if** $\mathcal{M}_E[\![\epsilon]\!]\,\rho\,\sigma = bool_v\,\mathsf{T}$

$\quad$ **then** $\mathcal{M}_{I*}[\![\langle\mathtt{goto}(1+\phi_2), \mathtt{label}\ \phi_2\rangle \,\frown\, instrOf(\mathcal{O}_C\{\gamma_2\}\,\rho_o\,\phi_1)$

$\qquad \frown\langle\mathtt{label}(1+\phi_2)\rangle]\!]\,\rho_\iota\,\vartheta\,\sigma_{\iota1}$

$\quad$ **else** $\mathcal{M}_I[\![\mathtt{label}(1+\phi_2)]\!]\,\rho_\iota\,\vartheta\,\sigma_{\iota2})$

$\quad$ **where** $\Re_S\,\rho_o\,\sigma_{\iota k} == \mathcal{M}_C[\![\gamma_k]\!]\,\rho\,\sigma$

$$= restrict(\rho_o, top, \qquad\qquad \text{[Aida 10.4.3]}$$

$\quad$ **if** $\mathcal{M}_E[\![\epsilon]\!]\,\rho\,\sigma = bool_v\,\mathsf{T}$

$\quad$ **then** $\rho_\iota[\![1+\phi_2]\!]\,\sigma_{\iota1}$

$\quad$ **else** $\mathcal{M}_I[\![\mathtt{label}(1+\phi_2)]\!]\,\rho_\iota\,\vartheta\,\sigma_{\iota2})$

$$= restrict(\rho_o, top, \qquad\qquad \text{[Aida 10.4.12]}$$

$\quad$ **if** $\mathcal{M}_E[\![\epsilon]\!]\,\rho\,\sigma = bool_v\,\mathsf{T}$ **then** $\vartheta\,\sigma_{\iota1}$ **else** $\vartheta\,\sigma_{\iota2})$

$\square$

So

$\Re_S\,\rho_o\,\sigma_\iota'$

$$= \Re_S\,\rho_o\,restrict(\rho_o, top, \sigma_\iota') \qquad\qquad \text{[lemma r2]}$$

$$= \Re_S\,\rho_o\,restrict(\rho_o, top, \qquad\qquad \text{[lemma]}$$

$\quad$ **if** $\mathcal{M}_E[\![\epsilon]\!]\,\rho\,\sigma = bool_v\,\mathsf{T}$ **then** $\sigma_{\iota1}$ **else** $\sigma_{\iota2})$

$$= \textbf{if } \mathcal{M}_E[\![\epsilon]\!]\,\rho\,\sigma = bool_v\,\mathsf{T}\textbf{ then }\Re_S\,\rho_o\,\sigma_{\iota1}\textbf{ else }\Re_S\,\rho_o\,\sigma_{\iota2} \qquad \text{[lemma r2]}$$

$$= \textbf{if } \mathcal{M}_E[\![\epsilon]\!]\,\rho\,\sigma = bool_v\,\mathsf{T} \qquad\qquad \text{[defn } \sigma_{\iota1}\ \sigma_{\iota2}]$$

$\quad$ **then** $\mathcal{M}_C[\![\gamma_1]\!]\,\rho\,\sigma$ **else** $\mathcal{M}_C[\![\gamma_2]\!]\,\rho\,\sigma$

$$= \mathcal{M}_C[\![\mathsf{choice}(\epsilon, \gamma_1, \gamma_2)]\!]\,\rho\,\sigma \qquad\qquad \text{[Tosca choice 8.5.6.4]}$$

$$= \sigma' \qquad\qquad \text{[defn } \sigma']$$

$\square$

13.7.7 Loop

Here $\gamma = \mathsf{loop}(\epsilon, \gamma)$. The expression induction hypothesis is assumed for the expression component, and the command induction hypothesis is assumed for the body subcommand.

Lemma:

$restrict(\rho_o, top, \vartheta\,\sigma_\iota')$

$\quad = restrict(\rho_o, top, \mathcal{M}_{I*}[\![instrOf(\mathcal{O}_C\langle\!|\mathsf{loop}(\epsilon,\gamma)\rangle\!|\,\rho_o\,\phi)]\!]\,\rho_\iota\,\vartheta\,\sigma_\iota)$ [defn σ_ι']

$\quad = restrict(\rho_o, top,$ [template 11.4.6]
$\qquad \mathcal{M}_{I*}[\![\langle\mathtt{label}\;\phi_1\rangle\frown\mathcal{O}_E\langle\!|\epsilon\rangle\!|\,\rho_o\;top$
$\qquad\qquad \frown\langle\mathtt{jump}(1+\phi_1)\rangle\frown instrOf(\mathcal{O}_C\langle\!|\gamma\rangle\!|\,\rho_o\,\phi)$
$\qquad\qquad \frown\langle\mathtt{goto}\,\phi_1,\mathtt{label}(1+\phi_1)\rangle]\!]\,\rho_\iota\,\vartheta\,\sigma_\iota)$

$\quad = restrict(\rho_o, top, \mathcal{M}_{I*}[\![\mathcal{O}_E\langle\!|\epsilon\rangle\!|\,\rho_o\;top]\!]\,\rho_\iota$ [Aida 10.4.12]
$\qquad (\mathcal{M}_{I*}[\![\langle\mathtt{jump}(1+\phi_1)\rangle\frown instrOf(\mathcal{O}_C\langle\!|\gamma\rangle\!|\,\rho_o\,\phi)$
$\qquad\qquad \frown\langle\mathtt{goto}\,\phi_1,\mathtt{label}(1+\phi_1)\rangle]\!]\,\rho_\iota\,\vartheta)\,\sigma_\iota)$

$\quad = restrict(\rho_o, top,$ [induction hyp.]
$\qquad \mathcal{M}_{I*}[\![\langle\mathtt{jump}(1+\phi_1)\rangle\frown instrOf(\mathcal{O}_C\langle\!|\gamma\rangle\!|\,\rho_o\,\phi)$
$\qquad\qquad \frown\langle\mathtt{goto}\,\phi_1,\mathtt{label}(1+\phi_1)\rangle]\!]\,\rho_\iota\,\vartheta\,\sigma_{\iota A})$
$\qquad \text{where } \sigma_{\iota A} == \sigma_\iota\boxplus\{A\mapsto\mathcal{M}_E[\![\epsilon]\!]\,\rho\,\sigma\}$

$\quad = restrict(\rho_o, top,$ [Aida 10.4.4]
$\qquad \textbf{if } \mathcal{M}_E[\![\epsilon]\!]\,\rho\,\sigma = bool_v\;\mathsf{F}$
$\qquad \textbf{then } \rho_\iota[\![1+\phi_1]\!]\,\sigma_{\iota A}$
$\qquad \textbf{else } \mathcal{M}_{I*}[\![instrOf(\mathcal{O}_C\langle\!|\gamma\rangle\!|\,\rho_o\,\phi)$
$\qquad\qquad \frown\langle\mathtt{goto}\,\phi_1,\mathtt{label}(1+\phi_1)\rangle]\!]\,\rho_\iota\,\vartheta\,\sigma_{\iota A})$

$\quad = restrict(\rho_o, top,$ [Aida 10.4.12]
$\qquad \textbf{if } \mathcal{M}_E[\![\epsilon]\!]\,\rho\,\sigma = bool_v\;\mathsf{T}$
$\qquad \textbf{then } \mathcal{M}_{I*}[\![instrOf(\mathcal{O}_C\langle\!|\gamma\rangle\!|\,\rho_o\,\phi)]\!]\,\rho_o$
$\qquad\qquad (\mathcal{M}_{I*}[\![\langle\mathtt{goto}\,\phi_1,\mathtt{label}(1+\phi_1)\rangle]\!]\,\rho_\iota\,\vartheta)\,\sigma_{\iota A}$
$\qquad \textbf{else } \vartheta\,\sigma_{\iota A})$

$\quad = restrict(\rho_o, top,$ [induction hyp.]
$\qquad \textbf{if } \mathcal{M}_E[\![\epsilon]\!]\,\rho\,\sigma = bool_v\;\mathsf{T}$
$\qquad \textbf{then } \mathcal{M}_{I*}[\![\langle\mathtt{goto}\,\phi_1,\mathtt{label}(1+\phi_1)\rangle]\!]\,\rho_\iota\,\vartheta\,\sigma_{\iota 1}$
$\qquad \textbf{else } \vartheta\,\sigma_{\iota A})$
$\qquad \text{where } \Re_S\,\rho_o\,\sigma_{\iota 1} == \mathcal{M}_C[\![\gamma]\!]\,\rho\,\sigma$

$$= restrict(\rho_o, top, \qquad\qquad\qquad\qquad\text{[Aida 10.4.3]}$$
$$\quad \textbf{if } \mathcal{M}_E[\![\epsilon]\!]\,\rho\,\sigma = bool_v\,\mathsf{T}$$
$$\quad \textbf{then } \mathcal{M}_{I*}[\![instrOf(\mathcal{O}_C \langle\!| loop(\epsilon, \gamma) |\!\rangle\,\rho_o\,\phi)]\!]\,\rho_\iota\,\vartheta\,\sigma_{\iota 1}$$
$$\quad \textbf{else } \vartheta\,\sigma_{\iota A})$$

$\square$

So

$\Re_S\,\rho_o\,\sigma_\iota'$

$$= \Re_S\,\rho_o\,restrict(\rho_o, top, \sigma_\iota) \qquad\qquad\qquad\text{[lemma } \mathbf{r2}]$$

$$= \Re_S\,\rho_o\,restrict(\rho_o, top, \qquad\qquad\qquad\qquad\text{[lemma]}$$
$$\quad \textbf{if } \mathcal{M}_E[\![\epsilon]\!]\,\rho\,\sigma = bool_v\,\mathsf{T}$$
$$\quad \textbf{then } \mathcal{M}_{I*}[\![instrOf(\mathcal{O}_C \langle\!| loop(\epsilon, \gamma) |\!\rangle\,\rho_o\,\phi)]\!]\,\rho_\iota\,\sigma_{\iota 1}$$
$$\quad \textbf{else } \sigma_{\iota A})$$

$$= \textbf{if } \mathcal{M}_E[\![\epsilon]\!]\,\rho\,\sigma = bool_v\,\mathsf{T} \qquad\qquad\qquad\text{[defn } \sigma_{\iota 1}, \sigma_{\iota A}]$$
$$\quad \textbf{then } \mathcal{M}_C[\![loop(\epsilon, \gamma)]\!]\,\rho\,(\mathcal{M}_C[\![\gamma]\!]\,\rho\,\sigma)$$
$$\quad \textbf{else } \sigma$$

$$= \mathcal{M}_C[\![loop(\epsilon, \gamma)]\!]\,\rho\,\sigma \qquad\qquad\qquad\qquad\text{[Tosca 8.5.7.4]}$$

$$= \sigma' \qquad\qquad\qquad\qquad\qquad\qquad\qquad\text{[defn } \sigma']$$

$\square$

13.7.8   Input

Here $\gamma = \mathsf{input}(\xi)$. This is a base case, so no induction hypothesis is needed.
  Lemma:

$\vartheta\,\sigma_\iota'$

$$= \mathcal{M}_{I*}[\![instrOf(\mathcal{O}_C \langle\!| \mathsf{input}\ \xi |\!\rangle\,\rho_o\,\phi)]\!]\,\rho_\iota\,\vartheta(\varsigma_\iota, \langle v \rangle \frown in, out) \qquad\text{[defn } \sigma_\iota']$$

$$= \mathcal{M}_{I*}[\![\langle \mathsf{input}, \mathtt{store}\,\rho_o[\![\xi]\!]\rangle]\!]\,\rho_\iota\,\vartheta(\varsigma_\iota, \langle v \rangle \frown in, out) \qquad\text{[template]}$$

$$= \mathcal{M}_I[\![\mathtt{store}\,\rho_o[\![\xi]\!]]\!]\,\rho_\iota\,\vartheta(\varsigma_\iota \oplus \{A \mapsto v\}, in, out) \qquad\text{[Aida 10.4.10]}$$

$$= \vartheta(\varsigma_\iota \oplus \{A \mapsto v, \rho_o[\![\xi]\!] \mapsto v\}, in, out) \qquad\qquad\text{[Aida 10.4.7]}$$

$\square$

So

$$\Re_S\,\rho_o\,\sigma_\iota{}'$$
$$= \Re_S\,\rho_o(\varsigma_\iota \oplus \{A \mapsto v, \rho_o[\![\xi]\!] \mapsto v\}, in, out) \qquad \text{[lemma]}$$
$$= (\varsigma \oplus \{\rho[\![\xi]\!] \mapsto v\}, in, out) \qquad \text{[defn } \Re_S, \sigma]$$
$$= \mathcal{M}_C[\![\text{input } \xi]\!]\,\rho(\varsigma, \langle v\rangle \frown in, out) \qquad \text{[Tosca 8.5.8.4]}$$
$$= \sigma' \qquad \text{[defn } \sigma']$$

□

13.7.9   Output

Here $\gamma = \text{output}(\epsilon)$. The expression induction hypothesis is assumed for the expression component.

Lemma:

$$restrict(\rho_o, top, \vartheta\,\sigma_\iota{}')$$
$$= restrict(\rho_o, top, \qquad\qquad\qquad\qquad\qquad \text{[defn } \sigma_\iota']$$
$$\quad \mathcal{M}_{I*}[\![instrOf(\mathcal{O}_C\langle\!\langle \text{output } \epsilon\rangle\!\rangle\,\rho_o\,\phi)]\!]\,\rho_\iota\,\vartheta(\varsigma_\iota, in, out))$$
$$= restrict(\rho_o, top, \qquad\qquad\qquad\qquad\qquad\qquad \text{[template]}$$
$$\quad \mathcal{M}_{I*}[\![\mathcal{O}_E\langle\!\langle\epsilon\rangle\!\rangle\,\rho_o\ top \frown \langle\text{output}\rangle]\!]\,\rho_\iota\,\vartheta(\varsigma_\iota, in, out))$$
$$= restrict(\rho_o, top, \qquad\qquad\qquad\qquad\qquad \text{[induction hyp.]}$$
$$\quad \mathcal{M}_I[\![\text{output}]\!]\,\rho_\iota\,\vartheta(\varsigma_\iota \oplus \{A \mapsto \mathcal{M}_E[\![\epsilon]\!]\,\rho\,\sigma\}, in, out))$$
$$= restrict(\rho_o, top, \qquad\qquad\qquad\qquad\qquad\qquad \text{[Aida 10.4.11]}$$
$$\quad \vartheta(\varsigma_\iota \oplus \{A \mapsto \mathcal{M}_E[\![\epsilon]\!]\,\rho\,\sigma\}, in, out \frown \langle\mathcal{M}_E[\![\epsilon]\!]\,\rho\,\sigma\rangle))$$

□

So

$$\Re_S\,\rho_o\,\sigma_\iota{}'$$
$$= \Re_S\,\rho_o\,restrict(\rho_o, top, (\varsigma_\iota, in, out)) \qquad \text{[lemma } \mathbf{r2}]$$
$$= \Re_S\,\rho_o\,restrict(\rho_o, top, \qquad\qquad\qquad\qquad \text{[lemma]}$$
$$\quad (\varsigma_\iota \oplus \{A \mapsto \mathcal{M}_E[\![\epsilon]\!]\,\rho\,\sigma\}, in, out \frown \langle\mathcal{M}_E[\![\epsilon]\!]\,\rho\,\sigma\rangle))$$
$$= \Re_S\,\rho_o(\varsigma_\iota, in, out \frown \langle\mathcal{M}_E[\![\epsilon]\!]\,\rho\,\sigma\rangle) \qquad \text{[defn. } restrict]$$
$$= (\varsigma, in, out \frown \langle\mathcal{M}_E[\![\epsilon]\!]\,\rho\,\sigma\rangle) \qquad \text{[defn } \Re_S, \sigma]$$
$$= \mathcal{M}_C[\![\text{output } \epsilon]\!]\,\rho\,\sigma \qquad \text{[Tosca 8.5.9.4]}$$
$$= \sigma' \qquad \text{[defn } \sigma']$$

□

13.7.10   Multiple commands

The definition of the translation for multiple commands follows the form of the definition of the meaning of multiple commands. Given the correctness of the single commands translation, and the unique allocation of labels, the multiple commands correctness follows directly.

13.8   Program

Given the correctness of the declaration translation and of the command translation, the Tosca program translation correctness follows directly.

Chapter 14

The Prolog Implementation

14.1   Necessary components

The Prolog implementation of the semantics specified so far needs several components over and above the translation of the various semantics into a DCTG. It also needs support for the DCTG operators themselves, a parser to convert Tosca's concrete syntax strings to an abstract syntax tree, and support for sets and set operations. These extra components are discussed below, and then the translation of the semantics is given.

14.2   Supporting constructs

14.2.1   DCTG support

Although standard Prologs have support built in for DCGs, they do not have such support for DCTGs. It is necessary to provide explicit support for converting a Prolog program written in DCTG form to ordinary Prolog clauses. [Abramson and Dahl 1989, Appendix II.3] gives a listing of such a Prolog interpreter for DCTGs.

14.2.2   Lexing and parsing

Prolog predicates to support lexing and parsing the input concrete syntax have to be written. Lexing breaks the input stream of individual characters into a stream of *tokens*: keywords, identifiers and operators; parsing builds the tokens into a tree structure as defined by the abstract syntax.

Prolog's pattern matching capabilities come into their own here, and a highly declarative definition of tokens, keywords and the structure of identifiers can be given. [Abramson and Dahl 1989, Chapter 9] includes the parser for a simple

DCTG. The compiler's lexing phase can be written to correspond closely with the concrete syntax definition of identifiers and keywords (not defined for Tosca).

14.2.3   Sets and set operations

The standard way to represent sets and tuples in Prolog is by using lists. Z functions are simply sets of pairs, and can be represented as lists of 2-element lists. So, for example, an environment such as

$$\{x \mapsto \text{integer}, b \mapsto \text{boolean}\}$$

can be represented in Prolog as

```
[ [x,int], [b,bool] ]
```

Sets of other compound elements, for example, the various *States*, can also be represented as lists of lists.

Many implementations of Prolog provide library support for set operations such as membership test, union and intersection. If not, these are quite simple to write. Special definitions do have to be written to support the more Z-specific operations such as function application (looking up a value), function overriding $\oplus$, and domain restriction $\lhd$. More definitions are needed to support those functions written specially for the semantics specification, such as *worseState*. These definitions are quite straightforward, and are not given below.

14.3   Translating the semantics

14.3.1   The approach

Translating the semantic meaning functions and the operational semantics needs to be done systematically, in order to provide the clearly visible path from the mathematics to the implementation.

Consider for the moment the dynamic meaning of the binary expression (section 8.4.5.4):

$$\mathcal{M}_E[\![\_]\!] : EXPR \nrightarrow Env \nrightarrow State \nrightarrow VALUE$$

$$\mathcal{M}_E[\![\text{binExpr}(\epsilon_1, \omega, \epsilon_2)]\!] \, \rho \, \sigma =$$

$$\mathcal{M}_B[\![\omega]\!](\mathcal{M}_E[\![\epsilon_1]\!] \, \rho \, \sigma, \mathcal{M}_E[\![\epsilon_2]\!] \, \rho \, \sigma)$$

This could be rewritten without the nested function calls as

$$\mathcal{M}_E[\![\_]\!] : EXPR \nrightarrow Env \nrightarrow State \nrightarrow VALUE$$

$$\exists\, v_1, v_2 : VALUE \mid$$
$$\qquad v_1 = \mathcal{M}_E[\![\epsilon_1]\!]\,\rho\,\sigma$$
$$\qquad \wedge\ v_2 = \mathcal{M}_E[\![\epsilon_2]\!]\,\rho\,\sigma\ \bullet$$
$$\quad \mathcal{M}_E[\![\mathsf{binExpr}(\epsilon_1, \omega, \epsilon_2)]\!]\,\rho\,\sigma = \mathcal{M}_B[\![\omega]\!](v_1, v_2)$$

This is translated into a Prolog DCTG as

```
expr ::= tLPAREN, expr^^E1, tBINOP^^O, expr^^E2, tRPAREN
<:>
    (meaning(Env, State, Value) ::-
        E1^^meaning(Env, State, Value1),
        E2^^meaning(Env, State, Value2),
        O^^meaning(Value1, Value2, Value)
    ).
```

The argument corresponding to the *EXPR* appears in the syntax definition part of the Prolog, before the `<:>`. Each of the other arguments, and the resulting value, are supplied as arguments to the `meaning` goal, in the same order as in the Z specification (for clarity). Its meaning (the resulting `Value`) is given in terms of the meaning of the operator when supplied with two arguments that are the meanings of the two subexpressions. These have to be pulled out as separate statements in the Prolog.

In the Z specification, the different dynamic meaning functions—for declarations, operators, expressions, and commands—have to be given different names, because they have different types. Prolog is an untyped language, so all the dynamic meaning clauses can have the same name, `meaning`, even though they may take different numbers of arguments. Prolog's pattern matching ensures the correct clauses are used.

These examples show the general form of the translation process.

1. The syntax part of the DCTG, before the `<:>`, follows the concrete syntax specification.

2. The arguments to the head of the Prolog statement (the part before the `::-`) correspond to the semantic arguments (state and environment as appropriate) and result of the meaning function. They are written in the same order in the Prolog as in the Z, for clarity.

3. The body of the Prolog statement (the part after the `::-`) corresponds to the specification of the meaning function. Nested function calls may have to be pulled out into separate statements.

14.3.2   Tosca's semantics as a DCTG

The following shows a summary of Tosca's DCTG. It has all five semantics attached to each node: the three non-standard static semantics (declaration-before-use checking `declcheck`, type checking `typecheck` and initialization-before-use checking `usecheck`), the dynamic semantics `meaning` and the operational semantics `code`. These provide the various static checkers, an interpreter, and a compiler, respectively.

In the example below, the dynamic state includes only the store component, and not the lists of input and output values. These latter components are represented during interpretation by prompting the user for keyboard input, and by writing the output to the screen, respectively. Hence, the dynamic store and state are identified in the Prolog version:

```
compile(Source) :-
      lexemes(Source, Tokens),
      tosca(Tree, Tokens, [ ]),
      Tree^^declcheck(DCheck),
      (    DCheck = checkWrong,
           fatalerror(['declaration(s) check wrong'])
      ;    DCheck = checkOK ),
      Tree^^typecheck(TCheck),
      (    TCheck = checkWrong,
           fatalerror(['type(s) check wrong'])
      ;    TCheck = checkOK ),
      Tree^^usecheck(UCheck),
      (    UCheck = checkWrong,
           fatalerror(['use(s) check wrong'])
      ;    UCheck = checkOK ),
      Tree^^meaning,
      Tree^^code(InstrList), formatcode(InstrList).
```

The `lexemes` goal splits the input source code, a stream of characters, into a list of Tokens (the definition of `lexemes` is not given here). The `tosca` goal parses these tokens into the abstract syntax `Tree`, by matching against the concrete syntax part of the DCTG. The definition of `tosca` in DCTG form is given in the next section; the one used here corresponds to the form after translation into plain Prolog (see section 3.3 for an example of the translation, which explains the form of the arguments to the `tosca` goal).

The three static checks are done by executing the `declcheck`, `typecheck` and `usecheck` semantics: the program stops with an error message if any of these semantics returns a `checkWrong` value. The interpreter runs by executing the `meaning` semantics, then the Aida abstract assembly code is obtained by executing the `code` semantics, then printed out in an appropriate form using `formatcode`. In practice, one or other of these last executions is commented out to provide either an interpreter or a compiler.

A full compiler also needs to report errors rather more informatively than Prolog's rather terse no. Extra goals are inserted into the relevant parts of the code to print out helpful diagnostics, for example, by formatting the various static states in a manner that shows which variables have been used improperly. However, these have not been included in the Prolog given here, since they tend to clutter the code.

14.3.3   Program

A Tosca program is a list of declarations, and a command. For each semantics, the meaning of the declaration list is evaluated in an initially empty environment (modelled by the empty list [ ]) to produce the relevant declaration environment. The meaning of the command is executed in this environment, with the appropriate state:

```
tosca ::= declList^^DL, tENDDECL, cmd^^C
<:>
      (declcheck(DCheck) ::-
            DL^^declcheck([ ], DEnv),
            C^^declcheck(DEnv, DCheck)
      ),
      (typecheck(TCheck) ::-
            DL^^typecheck([ ], TEnv),
            C^^typecheck(TEnv, TCheck)
      ),
      (usecheck(UCheck) ::-
            DL^^usecheck([ ], UEnv),
            C^^usecheck(UEnv, [[ ], checkOK], [_, UCheck])
      ),
      (meaning ::-
            DL^^meaning([ ], Env),
            C^^meaning(Env, [ ], _)
      ),
      (code(InstrList) ::-
            DL  code([ ], OEnv),
            olocn(OLocn), assert(top(OLocn)),
            C^^code(OEnv, 0, _, InstrList)
      ).
```

The various check results (DCheck, TCheck and UCheck) are used in the compiler goal to check for static errors, and to stop if any are found. They all have to have different names, as do the different environments and states, otherwise Prolog would attempt to unify them: to find a solution where they all have the same value. Such a solution is unlikely to exist.

The result of a use check is a use state: a pair, modelled as a two-component list, consisting of the use store and a check value. The use check status of a program depends only on the final check value, not the final use store. So the final use store argument in the `usecheck` goal is an 'anonymous variable', written as an underscore, indicating that its value is not used elsewhere.

Similarly, the final state from the dynamic `meaning` semantics is not needed; the dynamic meaning of a Tosca program is defined to be its output stream, irrespective of its final state. So this final state is indicated by an anonymous variable, too. Fortunately, Prolog does not attempt to unify anonymous variables; they can happily have different values.

The result from the `code` semantics is `InstrList`, a list of Aida instructions. This is printed out by the `compile` goal. The anonymous variable in the final `code` goal corresponds to the final 'next label' value, which is not needed. The value of `top` is asserted, so that it can be used when allocated temporary locations.

14.3.4   Declarations

A declaration declares a variable name to be of a particular type:

```
decl ::= tIDENT^^I, tCOLON, tTYPE^^T
<:>
    (declcheck(PreDEnv, PostDEnv) ::-
        I^^meaning(Id),
        override(PreDEnv, Id, checkOK, PostDEnv)
    ),
    (typecheck(PreTEnv, PostTEnv) ::-
        I^^meaning(Id),
        T^^meaning(Type),
        override(PreTEnv, Id, Type, PostTEnv)
    ),
    (usecheck(PreUEnv, PostUEnv) ::-
        I^^meaning(Id),
        gensym(uloc, ULocn),
        override(PreUEnv, Id, ULocn, PostUEnv)
    ),
    (meaning(PreEnv, PostEnv) ::-
        I^^meaning(Id),
        gensym(loc, Locn),
        override(PreEnv, Id, Locn, PostEnv)
    ),
```

```
(code(PreOEnv, PostOEnv) ::-
    I^^meaning(Id),
    gensym(oloc, OLocn),
    override(PreOEnv, Id, OLocn, PostOEnv)
).
```

The **meaning** of a name is simply the name itself. Similarly, the **meaning** of a type is (the name of) the type.

The predicate **override(Fun, X, Y, Fun1)** has to be specially written to implement the Z override, $\oplus$. Rather than taking a set of pairs, as in Z, the Prolog version takes a single pair as two separate arguments. So it succeeds if

$$\text{Fun} \oplus \{X \mapsto Y\} = \text{Fun1}$$

and uses the convention that the result is written as the last argument to the Prolog predicate.

Unique locations are generated using Prolog's built-in **gensym** predicate. Repeated use of **gensym(str, X)** gives X the value **str1**, **str2**, and so on.

14.3.5   Operators

14.3.5.1   Unary operators

```
tUNYOP ::= [unyop(tMINUS)]
<:>
    (typecheck(Type1, Type) ::-
        (   Type1 = int, Type = int
        ;   Type1 \= int, Type = typeWrong)),
    (meaning(X, Value) ::- Value = - X),
    (code(negate)).
```

Prolog's semicolon denotes the disjunction ('or-ing') of goals. So the type checking semantics reads 'Type1 is **int** and Type is **int**, or Type1 is not **int**, and Type is **typeWrong**'.

Note that there are no declaration or use checking semantics defined for operators:

```
tUNYOP ::= [unyop(tNOT)]
<:>
    (typecheck(Type1, Type) ::-
        (   Type1 = bool, Type = bool
        ;   Type \= bool, Type = typeWrong)),
    (meaning(X, Value) ::-
        (   X = bTRUE, Value = bFALSE
        ;   X = bFALSE, Value = bTRUE)),
    (code(not)).
```

14.3.5.2   Binary operators

Only one in each group of binary operators (arithmetic, comparison, logical) is shown below, the others are similar. Tosca's arithmetic and comparison operators can be implemented by using Prolog's built-in operators:

```
tBINOP ::= [binop('+')]
<:>
      (typecheck(Type1, Type2, Type) ::-
          (    Type1 = int, Type2 = int, Type = int
          ;    Type = typeWrong)),
      (meaning(X, Y, Value) ::- Value is X + Y),
      (code(add)).
```

Note that the type checking definition depends on the order in which goals are evaluated in Prolog: the goal written first in a disjunction is evaluated first, and so `Type` is set to `typeWrong` only if the first goal fails. If the order were not determined, if the two goals in the disjunction could be evaluated in either order, it would have to be written as

```
      Type1 = int, Type2 = int, Type = int
;     (Type1 \= int ; Type2 \= int), Type = typeWrong
```

The original version is clearer and more closely related to the corresponding Z specification:

$$\mathcal{T}_B[\![\mathsf{binArithOp}\,\omega_\alpha]\!] =$$

$$\mathbf{if}\ \tau_1 = \mathsf{integer} \land \tau_2 = \mathsf{integer}\ \mathbf{then}\ \mathsf{integer}\ \mathbf{else}\ \mathit{typeWrong}$$

The second Prolog version would be a better translation if the Z specification had been written, less clearly, as

$$(\tau_1 = \mathsf{integer} \land \tau_2 = \mathsf{integer} \land \mathcal{T}_B[\![\mathsf{binArithOp}\,\omega_\alpha]\!] = \mathsf{integer})$$

$$\lor\ ((\tau_1 \neq \mathsf{integer} \lor \tau_2 \neq \mathsf{integer}) \land \mathcal{T}_B[\![\mathsf{binArithOp}\,\omega_\alpha]\!] = \mathit{typeWrong})$$

```
tBINOP ::= [bin(le)]
<:>
      (typecheck(Type1, Type2, Type) ::-
          (    Type1 = int, Type2 = int, Type = bool
          ;    Type = typeWrong)),
      (meaning(X, Y, Value) ::-
          (    X =< Y, Value = bTRUE
          ;    Value = bFALSE)),
      (code(le)).
```

```
tBINOP ::= [bin(and)]
<:>
    (typecheck(Type1, Type2, Type) ::-
            (   Type1 = bool, Type2 = bool, Type = bool
            ;   Type = typeWrong)),
    (meaning(X, Y, Value) ::-
            (   X = bTRUE, Y = bTRUE, Value = bTRUE
            ;   Value = bFALSE)),
    (code(and)).
```

14.3.6 Expressions

14.3.6.1 Constant

```
expr ::= tCONST^^X
<:>
    (declcheck(_, checkOK)),
    (typecheck(_, Type) ::-
        X^^meaning(Value),
        (   (Value = bTRUE ; Value = bFALSE), Type = bool
        ;   Type = int )
    ),
    (usecheck(_, UState, UState)),
    (meaning(_, _, Value) ::- X^^meaning(Value)),
    (code(_, _, [loadConst(Value)]) ::- X^^meaning(Value)).
```

The various meanings of a constant expression are independent of any environment or state. Hence, these are all indicated by anonymous variables.

14.3.6.2 Named variable

```
expr ::= tIDENT^^I
<:>
    (declcheck(DEnv, DCheck) ::-
        I^^meaning(Id),
        domain(DEnv, DDom),
        (   member(Id, DDom), DCheck = checkOK
        ;   DCheck = checkWrong )
    ),
    (typecheck(TEnv, Type) ::-
        I^^meaning(Id),
        lookup(TEnv, Id, Type)
    ),
```

```
(usecheck(UEnv, PreUState, PostUState) ::-
    I^^meaning(Id),
    lookup(UEnv, Id, ULocn),
    PreUState = [PreUStore, PreUse],
    domain(PreUStore, UDom),
    (   member(ULocn, UDom),
        lookup(PreUStore, ULocn, Use),
        worse([PreUse, Use], PostUse),
        PostUState = [PreUStore, PostUse]
    ;
        override(PreUStore, ULocn, checkWrong, PostUStore),
        PostUState = [PostUStore, checkWrong]
    )
),
(meaning(Env, State, Value) ::-
    I^^meaning(Id),
    lookup(Env, Id, Locn),
    lookup(State, Locn, Value)
),
(code(OEnv, _, [loadVar(OLocn)]) ::-
    I^^meaning(Id),
    lookup(OEnv, Id, OLocn)
).
```

The Prolog predicate `member(Elem, Set)` implements 'element of'; it succeeds if $Elem \in Set$.

`domain(Fun, Dom)` finds the domain of a function; it succeeds if $Dom = dom$ Fun. `lookup(Fun, X, Y)` implements function application; it succeeds if $Fun(X) = Y$.

`worse([U1, U2, ..., Un], U)` implements the $\bowtie$ function; it succeeds if

$$U1 \bowtie U2 \bowtie \ldots \bowtie Un = U$$

14.3.6.3   *Unary expression*

```
expr ::= tUNYOP^^O, expr^^E
<:>
    (declcheck(DEnv, DCheck) ::- E^^declheck(DEnv, DCheck)),
    (typecheck(TEnv, Type) ::-
        E^^typecheck(TEnv, TypeE),
        O^^typecheck(TypeE, Type)
    ),
    (usecheck(UEnv, PreUState, PostUState) ::-
        E^^usecheck(UEnv, PreUState, PostUState) ),
```

```
(meaning(Env, State, Value) ::-
    E^^meaning(Env, State, ValueE),
    O^^meaning(ValueE, Value)
),
(code(OEnv, OLocn, [ExprCode, unyOp(Op)]) ::-
    E^^code(OEnv, OLocn, ExprCode),
    O^^code(Op)
).
```

Note that the declaration and use checking semantics are independent of the operator O.

14.3.6.4 *Binary expression*

```
expr ::= tLPAREN, expr^^E1, tBINOP^^O, expr^^E2, tRPAREN
<:>
    (declcheck(DEnv, DCheck) ::-
        E1^^declcheck(DEnv, DCheck1),
        E2^^declcheck(DEnv, DCheck2),
        worse([DCheck1, DCheck2], DCheck)
    ),
    (typecheck(TEnv, Type) ::-
        E1^^typecheck(TEnv, Type1),
        E2^^typecheck(TEnv, Type2),
        O^^typecheck(Type1, Type2, Type)
    ),
    (usecheck(UEnv, PreUState, PostUState) ::-
        E1^^usecheck(UEnv, PreUState, UState1),
        E2^^usecheck(UEnv, PreUState, UState2),
        worseState(UState1, UState2, PostUState)
    ),
    (meaning(Env, State, Value) ::-
        E1^^meaning(Env, State, Value1),
        E2^^meaning(Env, State, Value2),
        O^^meaning(Value1, Value2, Value)
    ),
    (code(OEnv, OLocn, [ExprCode2, store(OLocn), ExprCode1,
            binOp(Op,OLocn)]) ::-
        E2^^code(OEnv, OLocn, ExprCode2),
        OLocn1 is OLocn + 1,
        E1^^code(OEnv, OLocn1, ExprCode1),
        O^^code(Op)
    ).
```

`worseState(S1, S2, S)` implements the *worseState* function; it succeeds if

$$worseState(S1, S2) = S$$

14.3.7   Commands

14.3.7.1   *Block*

```
cmd ::= tBEGIN, cmdList^^CL, tEND
<:>
     (declcheck(DEnv, DCheck) ::- CL^^declcheck(DEnv, DCheck)),
     (typecheck(TEnv, TCheck) ::- CL^^typecheck(TEnv, TCheck)),
     (usecheck(UEnv, PreUState, PostUState) ::-
          CL^^usecheck(UEnv, PreUState, PostUState) ),
     (meaning(Env, PreState, PostState) ::-
          CL^^meaning(Env, PreState, PostState) ),
     (code(OEnv, PreLabel, PostLabel, InstrList) ::-
          CL^^code(OEnv, PreLabel, PostLabel, InstrList) ).
```

14.3.7.2   *Skip*

```
cmd ::= tSKIP
<:>
     (declcheck(_, checkOK)),
     (typecheck(_, checkOK)),
     (usecheck(_, UState, UState)),
     (meaning(_, State, State)),
     (code(_, Label, Label, [ ])).
```

14.3.7.3   *Assignment*

```
cmd ::= tIDENT^^I, tASSIGN, expr^^E
<:>
     (declcheck(DEnv, DCheck) ::-
          I^^meaning(Id),
          domain(DEnv, DDom),
          (    member(Id, DDom), DCheckI = checkOK
          ;    DCheckI = checkWrong ),
          E^^declcheck(DEnv, DCheckE),
          worse([DCheckI, DCheckE], DCheck)
     ),
     (typecheck(TEnv, TCheck) ::-
          I^^meaning(Id),
          lookup(TEnv, Id, TypeI),
          E^^typecheck(TEnv, TypeE),
          (    TypeI = TypeE, TypeE \= typeWrong, TCheck = checkOK
          ;    TCheck = checkWrong )
     ),
```

```
(usecheck(UEnv, PreUState, PostUState) ::-
    I^^meaning(Id),
    lookup(UEnv, Id, ULocn),
    E^^usecheck(UEnv, PreUState, MidUState),
    MidUState = [MidUStore,_],
    domain(MidUStore, UDom),
    (   member(ULocn, UDom), PostUState = MidUState
    ;   updateStoreU(MidUState, ULocn, checkOK, PostUState) )
),
(meaning(Env, PreState, PostState) ::-
    I^^meaning(Id),
    E^^meaning(Env, PreState, Value),
    lookup(Env, Id, Locn),
    updateStore(PreState, Locn, Value, PostState)
),
(code(OEnv, Label, Label, [InstrListE, store(OLocn)]) ::-
    top(TempLocn),
    E^^code(OEnv, TempLocn, InstrListE),
    I^^meaning(Id),
    lookup(OEnv, Id, OLocn)
).
```

updateStoreU(UState, L, C, UState1) implements $\boxplus_v$; it succeeds if

$$\text{UState} \boxplus_v \{\text{L} \mapsto \text{C}\} = \text{UState1}$$

updateStore(State, L, V, State1) implements $\boxplus$; it succeeds if

$$\text{State} \boxplus \{\text{L} \mapsto \text{V}\} = \text{State1}$$

14.3.7.4 Choice

```
cmd ::= tIF, expr^^E, tTHEN, cmd^^C1, tELSE, cmd^^C2
<:>
    (declcheck(DEnv, DCheck) ::-
        E^^declcheck(DEnv, DCheckE),
        C1^^declcheck(DEnv, DCheckC1),
        C2^^declcheck(DEnv, DCheckC2),
        worse([DCheckE, DCheckC1, DCheckC2], DCheck)
    ),
    (typecheck(TEnv, TCheck) ::-
        E^^typecheck(TEnv, TypeE),
        C1^^typecheck(TEnv, TCheckC1),
        C2^^typecheck(TEnv, TCheckC2),
        (   TypeE = bool, TCheckE = checkOK
        ;   TCheckE = checkWrong ),
        worse([TCheckE, TCheckC1, TCheckC2], TCheck)
    ),
```

```
(usecheck(UEnv, PreUState, PostUState) ::-
    E^^usecheck(UEnv, PreUState, MidUState),
    C1^^usecheck(UEnv, MidUState, UState1),
    C2^^usecheck(UEnv, MidUState, UState2),
    worseState(UState1, UState2, PostUState)
),
(meaning(Env, PreState, PostState) ::-
    E^^meaning(Env, PreState, Value),
    (    Value = bTRUE,
         C1^^meaning(Env, PreState, PostState)
    ;
         Value = bFALSE,
         C2^^meaning(Env, PreState, PostState) )
),
(code( OEnv, PreLabel, PostLabel,
        [TestCode, jump(L1), ThenCode, goto(L2),
            label(L1), ElseCode, label(L2)]) ::-
    top(TempLocn),
    E^^code(OEnv, TempLocn, TestCode),
    C1^^code(OEnv, PreLabel, MidLabel, ThenCode),
    C2^^code(OEnv, MidLabel, L1, ElseCode),
    L2 is L1 + 1,
    PostLabel is L1 + 2
).
```

14.3.7.5 *Loop*

```
cmd ::= tWHILE, expr^^E, tDO, cmd^^C
<:>
    (declcheck(DEnv, DCheck) ::-
        E^^declcheck(DEnv, DCheckE),
        C^^declcheck(DEnv, DCheckC),
        worse([DCheckE, DCheckC], DCheck)
    ),
    (typecheck(TEnv, TCheck) ::-
        E^^typecheck(TEnv, TypeE),
        C^^typecheck(TEnv, TCheckC),
        (    TypeE = bool, TCheckE = checkOK
        ;    TCheckE = checkWrong ),
        worse([TCheckE, TCheckC], TCheck)
    ),
    (usecheck(UEnv, PreUState, PostUState) ::-
        E^^usecheck(UEnv, PreUState, UStateE),
        C^^usecheck(UEnv, UStateE, UStateC),
        worseState(UStateE, UStateC, PostUState)
    ),
```

```
    (meaning(Env, PreStore, PostStore) ::-
        while(Env, PreStore, PostStore, E, C)
    ),
    (code(OEnv, PreLabel, PostLabel,
            [label(L1), TestCode, jump(L2), BodyCode,
            goto(L1), label(L2)]) ::-
        top(TempLocn),
        E^^code(OEnv, TempLocn, TestCode),
        C^^code(OEnv, PreLabel, L1, BodyCode),
        L2 is L1 + 1,
        PostLabel is L1 + 2
    ).
```

The dynamic meaning of the loop is pulled out as a separate clause, while, so that it can be consulted recursively. The copy_term is used to provide a copy of the tree that can be instantiated with values during one execution of the loop:

```
while(Env, PreStore, PostStore, E, C) :-
    copy_term(E, E1),
    E^^meaning(Env, PreStore, Value),
    (   Value = bTRUE,
        copy_term(C, C1),
        C^^meaning(Env, PreStore, MidStore),
        while(Env, MidStore, PostStore, E1, C1)
    ;
        Value = bFALSE,
        PostStore = PreStore
    ).
```

14.3.7.6 Input

```
cmd ::= tINPUT, tIDENT^^I
<:>
    (declcheck(DEnv, DCheck) ::-
        I^^meaning(Id),
        domain(DEnv, DDom),
        (   member(Id, DDom), DCheck = checkOK
        ;   DCheck = checkWrong )
    ),
    (typecheck(TEnv, TCheck) ::-
        I^^meaning(Id),
        lookup(TEnv, Id, Type),
        (   Type = int, TCheck = checkOK
        ;   TCheck = checkWrong )
    ),
```

```
(usecheck(UEnv, PreUState, PostUState) ::-
    I^^meaning(Id),
    lookup(UEnv, Id, ULocn),
    PreUState = [PreUStore, _],
    domain(PreUStore, UDom),
    (    member(ULocn, UDom), PostUState = PreUState
    ;    updateStoreU(PreUState, ULocn, checkOK, PostUState) )
),
(meaning(Env, PreState, PostState) ::-
    I^^meaning(Id),
    writel(['input:  ', Id, ' :  ']), read(Value),
    lookup(Env, Id, Locn),
    updateStore(PreState, Locn, Value, PostState)
),
(code(OEnv, OLocn, OLocn, [input, store(IdLocn)]) ::-
    I^^meaning(Id),
    lookup(OEnv, Id, IdLocn)
).
```

The dynamic semantics is interpreted slightly differently in the Prolog. Rather than having an initial input stream, and taking the first item from it on each input command, instead the interpreter prompts the user to type the input, and reads the input value from the keyboard.

14.3.7.7 Output

```
cmd ::= tOUTPUT, expr^^E
<:>
    (declcheck(DEnv, DCheck) ::- E^^declcheck(DEnv, DCheck)),
    (typecheck(TEnv, TCheck) ::-
        E^^typecheck(TEnv, Type),
        (    Type = int, TCheck = checkOK
        ;    TCheck = checkWrong )
    ),
    (usecheck(UEnv, PreUState, PostUState) ::-
        E^^usecheck(UEnv, PreUState, PostUState) ),
    (meaning(Env, PreState, PostState) ::-
        E^^meaning(Env, PreState, Value),
        PostState = PreState,
        writel(['output :  ', Value, nl])
    ),
    (code(OEnv, OLocn, OLocn, [ExprCode, output]) ::-
        top(TempLocn),
        E^^code(OEnv, TempLocn, ExprCode)
    ).
```

The dynamic semantics is interpreted slightly differently in the Prolog. Rather than storing all the outputs up into a final output stream, the interpreter writes the outputs to the screen on each output command.

Part IV

Winding Up

Chapter 15

Further Considerations

15.1 One small step

Tosca is very similar to the classic tutorial language of 'while' programs, but here much more emphasis has been placed on static semantics. Although languages almost as small as Tosca are actually used in developing some high integrity applications, the reason is not that they are particularly appropriate, but simply that larger languages are not considered safe, for the reasons outlined in Chapter 1. Tosca is merely a first small step away from assembly language.

There are a variety of concerns that need to be addressed for developing a compiler for a 'full' language. These range from theoretical concerns about what language features should be supported, to pragmatic ones of how to manage the development process in practice. Some of these are discussed below.

15.2 Other language features

Tosca lacks some of the language features needed to support good software engineering practice, and treats others in a less than satisfactory manner. Some of these are discussed below.

Note that as more sophisticated features are added, the approach of sets and partial functions taken in this book becomes inadequate. The full power of domain theory is required. However, the approach described here (separate static semantics, proof by structural induction, and implementation as a DCTG) is just as applicable in the more powerful mathematical formalism.

15.2.1   Data structures: arrays and records

Data structures appropriate to the application, not to the hardware, are one of the first features that need to be supplied. More than integers and booleans are needed. Statically bounded arrays and non-recursive record structures (exactly the kind of restrictions usually required of a high integrity language) are relatively straightforward to specify and prove.

The introduction of arrays begs for the introduction of a **for** loop, too, to iterate over them. This is also quite straightforward: simpler than a **while** loop in many respects.

A good, careful, specification of the type checking semantics of record types is needed to curtail those interminable traditional discussions of whether **foo** and **baz** have the same type or not in a declaration such as

    foo : record(x:int ; y:int) ;
    baz : record(x:int ; y:int) ;

15.2.2   Functions and procedures

Tosca's main disadvantage is the lack of an abstraction mechanism. Procedures or functions are essential for modularizing large programs.

Most traditional books on compiler writing give informal descriptions of algorithms for compiling procedures and functions. The challenge for a high integrity compiler specifier is not only to formalize such an algorithm, but to formalize it in such a way that it is possible to prove it correct against the dynamic semantics specification.

15.2.3   Recursion

Recursion (both in procedure calls and data structures) is usually forbidden in high integrity languages, because of the danger that an embedded processor could run out of memory during program execution. For a non-recursive language such as Tosca, it is possible to work out at compile time how much memory a program requires, and so to check that the proposed target machine has enough memory to run it.

But there are critical applications that are not embedded, and where it is perfectly allowable for them to stop and complain that they have run out of memory, provided they do not produce any partial, incorrect output. An example of such an application is a compiler for a high integrity language! Recursion is allowable (and in fact highly desirable) in a high integrity development language.

15.2.4   Separate compilation

Once procedures and functions have been added to the language, separate compilation becomes a possibility. As much care needs to be taken over specifying the meaning of separate modules as on any other language feature. On the dynamic side, the initial environment can be taken as non-empty, but rather containing the relevant procedures. On the static side, careful definitions are needed to provide safe separate compilation.

From the high integrity perspective, there is an extra potential for errors introduced by separate compilation. The configuration system needs to ensure that the correct versions of modules are provided for linking. The newly needed linker needs to be proved correct, too, which can be done using the same techniques as described here for the compiler.

15.3   Tool support

Tosca is small enough that the specification, proof and translation work can feasibly be done by hand. As the language grows, tool support at all stages of the process becomes imperative.

There are tools to support writing and checking Z specification. But set-based Z is not appropriate for larger languages, and so tool support for domain theory based specifications is necessary. Both the correctness proofs and the translation into executable form are highly stylized, so tool support for these should also be feasible.

15.4   Optimization

Optimization can be dangerous. It can produce obscure code, and it can introduce bugs. Hence the traditional motto runs: *First law of optimization: don't do it. Second law of optimization (for experts only): don't do it yet.*

15.4.1   Of the compiler

It is highly inadvisable to optimize the performance of the compiler. One of the requirements of the method advocated in this book is that there be a clear, visibly correct, translation from the mathematical definition of the semantics to the Prolog DCTG implementation. Optimization could only compromise this visibility.

15.4.2   Of the target code

One of the requirements for a high integrity compiler is that there be a clear mapping between each fragment of target code and its corresponding source code. This would seem to rule out optimization, which tends to obscure any such correspondence. However, the reason for this requirement is that the compiler is not trusted, and so this correspondence is required to enable an extra validation step to be performed. When the compiler can be trusted, this validation will not be required, and optimization becomes possible.

All optimizations must be performed with the same care and proof work as the compiler development, to ensure that no bugs are introduced. The semantics of the language should be used to prove that any proposed optimization is a *meaning preserving* transform.

15.5   Axiomatic semantics

As stated in Chapter 1, one issue not addressed here is the problem of how one would go about proving that a high integrity application written in the source language is itself correct. In fact, denotational semantics is not the most appropriate formalism for reasoning about the properties of a program; axiomatic semantics is a better approach.

The axiomatic semantics of a language should, however, be proved *sound* against the denotational semantics: that everything provable using the axiomatic semantics is in fact true. The logic for Z itself has been proved sound against its denotational semantics in such a manner.

15.6   Testing

The process of proving the compiler correct is a process of greatly increasing assurance in its correctness, not a process of providing absolute certainty. Just because the operational semantics templates have been proved correct, and the translation performed in a clear and visible manner, does not mean that the resulting compiler is infallible. There are many possible sources of bugs still around. Some of these are discussed below.

There could be an error in the proof. If a proof is done by hand, certain 'obvious' steps tend to be left out, for brevity. This could introduce an error, as could a simple mistake in copying from one line to the next. Cutting out the human step, and using a machine-based proof assistant, removes one class of errors and introduces another: there might be a bug in the proof tool. Since machine-produced proofs tend to be exceedingly long and dull (no steps are left out, and the steps tend to be smaller) there is less chance that a human reviewer might catch the error. Assurance can be increased by checking the proof produced by one tool with a separately developed tool, the hope being that if the second tool also has bugs, they might be different bugs.

There could be an error in the translation from Z to Prolog. Again, this could be due to a transcription error if done by hand, or a programming error in an automated translator. Some of the more trivial typographical errors are detected as syntax errors by the Prolog system when the compiler is run. But some errors might slip through.

There could be an error in the development environment. This includes the possibility of errors in the DCTG implementation, in the Prolog system itself, in the underlying operating system, and in the underlying hardware.

There could be an error in the formal semantics of the target microprocessor because the action of its instructions has been misunderstood, and formalized incorrectly.

The moral of this tale is that, no matter how much mathematical specification and proof is carried out, good old-fashioned testing still has a role to play. It provides yet another degree of increased assurance. But remember Dijkstra's famous aphorism: *Program testing can be used to show the presence of errors, but never to show their absence!*

15.7 Validation versus verification

Yet another potential source of bugs is that there could be an error in the target microprocessor so that it does not implement its specified semantics. There is a subtle difference from the last point made in the previous section, and arises from the difference between verification and validation.

Verification is the process of proving some property of a piece of mathematics, for example, that one specification is a correct refinement of another, or that a specification exhibits certain properties expressed in a theorem. Verification is a formal, mathematical process.

Validation is the process of demonstrating that a model (here assumed to be a mathematical model) has the desired properties, for example, that it suitably captures the system requirements, or adequately models the operation of a physical device. Validation is inherently informal, and cannot even in principle be a mathematical process, because it is attempting to demonstrate some correspondence between a piece of mathematics and the physical real world. It is impossible to *prove* a mathematical model faithfully reflects the physical system it is modelling, that is, to prove that everything that needs to be modelled has been modelled, and that what has been modelled has been done so accurately. So, to return to the example that started this discussion, it is impossible ever to prove, in the mathematical sense of the word, that a given microprocessor implements its mathematical semantics. This argument holds for any applications that interact with or control aspects of the real world. No less a person than Einstein said: *As far as the laws of mathematics refer to reality, they are not certain, and as far as they are certain, they do not refer to reality.* There is always a need to validate the formal mathematical specification against informal requirements or behaviour of a physical device. Validation is a fancy name for testing.

This point is laboured because there is frequently misunderstanding about what a formal specification provides. It provides greatly increased assurance, but it does not provide certainty. This is not a failing peculiar to mathematics, however. Nothing provides certainty.

15.8   Further reading

A catalogue of the various tools currently available for supporting Z can be found in [Parker 1991].

[Tennent 1991] describes how to prove the soundness of an axiomatic semantics against the denotational semantics of a programming language. [Woodcock and Brien 1992] describe a logic for Z, and discuss its soundness proofs.

For a thought-provoking argument on what constitutes a valid proof, and how much assurance the existence of a proof actually gives, see [De Millo *et al.* 1979].

Chapter 16

Concluding Remarks

16.1 Summary of the approach

In summary, the approach to building a high assurance compiler described in this book has the following steps.

1. Specify a denotational semantics for the source language. Many problems and ambiguities arising in the language definition can be resolved at this stage. This specification should include both dynamic and static semantics.

2. Write each semantics as a Prolog DCTG. Each static semantics provides the relevant checker (for example, type checker, declaration checker). The dynamic semantics provides an interpreter that can be used to provided further validation for the proposed semantics.

3. Specify a denotational semantics for the target language.

4. Specify an operational semantics of the source language as code templates in the target language. This specification is an algorithm for the compiler.

5. Calculate the meaning of these templates, using the target language semantics, to prove that they have the same meaning as the corresponding source language constructs. This proves that the proposed compiler performs a correct (meaning preserving) translation.

6. Write the operational semantics as a DCTG. This provides a compiler.

16.2   The criteria for high assurance compilation

How does this approach fit the criteria laid out for a high assurance compiler in Chapter 1?

1. *The high level source language must have a target-independent meaning.* The denotational semantics definition provides this meaning. The calculation of the meaning of a program can proceed manually from the semantics, as shown in the 'square' example of Chapter 9, or mechanically by using the target-independent interpreter.

2. *The source language must have a mathematically defined semantics.* The denotational semantics definition of Tosca is a mathematical definition, and hence, can be reasoned about.

3. *The target language must also have a mathematically defined semantics.* The denotational semantics definition of Aida is a mathematical definition.

4. *The compiler ... must be correct.* Each Aida template has been proved to have the same meaning as the corresponding Tosca statement.

5. *[The compiler] must be written clearly, and must be clearly related to the semantics.* The Prolog DCTG approach allows a clear one-to-one mapping between the mathematical definition and its implementation.

6. *The target code produced by the compiler must be clear, and easily related to the source code.* The template style and lack of optimization allows a clear mapping from target code to the corresponding source code. If a clearer correspondence is needed, it is a simple job to make the compiler annotate the target code.

7. *The semantics ... must be made available for peer review and criticism.* See the descriptions in sections 8.2–8.6 and Chapter 10.

The small languages and the compiler described in this book were developed as a prototype demonstration, and it would not be surprising if mistakes are found in either the semantics or the compiler. Indeed, since one of the aims of the approach described here is to produce a specification and implementation of sufficient clarity to facilitate the discovery of such errors, it would be disappointing if they were not discovered!

Part V

Appendices

Appendix A

Bibliography

[Abramson and Dahl 1989]
Harvey Abramson and Veronica Dahl. *Logic Grammars*. Symbolic Computation series. Springer Verlag, 1989.

[Aho and Ullman 1977]
Alfred V. Aho and Jeffrey D. Ullman. *Principles of Compiler Design*. Addison-Wesley, 1977.

[Aho *et al.* 1988]
Alfred V. Aho, Brian W. Kernighan, and Peter J. Weinberger. *The AWK Programming Language*. Addison-Wesley, 1988.

[Allison 1986]
L. Allison. *A Practical Introduction to Denotational Semantics*. Cambridge University Press, 1986.

[Andrews *et al.* 1991]
Derek Andrews, Don Ward, Roger Henry, *et al.* CD10514-2(draft):1991 fourth working draft Modula-2 standard, 1991.

[Austin 1976]
J. L. Austin. *How to do Things with Words*. Oxford University Press, 2nd edition, 1976.

[Bergeretti and Carré 1985]
J. F. Bergeretti and B. Carré. Information flow and data flow analysis of while programs. *ACM Transactions on Programming Languages and Systems*, 7:37–61, 1985.

[Bramson 1984]
B. D. Bramson. Malvern's program analysers. *RSRE Research Review*, 1984.

[Carré 1989]
> Bernard A. Carré. Reliable programming in standard languages. In Chris T. Sennett, editor, *High-integrity Software*. Pitman, 1989.

[Clocksin and Mellish 1987]
> W. F. Clocksin and C. S. Mellish. *Programming in Prolog*. Springer Verlag, 3rd edition, 1987.

[Cohn 1979]
> A. Cohn. *Machine Assisted Proofs of Recursion Implementation*. PhD thesis, University of Edinburgh, 1979.

[Cousot and Cousot 1977]
> P. Cousot and R. Cousot. Abstract interpretation: a unified lattice model for static analysis of programs by construction or approximation of fixed points. In *Proceedings of the Fourth Annual ACM Symposium on the Principles of Programming Languages*. ACM, 1977.

[De Millo *et al.* 1979]
> R. A. De Millo, R. J. Lipton, and A. J. Perlis. Social processes and proofs of theorems and programs. *Communications of the ACM*, 22(5):271–280, 1979. see also 'ACM Forum', 22(11):621–630.

[Gordon 1979]
> Michael J. C. Gordon. *The Denotational Description of Programming Languages — An Introduction*. Springer Verlag, 1979.

[Hall 1990]
> J. Anthony Hall. Seven myths of formal methods. *IEEE Software*, pages 21–28, September 1990.

[Hayes 1987]
> Ian J. Hayes, editor. *Specification Case Studies*. Prentice Hall, 1987.

[Hoare 1991]
> C. A. R. Hoare. Refinement algebra proves correctness of compiling specifications. In C. Carroll Morgan and James C. P. Woodcock, editors, *3rd BCS-FACS Refinement Workshop*, Workshops in Computing, pages 33–48. Springer Verlag, 1991.

[Hoare and Jones 1989]
> C. A. R. Hoare and Cliff B. Jones. *Essays in Computer Science*. Prentice Hall, 1989.

[Kernighan and Pike 1984]
> Brian W. Kernighan and Rob Pike. *The Unix Programming Environment*. Prentice Hall, 1984.

[Knuth 1968]
> Donald E. Knuth. Semantics of context-free languages. *Mathematical Systems Theory*, 2(2):127–145, 1968. correction, 5(1):95–96, 1971.

[Lee 1989]

Peter Lee. *Realistic Compiler Generation.* Foundations of Computing series. MIT Press, 1989.

[McCarthy and Painter 1966]

J. McCarthy and J. Painter. Correctness of a compiler for arithmetic expressions. Technical Report AIM-40, Stanford University, 1966.

[Meyer 1985]

Bertrand Meyer. On formalism in specifications. *IEEE Software*, 2:6–26, January 1985.

[Meyer 1990]

Bertrand Meyer. *Introduction to the Theory of Programming Languages.* Prentice Hall, 1990.

[Milner and Weyhrauch 1972]

Robin Milner and R. Weyhrauch. Proving compiler correctness in a mechanized logic. *Machine Intelligence*, 7, 1972.

[Morris 1973]

F. L. Morris. Advice on structuring compilers and proving them correct. In *Proceedings of the First Annual ACM Symposium on Principles of Programming Languages*, pages 144–152. ACM, 1973.

[Mosses 1975]

Peter D. Mosses. *Mathematical Semantics and Compiler Generation.* PhD thesis, University of Oxford, 1975.

[Neumann 1985]

Peter G. Neumann. Some computer-related disasters and other egregious horrors. *ACM SIGSOFT Software Engineering Notes*, 10(1):6, 1985.

[Parker 1991]

Colin E. Parker. Z tools catalogue. ZIP document ZIP/BAe/90/020, British Aerospace, Warton, May 1991.

[Paulson 1981]

L. Paulson. *A Compiler Generator for Semantic Grammars.* PhD thesis, Stanford University, 1981.

[Paulson 1982]

L. Paulson. A semantics-directed compiler generator. In *Proceedings of the Ninth Annual ACM Symposium on Principles of Programming Languages*, pages 224–239. ACM, 1982.

[Polak 1981]

Wolfgang Polak. *Compiler Specification and Verification*, volume 124 of *Lecture Notes in Computer Science*. Springer Verlag, 1981.

[Potter *et al.* 1991]

    Ben Potter, Jane Sinclair, and David Till. *An Introduction to Formal Specification and Z.* Prentice Hall, 1991.

[Schmidt 1988]

    David A. Schmidt. *Denotational Semantics: A Methodology for Language Development.* Wm. C. Brown Publishers, 1988.

[Spivey 1992]

    J. Michael Spivey. *The Z Notation: a Reference Manual.* Prentice Hall, 2nd edition, 1992.

[Stepney and Lord 1987]

    Susan Stepney and Stephen P. Lord. Formal specification of an access control system. *Software—Practice and Experience*, 17(9):575–593, 1987.

[Stepney *et al.* 1991]

    Susan Stepney, Dave Whitley, David Cooper, and Colin Grant. A demonstrably correct compiler. *BCS Formal Aspects of Computing*, 3:58–101, 1991.

[Sterling and Shapiro 1986]

    Leon Sterling and Ehud Shapiro. *The Art of Prolog: Advanced Programming Techniques.* MIT Press, 1986.

[Stoy 1977]

    Joseph E. Stoy. *Denotational Semantics and the Scott-Strachey Approach to Programming Language Theory.* MIT Press, 1977.

[Tennent 1991]

    R. D. Tennent. *Semantics of Programming Languages.* Prentice Hall, 1991.

[Tofte 1990]

    Mads Tofte. *Compiler Generators: what they can do, what they might do, and what they will probably never do*, volume 19 of *EATCS Monographs on Theoretical Computer Science.* Springer Verlag, 1990.

[Wand 1984]

    M. Wand. A semantic prototyping system. *Proceedings of the SIGPLAN 84 Symposium on Compiler Construction; ACM SIGPLAN Notices*, 19(6):213–221, 1984.

[Warren 1980]

    David H. Warren. Logic programming and compiler writing. *Software—Practice and Experience*, 10:97–125, 1980.

[Woodcock and Brien 1992]

    James C. P. Woodcock and Stephen M. Brien. $\mathcal{W}$: A logic for Z. In John E. Nicholls, editor, *Proceedings of the 6th Annual Z User Meeting, York*, Workshops in Computing, pages 77–96. Springer Verlag, 1992.

Appendix B

Recursive Definition of Loops

In section 8.5.7.4, the semantics of the while loop was defined recursively, in terms of itself. A non-recursive formulation of the semantics is possible, but it is less convenient for implementing the interpreter. Consider the following, which specifies an infinite family of functions $\mathcal{W}$, whose members are defined in terms of earlier members of the family, *not* in terms of themselves:

$$
\begin{array}{|l}
\mathcal{W} : \mathsf{N} \longrightarrow (CMD \times EXPR) \longrightarrow Env \twoheadrightarrow State \twoheadrightarrow State \\[2mm]
\hline
\forall\, n : \mathsf{N};\; \gamma : CMD;\; \epsilon : EXPR;\; \rho : Env;\; \sigma : State \bullet \\[2mm]
\quad \mathcal{W}_0(\gamma, \epsilon)\,\rho = \varnothing[State \times State] \\[2mm]
\quad \wedge\; \mathcal{W}_{n+1}(\gamma, \epsilon)\,\rho\,\sigma = \\
\qquad \mathbf{if}\; \mathcal{M}_E[\![\epsilon]\!]\,\rho\,\sigma = bool_v\; \mathsf{T}\; \mathbf{then}\; \mathcal{W}_n(\gamma, \epsilon)\,\rho(\mathcal{M}_C[\![\gamma]\!]\,\rho\,\sigma)\; \mathbf{else}\; \sigma
\end{array}
$$

$\mathcal{W}_0(\gamma, \epsilon)\,\rho$ is the empty function. There is no state that is in its domain. Since the possibility of a non-terminating loop is being modelled by using a *partial* state transition function, the empty function can be interpreted as the specification of a non-terminating loop.

Each successive $\mathcal{W}_n$ executes the body command one more time before it becomes the empty non-terminating function. So $\mathcal{W}_n$ has the same behaviour as a loop that executes less than n times before terminating. For any particular loop that terminates, it is possible to find a particular value of n sufficiently large.

So $\mathcal{W}_{n+1}$ has a larger domain than $\mathcal{W}_n$ (it also includes loops that execute n times), but where their domains overlap (on loops that execute less than n times), their results agree. Hence we can take the union of all these $\mathcal{W}_n$ and define the meaning of a general loop non-recursively as

$$
\big|\quad \mathcal{M}_C[\![\mathsf{loop}(\epsilon, \gamma)]\!] = \bigcup\{\, n : \mathsf{N} \bullet \mathcal{W}_n(\gamma, \epsilon) \,\}
$$

Appendix C

Z's Free Type Construct

Z uses fairly standard mathematical notation for most of its constructs, but its free type (disjoint union) needs a little more explanation.

A disjoint union is a way of combining two sets into a new set so that all the elements of the new set 'know' which of the old sets it came from. The simplest way to do this is to tag every element. So, for example, the disjoint union of $A = \{a, b, c\}$ and $B = \{c, d, e\}$ could be written as $\{(a,1), (b,1), (c,1), (c,2), (d,2), (e,2)\}$. By examining its tag, it is possible to discover if any particular c comes from A or from B.

In mathematics, a disjoint union is often written as $A + B$, and the tags are often omitted, since the sets being unioned are often disjoint in the first place. So it is quite possible to see expressions like $VALUE = NAT + BOOL$.

Z does not have this luxury. It is based on *typed* set theory, and its type rules do not permit sets of different types to be combined in this way. A more elaborate approach is used: free type definitions. A simple example is

$$IDCHAR ::= uscore$$
$$\mid d\langle\!\langle DIGIT \rangle\!\rangle$$
$$\mid a\langle\!\langle ALPHA \rangle\!\rangle$$

which introduces the set $IDCHAR$, and puts some constraints on its members, given that $DIGIT$ and $ALPHA$ are sets introduced elsewhere. d and a act the part of tags: they are functions that map elements of $DIGIT$ and $ALPHA$ to members of $IDCHAR$. These constructor functions are total injections (one-to-one functions); they map every element in their domain to a different element of $IDCHAR$. $uscore$ is a single element of $IDCHAR$. Extra conditions ensure that all these constructed elements of $IDCHAR$ are distinct (that $uscore$ and the ranges of a and d do not overlap), and that there are no other elements in $IDCHAR$ (it is the smallest set containing these constructed elements). The construction is summarized in Figure C.1. An equivalent Z form is

$$[IDCHAR]$$

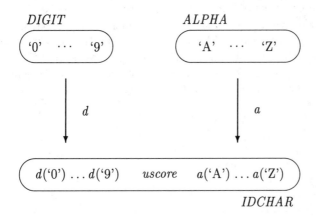

Figure C.1 Construction of a free type

$uscore : IDCHAR$
$d : DIGIT \rightarrowtail IDCHAR$
$a : ALPHA \rightarrowtail IDCHAR$

$\langle\{uscore\}, \text{ran } d, \text{ran } a\rangle$ partition $IDCHAR$

A consequence of using free types is that definitions tend to be splattered with the names of these tag functions. For example, given a *DIGIT* called δ, the corresponding *IDCHAR* is $d(\delta)$; given an *IDCHAR* called ι that is in the range of d, it corresponds to the *DIGIT* $d^\sim(\iota)$ (where the function $d^\sim$ is the inverse of the function d).

Free type definitions may also be recursive. In such a case there must be at least one non-recursive base case, to allow the recursion to terminate (or, from a more constructive viewpoint, to allow the construction to begin). For example, it is possible to define a recursive *LIST* type as

$LIST ::= nil$
$\qquad | \quad cons\langle\!\langle \mathbb{N} \times LIST\rangle\!\rangle$

which is shorthand for

$[LIST]$

$nil : LIST$
$cons : \mathbb{N} \times LIST \rightarrowtail LIST$

$\langle\{nil\}, \text{ran } cons\rangle$ partition $LIST$

The base element of *LIST* is *nil*. Using the constructor function with *nil* as its list argument constructs the further elements $cons(0, nil)$, $cons(1, nil)$, $cons(2, nil)$, ... Using *cons* with one of these 'one-element lists' constructs 'two-element lists' such as $cons(0, cons(0, nil))$, $cons(1, cons(0, nil))$, $cons(2, cons(0, nil))$, ..., $cons(0, cons(1, nil))$, $cons(1, cons(1, nil))$, $cons(2, cons(1, nil))$, ... And so on.

A recursive free type has an infinite number of elements, because it is always possible to use one of its constructor functions to make a new element from existing ones.

Appendix D

Glossary of Notation

In order to reduce the number of declarations needed in definitions, most of them have been made implicit, and the same symbol consistently used for the same type of variable. These are summarized below.

D.1 Syntactic variables

Name	Z type	Variable
command	CMD	γ
command list	seq CMD	Γ
declaration	$DECL$	δ
declaration list	seq $DECL$	Δ
expression	$EXPR$	ϵ
instruction	$INSTR$	ι
instruction list	seq $INSTR$	I
operator, binary	BIN_OP	ω
operator, binary arithmetic	BIN_ARITH_OP	ω_α
operator, binary comparison	BIN_COMP_OP	ω_χ
operator, binary logic	BIN_LOGIC_OP	ω_λ
operator, unary	UNY_OP	ψ
operator, unary arithmetic	UNY_ARITH_OP	ψ_α
operator, unary logic	UNY_LOGIC_OP	ψ_λ

D.2   Semantic variables

Name	Z type	Variable
boolean	*Boolean*	b
check	*CHECK*	c
constant value	*VALUE*	χ
continuation	*Cont*	ϑ
environment	*Env*	ρ
integer	$\mathbb{Z}$	n
label	*Label*	ϕ
location	*Locn*	λ
name, identifier	*NAME*	ξ
store	*Store*	ς
state	*State*	σ

D.3   Use of subscripts

Subscripts are used to distinguish different, but related, variables:

- Any variable can take a numerical subscript

- Declaration-before-use types have a subscript D, variables a subscript δ

- Type-checking types have a subscript T, variables a subscript τ

- Initialization-before-use types have a subscript U, variables a subscript υ

So, for example, ϕ, ϕ_4 represent variables of type *Label*, and $\sigma_\upsilon, \sigma_{\upsilon 2}$ represent variables of type *State$_U$*.

Index

S